Studies in Economic Transition

General Editors: **Jens Hölscher**, Reader in Economics, University of Brighton; and **Horst Tomann**, Professor of Economics, Free University Berlin

This series has been established in response to a growing demand for a greater understanding of the transformation of economic systems. It brings together theoretical and empirical studies on economic transition and economic development. The post-communist transition from planned to market economies is one of the main areas of applied theory because it is in this field that the most dramatic examples of change and economic dynamics can be found. The series aims to contribute to the understanding of specific major economic changes as well as to advance the theory of economic development. The implications of economic policy will be a major point of focus.

Titles include:

Lucian Cernat
EUROPEANIZATION, VARIETIES OF CAPITALISM AND ECONOMIC PERFORMANCE IN CENTRAL AND EASTERN EUROPE

Bruno Dallago and Ichiro Iwasaki (*editors*)
CORPORATE RESTRUCTURING AND GOVERNANCE IN TRANSITION ECONOMIES

Bruno Dallago (*editor*)
TRANSFORMATION AND EUROPEAN INTEGRATION
The Local Dimension

Hella Engerer
PRIVATIZATION AND ITS LIMITS IN CENTRAL AND EASTERN EUROPE
Property Rights in Transition

Saul Estrin, Grzegorz W. Kolodko and Milica Uvalic (*editors*)
TRANSITION AND BEYOND

Daniela Gabor
CENTRAL BANKING AND FINANCIALIZATION
A Romanian Account of how Eastern Europe became Subprime

Oleh Havrylyshyn
DIVERGENT PATHS IN POST-COMMUNIST TRANSFORMATION
Capitalism for All or Capitalism for the Few?

Iraj Hoshi, Paul J.J. Welfens and Anna Wziatek-Kubiak (*editors*)
INDUSTRIAL COMPETITIVENESS AND RESTRUCTURING IN ENLARGED EUROPE
How Accession Countries Catch Up and Integrate in the European Union

Mihaela Keleman and Monika Kostera (*editors*)
CRITICAL MANAGEMENT RESEARCH IN EASTERN EUROPE
Managing the Transition

David Lane (*editor*)
THE TRANSFORMATION OF STATE SOCIALISM
System Change, Capitalism, or Something Else

David Lane and Martin Myant (*editors*)
VARIETIES OF CAPITALISM IN POST-COMMUNIST COUNTRIES

Jens Lowitzsch
FINANCIAL PARTICIPATION OF EMPLOYEES IN THE EU-27

Enrico Marelli and Marcello Signorelli (*editors*)
ECONOMIC GROWTH AND STRUCTURAL FEATURES OF TRANSITION

Tomasz Mickiewicz
ECONOMIC TRANSITION IN CENTRAL EUROPE AND THE COMMONWEALTH OF INDEPENDENT STATES

Tomasz Mickiewicz
ECONOMICS OF INSTITUTIONAL CHANGE
Central and Eastern Europe Revisited

Milan Nikolić
MONETARY POLICY IN TRANSITION
Inflation Nexus Money Supply in Postcommunist Russia

Julie Pellegrin
THE POLITICAL ECONOMY OF COMPETITIVENESS IN AN ENLARGED EUROPE

Stanislav Poloucek (*editor*)
REFORMING THE FINANCIAL SECTOR IN CENTRAL EUROPEAN COUNTRIES

Johannes Stephan (*editor*)
TECHNOLOGY TRANSFER VIA FOREIGN DIRECT INVESTMENT IN CENTRAL AND EASTERN EUROPE

Horst Tomann
MONETARY INTEGRATION IN EUROPE

Milica Uvalic
SERBIA'S TRANSITION
Towards a Better Future

Hans van Zon
RUSSIA'S DEVELOPMENT PROBLEM
The Cult of Power

The full list of titles available is on the website:
www.palgrave.com/economics/set.asp

Studies in Economic Transition
Series Standing Order ISBN 978–0–333–73353–0
(outside North America only)

You can receive future titles in this series as they are published by placing a standing order. Please contact your bookseller or, in case of difficulty, write to us at the address below with your name and address, the title of the series and the ISBN quoted above.

Customer Services Department, Macmillan Distribution Ltd, Houndmills, Basingstoke, Hampshire RG21 6XS, England

Central Banking and Financialization

A Romanian Account of how Eastern Europe became Subprime

Daniela Gabor

palgrave
macmillan

Softcover reprint of the hardcover 1st edition 2011 978-0-230-27615-4

First published 2011 by
PALGRAVE MACMILLAN

Palgrave Macmillan in the UK is an imprint of Macmillan Publishers Limited, registered in England, company number 785998, of Houndmills, Basingstoke, Hampshire RG21 6XS.

Palgrave Macmillan in the US is a division of St Martin's Press LLC, 175 Fifth Avenue, New York, NY 10010.

Palgrave Macmillan is the global academic imprint of the above companies and has companies and representatives throughout the world.

Palgrave® and Macmillan® are registered trademarks in the United States, the United Kingdom, Europe and other countries.

ISBN 978-1-349-32505-4 ISBN 978-0-230-29504-9 (eBook)
DOI 10.1057/9780230295049

This book is printed on paper suitable for recycling and made from fully managed and sustained forest sources. Logging, pulping and manufacturing processes are expected to conform to the environmental regulations of the country of origin.

A catalogue record for this book is available from the British Library.

A catalog record for this book is available from the Library of Congress.

10 9 8 7 6 5 4 3 2 1
20 19 18 17 16 15 14 13 12 11

Contents

Illustrations

Tables

Figures

Acknowledgements

I am indebted to Sheila Dow, Victoria Chick, the late Dipak Ghosh, Peter Howells, Gary Dymski, Howard Nicholas, Anca Paliu and Irina Racaru for stimulating comments, guidance and support. I wish to acknowledge the support of the Funds for Women Graduates of the British Federation of Women Graduates. I am grateful to the National Bank of Romania for permission to reproduce its figures with output gap forecasts from the Inflation Reports.

1 Introduction

February 2009 was an unusual month for Central and Eastern Europe. (CEE). First, the international press started referring to it as the subprime region (Ahamed 2009). The association to the infamous subprime mortgage market in the USA described the same process with different actors. In the USA, NINJA (no income no job no assets) borrowers and imprudent banks together created an explosive cocktail that nearly destroyed international financial markets. The CEE countries similarly borrowed beyond their means to finance a fast process of convergence with their neighbouring European countries, mostly through Western European banks present in their banking systems. Austrian banks, for instance, had outstanding loans to the region amounting to 70 percent of Austria's gross domestic produce (GDP). As the collapse of Lehman Brothers in September 2008 saw European bank losses spiral, nothing seemed far-fetched, not even the possibility that these would abandon the region. In the event, global finance faced, according to *The Economist* (2009), a shock at least comparable to the US subprime mortgage market debacle. Second, the central banks of the Czech Republic, Romania, Poland, and Bulgaria accused the foreign-owned banks of speculating in currency markets and amplifying the negative effects of the international financial crisis. While concerns about speculative activity had been expressed on an individual basis during October 2008 (most vocally by the Central Bank of Romania), the coordinated public statement was unprecedented. Poland went further, calling developed countries to carefully assess the bailout strategies for Western banks operating in Eastern Europe. These, the governor of the Polish central bank charged, were using the bailout liquidity to speculate in CEE currency markets rather than to restart lending in home countries (Kaminska 2009).

Yet, by the end of 2009, the doom-and-gloom atmosphere seemed a bad dream. In a spectacular reversal, the CEE became the strongest performing region in the world.

This book sets out to explore how these events are connected. It focuses on central banks as key actors of the account; it treats central banking as a deeply political process; and it approaches it from the standpoint of neoliberalism and financialization.

Financialization and neoliberalism in Central and Eastern Europe

Financialization is a relatively new concept used to explain the quantitative and qualitative shifts in financial systems associated with financial liberalization and international deregulation. Krippner's (2005) popular definition focuses on the increasing importance of financial activities, rather than commodity production or trade, in generating profits. Crotty (2003) further describes a qualitative shift toward "impatient" finance that increasingly replaces the traditional long-term financing of productive activities with short-term market activities. Financialization is juxtaposed with neoliberalism in response to recent pleas for expanding analytical attention beyond the traditional treatment of neoliberalism as free-market ideology (Krippner 2007) or as a static project driven by a singular anti-state logic (Hay 2004). Neoliberalism is approached as ideology and practice, with shifting underlying rationalities: from the destructive attack on the state to a normalized mode where economic and financial relations are redefined through processes of financialization (Peck and Tickell 2002).

An increasingly large and multidisciplinary literature argues that neoliberalism in its financialized stage permeates and reconstructs policy spaces and economic and social relations (Goldstein 2009). Central and Eastern Europe offers an interesting terrain to explore this process, unique because of its historical engagement with neoliberalism after the collapse of socialism. Its transformation from a planned system has been scripted (with different degrees of success, depending on national configurations) by neoliberal insistence on market optimality, deregulation, and (financial) liberalization. By 2008, the International Monetary Fund (IMF) commended the region for successfully harnessing financialized globalization to growth priorities (Fabrizio 2008). In other words, it is no historical accident that the CEE, and not East Asia or Latin America, became "subprime" during the 2007–2009 crisis of finance-led growth regimes and that a large number of countries had to turn to the IMF for emergency support (Hungary, Latvia, Romania, Ukraine, Serbia, and Poland).

Formerly planned economies offer an ideal example of how central banks participated and were in turn structured by financialization. As will be shown, neoliberal approaches to macroeconomic management, built on monetarist economic theories, assigned the central bank a key role in redefining economic relations after the collapse of socialism. Since the superiority of neoliberalism was predicated on the superiority of the market, policy advice prescribed the depoliticization of economic decisions and the institutionalization of "a technical set of devices" for managing increasingly interdependent economies (Hay 2004). This naturalized the central bank as the institution par excellence fit to design, and ensure the deployment of, such devices.

Why Romania, and to what extent is it representative of regional dynamics? The focus on the specific dynamics of the Romanian policy space arises from conceptual and personal considerations. Following Karl Niebyl (1946), the political economy of central banking must pay equal attention to policy argumentation and institutional configurations. Data is important but requires interpretation, and there is seldom one interpretation that commands support from all policy actors. An analytical distinction between competing policy narratives and practices of central banking then requires the analysis to be restricted to the historical evolution of a single central-bank policy space. I have chosen Romania because my command of the language allowed me access to policy documents, speeches, and controversies that otherwise would be more difficult to map. However, the book is built on the premise that the institutionalization of central banks in relation to wider processes of neoliberalization and financialization is no longer a "national" affair. If globalization vs. nation-state dichotomies are abandoned, as Sassen (2003) persuasively argues, then certain components of the nation-state become denationalized. To apply Sassen's arguments in this context, the central bank offers an "institutional home" to global forces, and practices of central banking are reoriented to the requirements of financialization, embedded into complex networks of global governance alongside other supranational (the IMF) or private entities (commercial banks). Such a perspective rescues the analysis from remaining a (hopefully) interesting yet singular case study. Instead, Romania's experience between 1990 and 2008 is useful to identify the features of a financialized approach to monetary management and its inbuilt vulnerabilities that has consolidated in broadly similar forms throughout the region. Furthermore, a comparison of policy responses to crisis in Hungary and

Romania throughout 2009 allows for a reflection on possible politics of resistance to financialized practices.

The politics of central banking: An epistemological note

To argue that monetary policy is political makes no claim to originality. Even Alan Greenspan recognized this in late 2008 when he gave a positive answer to an extraordinary question: "Do you feel that your ideology pushed you to make decisions that you wish you had not made?"[1]. The question (and a positive answer) was extraordinary not only because the "maestro" had a near-mythical status in financial markets but also because it challenged a fundamental premise in monetary policy: the objectivity of technocratic policy-makers. It suggested that, under that cloak of objectivity surrounding monetary policy, lurk questions of power, ideology, and politics.

Furthermore, the political dimension of central banking has been analyzed from different theoretical traditions: from the Marxist approaches embedded in the work of Epstein (2005) or D'Arista (2005) to the neoclassical tradition otherwise impervious to institutional analysis (Alesina 1994). Yet the book approaches the political economy of central banking from a distinct position, seeking to transcend the dichotomy formulation–implementation usually deployed in monetary-policy analysis. Milton Friedman, that anti-government man, saw political interference, usually—although not exclusively—at the stage of implementation, as the greatest threat to rational monetary policy, essentially transgressing a necessary separation between the economic and political spheres. But monetary policy is not political because governments might impose political agendas onto an otherwise objective field of policy formulation, a problem solvable by ensuring adequate central-bank independence (the neoclassicals) or prioritizing the interest of labour (the Marxists). Politics and power are not grafted onto policy but constitutive of it, through processes with actors that mobilize and pursue competing agendas and interests (Keely and Scoones 1999).

The journey of this book started with my interest in central banking in post-socialist Romania. A first question to tackle was how to approach the analysis of monetary policy in a context so profoundly marked by system dislocation. What initially appeared to be a methodological question quickly acquired epistemological dimensions. The challenge was that monetary-policy analysis for Romania resisted the methods deployed in typical economic-policy analysis. Causal relations between relevant variables were difficult to establish empirically since the attempts to construct a capitalist system of production had resulted in repeated economic crisis, as shown in the lengthy relationship with the IMF. Before 1997, for instance, four stand-by arrangements (SBAs) went off-track in less than a year after signing. The SBAs assigned monetary policy an essential role in tackling the crisis; the common explanation of failure contrasted a reform-orientated central bank with vested (political) interests capturing policy implementation (Dragulin and Radulescu 1999).

I was thus searching for an approach that could shed some understanding on these recurrent episodes of crisis and on the role monetary policy had played before, during, and after, particularly against the wider processes of reorganizing the logic of economic production once the Central Plan, the mechanism for allocating resources in socialism, disappeared.

Encountering the work of Karl Niebyl on theories of money provided a first guiding step. An (unjustly) all-but-forgotten economist, in his 1946 *Studies on the Classical Theories of Money,* Niebyl suggested an interesting and innovative historical approach. Any account of central banking should involve three necessary dimensions: monetary theorizing, policy-making, and reality. In a capitalist system of production, Niebyl claimed, monetary theories and policies are embedded in particular institutional structures of the productive and financial sectors. The continuity of an economic doctrine depends on its capacity to anchor itself in the "continuity of reality," in satisfactorily representing and explaining this reality. However, he did not imply that a dominant theory at any one time would necessarily best represent those particular economic conditions: interests and power had to be considered in the process of doctrine formation. In other words, specific institutional configurations, rather than some objective criteria, might shape the theory and policy prescriptions applied to an economic problem[2].

In his methodological approach, Karl Niebyl was a pioneer not only in economics (Chick 1999) but also in policy studies. Indeed, it would be another forty years until questions of interests and power would be systematically addressed in policy analysis. Traditionally, an instrumental view represented policy as a rational problem-solving exercise and attributed to policy-makers control over other policy actors (Mosse 2005). Policy implementation follows the policy model in a linear fashion. Two alternative conceptualizations emerged to question this rationalist representation (Keely and Scoones 1999). The incrementalist perspective depicts policy as the "science of muddling through" through a continuous process of negotiation and bargaining, a perspective that retains the central role of models but acknowledges that implementation might be more complex than initially assumed. A second, more radical view, explicitly links policies with struggles over meaning and interpretation. Drawing on interpretative and critical traditions, this epistemological stance argues that social (and policy) inquiry be conducted through a broader interpretative framework (Fischer 1998).

Indeed, what Fischer calls the argumentative turn in policy analysis emerged in the 1980s against the growing discontent with the rationality project in policy analysis and its "common mission of rescuing public policy from the irrationalities and indignities of politics" (Stone 1988: 12). Under the positivist banner, policy was understood as a "science" concerned with generating predictive generalization and working according to a universal logic of scientific enquiry. Thus policy interventions, "based on causal laws of society and verified by neutral empirical observation" (Dyrzek 1982: 310), would consist of manipulating an array of variables toward achieving certain ends. To ensure a genuine "scientific" approach, empirical enquiry should be stripped of all normative dimensions and rigorously conducted according to the "fact-value dichotomy" by hypothesis testing, data collection, statistical analysis, and value-neutrality (Hawkesworth 1988). Rational policy engineers, technocrats, thus anchor policy knowledge in the confirmation of empirical experience, achieving what Habermas (1989) called the "scientization of politics" or the depoliticization of politics.

Depoliticization works to disguise the importance of discursive struggles in producing policies. Discourse is defined here as "an ensemble of ideas, concepts and categories through which meaning is given to phenomena" (Hajer 1995: 45), that shape and are shaped by social practices and institutions. A dominant interpretation requires a system of inclusion and exclusion: "discourses frame certain problems; that is to say, they distinguish some aspects of the situation rather than others" (Hajer 1995: 45). For instance, monetarist discourses, the economic theory underlying neoliberal approaches to macroeconomic management, view inflation as the consequence of excessive money creation by the central bank (rather than conflicts over the distribution of income or increases in the price of oil), fiscal activism as irremediably inflationary and distortive (rather than a legitimate policy response during crisis of private sector demand), central-bank support of public debt dynamics as inherently inflationary (rather than stabilizing the price of other assets) because it interferes with market allocation, and a tight monetary policy as corrective of price distortions (with little negative impact on output).

That policy is the product of discursive struggles is most apparent during times of crisis. Crises, according to the Slovenian philosopher Slavoj Žižek (2009), are moments of extraordinary politics that disrupt "existing cognitive mappings," leaving instead an ideological struggle over how to interpret events and think about solutions. In other words, policy responses do not develop out of technical, objective analysis of options but are the result of a political struggle over representing the crisis. Hay (1999) drew a Kuhnian analogy between periods of "exceptional" policy-making, when the parameters of what previously defined rational policy change, followed by periods of "normal" policy-making, when a dominant interpretation draws the boundaries of what is possible in policy.

Crisis is thus useful as a conceptual category to map how a dominant construction of the "problem" is stabilized and becomes hegemonic. As the "legitimate" policy issues come under increased contestation, it becomes increasingly apparent that policies are "shaped by competing narratives, informed by divergent interests" (Scoones 2003: 1). Indeed, narratives, defined as vehicles "for transmitting and making accessible a framework of meaning, that is discourse" (Hajer 1995: 23) have long been advocated as a valuable analytical tool for exploring moments of dislocation (Roe 1991). Framing is essential in all policy-making, providing the tools with which narratives are constructed and "cannot be settled by instrumental rationality precisely because it frames that" (Apthorpe and Gasper 1996: 6). By imposing a certain meaning and order onto a series of disjointed events, policy narratives provide a method for creating categories and spaces amenable for interventions, stabilizing the assumptions needed for policy-making while marginalizing competing approaches and closing down policy spaces (Keely 1997). Essential to any policy narrative is its complicity with politics, what Currie (1998) called the ideological function: not what it includes, but what it leaves out of the story.

Thus, Niebyl's (1946) approach will be modified to retrieve the politics of central banking from rationalist representations. Indeed, there is an interesting connection between Karl Niebyl's method of triangulating theory, policy, and reality and discursive approaches to policy analysis. Both view policy as contingent, consolidating through processes that reflect particular institutional configurations, rather than the inevitable product of a rational exercise. Where they differ is in the understanding of "reality," a discrepancy essentially arising from the different role accorded to language and meaning. Niebyl did not consider the politics of meaning in either theorizing or policy, an understandable omission since the foundations of the language turn in philosophy had just been laid by Wittgenstein (Fischer 1998) when Niebyl published his book. For Wittgenstein, language functions as a structuring agent: in other words, it constitutes "reality" rather than describes it. From this perspective, Niebyl's claim that "reality" represents the institutions of finance and production existing at any particular point in time is problematic because it presumes "an objective reality" and "disengaged spectators" as policy-makers and analysts (Howarth 2000). It underestimates how policies structure and are in turn influenced by institutional setups. Instead, critical approaches argue for a more complex relationship between discourses and "reality," where policy discourses have important institutional effects ([re] configuring relations of power or institutional practices) and ideological effects (privileging a particular understanding by casting policy in the neutral language of science) (Mosse 2005).

However, Mosse warns, this does not imply that the implementation "black box" of instrumentalist approaches can be unpacked by an approach that reduces explanations to the all-powerful operation of a hegemonic discourse. In fact, while a particular policy narrative might offer control over the interpretation of events, it is not necessary that the underlying model will be fully translated in practice. An important implication of allowing for the influence of institutional structures is that no one-to-one relationship can be presumed between theory, policy narratives, and central-bank practices, as Niebyl would probably have written today. In other words, *pace* Niebyl, policy models (informed by a particular theoretical conceptualization) might not shape practice in the way they claim, nor provide a guide to policy action. In fact, Mosse argued, the causality might be completely reversed: the endurance of certain policy models arises precisely from their capacity to legitimize certain practices. Central banks, from this perspective, then have to be understood through both what they say (the policy narratives) and what they do (practices of monetary management). And here "traditional tools" for the economist—empirical analysis—are essential in producing an account of practices (and their reconfiguration) in the policy space.

The Romanian case offers a good case study of the politics of monetary policy processes precisely because policy argumentation linked policy success to depoliticization and consistency with "objective" monetarist principles prescribed by international policy advice and conditionality. Indeed, the dominant account of the National Bank of Romania's (NBR) role goes as follows. The success of reform was conditional on policy commitments to neoliberal recipes for reform (Pop 2006). The neo-Communist governments of 1990–1996 failed to uphold these commitments, politically validating a Communist economic legacy, the soft budget constraint. Vested industrial interests were allowed to capture policy implementation against the rational policies agreed in repeated programs with the IMF, in two essential domains of economic reform: monetary policy and exchange-rate policy (IMF 1997a). Politicized economic decisions prevented the central bank, despite its best efforts, from ensuring the macroeconomic stability necessary for a successful marketization. The 1997 election of a right-wing government of declared neoliberal persuasion, applauded as such by international institutions, radically modified the approach to reform. Increasingly, though not consistently, the new government succeeded in separating the economic and political spheres. This allowed an objective formulation and implementation of stability-orientated monetarist policies. Temporary set-backs produced by divisive politics were finally resolved in late 1999, when the President of the country designated the governor of the central bank, Mugur Isărescu (governor since 1990) to become prime minister in a bid to end the bitter infighting of the ruling coalition. Since then, and until the 2008–2009 crisis, Romania became a growth star in the region, finally succeeding in its bid to join the European Union (EU) in January 2007. The 11-month premiership is broadly credited to have made a decisive break with the past and to have contributed to the creation of a near-mythical image of the governor as a competent, apolitical technocrat to whom public opinion turns at every moment of frustration with incompetent politics. As a testimony to the influence he commands in domestic politics, Mugur Isărescu remains governor of the central bank to date (2010), the world's longest-standing bank governor. The adoption of inflation-targeting in August 2005 further strengthened the commitments to sound economic principles and also contributed to sheltering Romania from the initial manifestations of the financial crisis affecting developed economies from 2007. While the crisis was to eventually hit Romania toward the end of 2008, it was an unavoidable consequence of the increasing interdependencies in the world economy. The central bank governor confidently stated that Romania was in a good position, better than ever before, to weather the crisis, because of its record of careful monetary management and the credibility conferred by the inflation-targeting regime (Isărescu 2008a).

This book will propose a different account. It concurs with Pop (2006) that it is misleading to suggest that neoliberalism gained ground only after the 1997 shift in the political will to reform. Instead, the entire period under analysis can be mapped as an ongoing process of neoliberalization with shifting characteristics. Hay (2004) or Peck and Tickell (2002) have convincingly argued that neoliberalism(s), while variegated in their localized manifestations, have shared an underlying logic of change: from the destructive attack on the Keynesian state (Peck and Tickell 2002) during years of exceptional politics (Hay 2004) to a constructive mode of normalized neoliberalism where the political construction of markets is mediated by the patterns of integration in international financial markets. This logic of change has also been at play in the CEE region, and it is the contribution of the book to the growing financialization literature to map how central banks have become increasingly embedded in neoliberal paradigms and networks of economic governance.

Structure of the book

To develop the above arguments, the book is divided in two main parts. Part I, 'The Political Economy of Central Banking', discusses the conceptual underpinnings of a post-Niebylian approach that emphasizes discursive struggles in the policy space. The policy advocacy of two important monetary theorists, John Maynard Keynes and Milton Friedman—and the replacement of monetarism with inflation-targeting—illustrates well that monetary policies have a necessary political dimension, more apparent during times of exceptional politics and better disguised during periods of "normal" policy-making. The attention to historical detail is not exhaustive but instead has two broader aims. A first aim acknowledges that the central-banking literature does not usually make for compelling reading because it is couched in highly technical terms. Yet, since the 2007 crisis in the US subprime market, the dynamics of interbank money markets came under unprecedented scrutiny in public arenas. The chapter seeks to harness this unusual willingness to engage with the jargon of central banking because the analysis of neoliberalism and financialization lose analytical strength without understanding the argumentative texture behind monetary policy. Second, the history of central banking throughout the 20th century is a story of shifting allegiances, voluntary or imposed, between states and markets. The battles fought have been strikingly similar, even if now they involve different actors and more complex practices. While some of the crisis responses between 2007 and 2009 brought macroeconomic policy back to elementary Keynesianism (quantitative easing and fiscal activism in developed countries), the spread of sovereign debt problems throughout the EU triggered calls for fiscal retrenchments echoing Milton Friedman's distaste for government. Indeed, Keynes's influential policy advocacy succeeded in subordinating monetary policy to the imperatives of public debt sustainability and identified the Treasury as the locus of economic competence, an uneasy position for the Bank of England. With the demise of Keynesianism, monetarism changed the image of competent economic policy-makers: governments lost credibility, to be replaced by markets and a central bank that ensured the stability necessary for markets to allocate resources efficiently. The ascendance of monetarism in international development discourse, particularly in the IMF's crisis interventions, was instrumental in spreading the neoliberal economic management model to developing countries, the CEE region included. When even the immense ideological appeal could not hide the empirical problems and policy uselessness underlying monetarism, inflation-targeting articulated a new vision of policy devolved to (and in some extreme cases working with) markets—which, political economists pointed out, was a neutral way of describing the unprecedented influence financial markets played in policy formulation.

The second part turns to monetary policy processes in Central and Eastern Europe. O'Neill's (1997) question is reformulated to ask: What does the central bank do when the state, defined through its central planning legacy, "retreats" from the market? The focus on power and politics in the policy space prompts a different set of reflections on the role of the central bank in the reconstitution of the post-socialist Romanian economy as neoliberal economy. Two broad periods are described through post-Niebylian lenses (see Table 2.2).

In the period of roll-back neoliberalism (1990–1996), through a combination of divisive politics, repeated economic crisis, and a singularly intense relationship with the IMF, the central bank was instrumental in the redefinition of the relationship between state-owned production and state-owned banks along "impatient finance" lines. The repeated failures to uphold commitments with the IMF should not be interpreted as an indication that Romanian politics were singularly ill equipped to deal with the discipline of austerity. Instead the representation "good policies" vs. "bad politics" had a clear ideological function: to sideline the role played by monetary policy decisions in redefining the relationship between finance and state-owned enterprises (SOEs).

The opening to global financial markets during the period of roll-out neoliberalism (after 1997) brought about institutional changes that saw Romania increasingly resemble neighbouring countries. Similar to other CEE countries, policy innovations were introduced to respond to, and attract, foreign capital flows. As bank privatization changed the patterns of ownership from state to private and from national to foreign, the central bank's strategies of exchange rate and liquidity management contributed to the financialization of banking-sector activity, of money markets, and of currency markets, the last accelerated by the entry of nonresident investment activity. This left Central and Eastern Europe highly vulnerable to volatility in international financial markets. The crisis responses in Romania and Hungary, both forced by global deleveraging to request IMF emergency assistance, indicate that it would be misleading to treat central banks as simple vehicles for neoliberal intentions and financialized practices. While the agreements rearticulated policy commitments to financialization, practices of central banking in Romania have sought to redefine the rules of engagement with international financial markets. A successful politics of resistance, the book concludes, will require central banks to renounce neoliberal suspicions, to prioritize public debt sustainability and to eventually turn, as the United Nations Conference on Trade and Development (UNCTAD) (2007) advised, to East Asian style of heterodox macroeconomic policies as alternative to neoliberal macroeconomic policies.

Part I

The Political Economy of Central Banking

2
The Political Economy of Central Banking: From Keynesianism to Inflation-targeting

Central banks, as Charles Goodhart (1988) put it, are institutions best described by the Chinese curse "May you live in interesting times." Indeed, one recurring theme of economic policy discussions throughout the 20th century, intensely debated during times of crisis, focused on the relationship between central banks, governments, and financial markets: should or indeed could central banks stay above politics? Was there a special case to be made for central-bank intervention during crisis, and what form should those interventions take?

During severe economic dislocations, "extraordinary" policy measures prepare the ground for contesting paradigms of central banking. Whether the paradigm can ride the storm or whether the crisis brings theoretical and institutional change is a question of politics rather than theoretical relevance: it depends on conflicting narrations of the crisis and the political power of the "discourse coalitions" sustaining a particular narration. In other words, the nexus theory–practice of central banking is not an evolutionary process of improvement guided by the development of academic scholarship.

Three narratives of monetary policy, and the transition from one to another, will be discussed to explore how the relationship between central banking, markets, and governments has changed over time. The first starts with Keynes's policy advocacy during the tumultuous 1930s and ends with the political demise of the Keynesian welfare state during the 1970s. Its successor, Chicago School monetarism, offers an interesting instance of a theory with at best a transitory influence on practices of central banking but immense ideological appeal. The foundational status of monetarism cannot be understood outside its articulation with the hegemony of neoliberalism as a paradigm of economic management. When mainstreamed into the IMF's stabilization strategy, monetarism became instrumental in the extension of the neoliberal paradigm of economic management to Central and Eastern European post-socialist transformations. Once monetarism outlived its usefulness in the political economy of neoliberalism, it was replaced with inflation-targeting – a policy strategy derived from New Keynesian economics that seeks to overtly enlist the market in the conduct of monetary policy. The increasing dominance of this policy regime raised analytical challenges for the study of economic policy under neoliberalism, so far unresolved. While it is accepted that inflation-targeting offers a policy regime better suited than monetarism to articulate the concerns of an increasingly financialized regime of accumulation, the actual operation of inflation-targeting in the political economy of financialization, and the geopolitical dimensions of this link, have not yet received much attention.

2.1 The Keynesian narrative of monetary policy discretion

The Keynesian paradigm of economic policy is commonly described as a "victory" of fiscal activism in the pursuit of full employment that assigned monetary policy a secondary, supporting role shaped by a "cheap money policy" (Friedman 1978; Hall 1999). Such an ordering of policy priorities arises from Keynesian narrations of economic crisis: namely that these are produced by unfettered market forces (in a system dominated by classical economics), to be addressed by strong states. However, both Keynes's journey to the "depression economics" of *The General Theory of Employment, Interest and Money* and the Bank of England's struggles with the image of an institution "selflessly working for the public good" (Goodhart 1989: 296) defined through the concerns of welfare capitalism suggests more complex, and at times overtly conflicting, relationships and policy processes. While the policy innovations from *A Tract on Monetary Reform* (1923) to *A Treatise on Money* (1930) and then *The General Theory of Employment, Interest and Money* (1936) show, at first sight, the abandonment of monetary policy as the tool to fight pessimistic expectations, the effectiveness of postwar Keynesianism depended in the first instance on macroeconomic policy coordination. In other words, the Keynesian paradigm of economic management redefined rather than marginalized the role of the central bank: the monetary activism associated with the use of the interest rate is replaced with the prioritizing of public debt sustainability through sophisticated debt management techniques (Kennedy 1962; Gowland 1984).

2.1.1 A Ricardian and Wicksellian prelude: Theoretical and institutional innovations

Keynes's engagement with monetary theory drew on two key figures of monetary theory: David Ricardo and Knut Wicksell. The first dominated British monetary thought and policy throughout the 19th century, at least until Keynes's re-reading of Wicksellian arguments helped monetary theory break its way out of the Ricardian spell.

Ricardian monetary theory developed during the Bullionist Controversies in the early 19th century, based on an unshaken faith in the virtues of the Gold Standard. It conceptualized an economic system governed by equilibrium forces and a sound financial system based upon and restrained by gold reserves (Viner 1955). The equilibrating forces of a gold-based monetary system were derived from an automatic adjustment mechanism produced by international commodity trade: any excess of gold, brought about by a general fall in the aggregate exchange value of commodities or the discovery of new mines, would drive its price below metallic value and increase commodity prices. The subsequent export of gold would see a fall in commodity prices that restored equilibrium.

The quantity theory of money causality embedded in the Ricardian narrative (a change in the quantity of money translates into price adjustments) offered an unambiguous view of central banking: significant disturbances would appear where the Bank of England printed paper money in excess of gold reserves, as was the case after the 1796 suspension of the convertibility of bank notes into gold. The suspension sought to avoid the threat that the wars with France, a commercial crisis, and the attending pressures on gold reserves would produce a major financial crisis (Viner 1955). While formally it applied only to Bank of England notes and maintained other issuing financial institutions under obligation to redeem notes in gold, in practice the suspension acquired a general character because of the role of the Bank of England in the financial system. Traditionally, London had been the dominant centre of finance as the residence of most major merchants (Cameron 1967). The Bank of England was set up in 1694, both as a bank to the government and as an institution to cater to the financial affairs of trade capitalism. It provided loans and discounted bills of exchange and promissory notes for London merchants. By the end of the 18th century, the Bank of England increased its strategic importance by becoming a de-facto monopoly issuer of paper means of payment in the London area. The competitive advantage of its position as the banker of the government had driven all London private banks to cease paper issuing by 1750, and, as a consequence, all large transactions were settled in Bank of England banknotes. Despite holding the country's gold reserves, the Bank of England had not assumed, however, what would later be identified as the distinguishing features of a central bank: it did not engage in discounting operations with private banks, nor did it allow all banks to hold deposit accounts (reserves).

While the extensive use of paper money triggered the first large-scale investigation in monetary matters, the laws governing commodity circulation dominated the Bullionist debate. Ricardo challenged the Bank of England lending strategy below "the rate of profit which can be made by the employment of capital".[3] The ensuing unlimited demand for paper money undermined the strict correspondence to gold and distorted the automatic adjustment: "If profits be high, and the Bank is willing to lend at low interest, can there be any conceivable number of bank notes which may not be applied for?" To restore the mechanism, Ricardo insisted that new forms of money must be forced to behave according to the laws governing commodity money, removing the temptation for Bank of England to create money in excess of gold reserves even during times of crisis.

British monetary legislation during the 19th century thus sought to establish a blueprint for institutional change derived from Ricardian economic ideas (Niebyl 1946). The 1844 Bank Charter Act gave legal standing to Ricardo's idea that the Bank of England had to be prevented from acting as a lender of last resort. It separated its Banking Department – envisaged to act as any other private banking institution – from the Issue Department, now an automatic exchange "bureau" from paper to gold and vice versa.[4] Moreover, by restricting access to the gold reserves in the Issue Department for external payments, it left the Banking Department with little resources to deal with situations of crisis.

Initially, the Bank of England quietly endorsed the Ricardian-inspired Peel Act because it allowed it to pursue its discount business without having to worry about its role (or accountability) for the functioning of the Gold Standard (Viner 1955). Yet competing pressures for institutional change arose from the increasingly complex financial relationships driven by industrialization. A succession of financial panics made it clear that the multiple functions of the financial system, combining lending to production with a range of speculative activities, required an institution willing to supply emergency liquidity to banks during panics and to protect gold reserves[5] (Thornton 1802; Bagehot 1876). Against Ricardian suspicions, the Bank Charter Act had to be suspended repeatedly to allow the Bank of England to exercise the lender-of-last-resort function.

Thus, throughout the 19th century, Bank of England institutional practices became increasingly embedded in the operations of the Gold Standard, both as lender of last resort and in the relationship with the banks. The increasing monetization attending industrialization saw the London Discount Market – an institutional structure composed of discount houses approximating today's wholesale/interbank market where banks trade liquidity with each other – gradually emerging as central to practices of monetary management. An increasingly integrated banking sector could mobilize capital more easily so that the practice of trading bills was extended to lending money with bills as collateral, an innovation that would greatly simplify the process of obtaining liquidity in a system somewhat constrained by the rigid time-consuming process of trading bills or holding large cash reserves (Niebyl 1946). The growing liquidity and volume of the interbank market had conflictive implications for the Bank of England operations. While the remarkable expansion in (joint-stock) banking threatened its discount business, gold movements responded to interbank interest rates rather than its own discount rate (Niebyl 1946). The functioning of the Gold Standard, that beacon of free-market ideology, required the development of institutional mechanisms that strengthened the central bank's control over money-market interest rates – in the language of the time, the institutional changes were described as "bringing the market into the Bank," a policy practice that has maintained its relevance ever since.

The pressures to reconcile private and public interests became apparent: the Bank of England's lending operations positioned it in direct competition with the discount banks it was expected to rescue during panics, a dilemma it also faced when it had to raise interest rates to restrain the gold outflows. Commercial banks' increased ability to mobilize liquidity, fostered by innovations that replaced banknotes with bills of exchange and bank deposits as instruments of credit, reduced dependence on liquidity from the Bank of England. By the late 1890s, the Bank of England had serious difficulties in influencing market rates. On several occasions, it raised the interest rate without attracting gold, as it failed to affect the interbank market.

In response, a radical overhaul in practices signalled the acceptance of the Bank of England's role in the Gold Standard. The 1890 introduction of open-market operations (OMOs) instituted interventions on the money market through the purchase or sale of debt instruments to increase or decrease liquidity and to bring market interest rates in line with the bank rate (Sayers 1976). OMOs had an asymmetric character, undertaken predominantly to defend gold reserves through a tightening of money market liquidity that raised interest rates. The Bank of England also institutionalized discount window lending, an extension of the lender-of-last-resort facility that allowed banks to borrow against collateral at any time rather than only during a crisis. From its early competitive position, the Bank of England realigned its interests with those of the financial sector.

Despite such a rapid pace of institutional change, most theoretical innovations after 1850 failed to move away significantly from the commodity money story. Menger's famous integration of money in the marginalist revolution was entirely based on commodity money (Ingham 1999)[6], a testimony to the strength of the Ricardian narrative.

Indeed, the narrative of automatic adjustment successfully simplified complex monetary processes while paying little analytical attention to the fast industrial expansion. It first imposed a strict definition of money as a commodity and thus refused to accept that the laws governing its circulation might follow a different logic. Aside from gold, it defined bank notes as the only legitimate form of money, as gold certificates rather than instruments of credit. The implications of either the widespread use of bills of exchange, which tended to adjust to the financing needs of the system in times of liquidity shortages, or bank deposits had not been addressed because of the challenges these raised to the automatic adjustment mechanism (Niebyl 1946).

Knut Wicksell, a quantity theorist of the late 19th century, sought to challenge what he viewed as an outdated depiction of the relationship between finance and production. Whereas Ricardian theory insisted on gold (and gold-based paper money), he held that the widespread use of instruments of credit as means of payment freed the banking system from the scarcity constraints of the gold reserves and, more fundamentally, broke down the quantity-theory relationship between the quantity of money and prices (Wicksell 1962: 76).

Wicksell's account constructed a credit-only economy, where transactions were settled through bank deposits[7], with no possible interference from cash (both coin and paper) governed by quantity-theory logic. At the centre of the Wicksellian story are two interest rates: a (bank) monetary rate and a natural rate (real, governed by the productivity of capital). Their divergence triggers a cumulative process of price movements.

The money rate, i.e. the rate charged on loans to entrepreneurs, is set within the credit economy by the banking system[8]. On the contrary, the natural rate of interest is determined in equilibrium by the supply and demand for capital in a system without money or credit where all lending is done in the form of real capital goods[9]. When the bank rate is equal to the natural one, there is no credit creation in the economy. This only occurs when the banks' rate falls below the natural rate, ultimately resulting in an increase in prices. Essentially, it is not the mere divergence from natural levels that brings about the change in prices but rather that the banking system has it in its power to maintain the short-term rate at a level low enough and for long enough to influence the long-term rate (i.e. bond rate). The transmission mechanism, later echoed by New Keynesian theories, links long-term interest rates with spending and investment decisions, an aggregate demand explanation of inflationary pressures[10]. There is a further cumulative element in the upward price movement, as bank rates below equilibrium levels induce business to repeatedly set their production plans higher and thus increase the demand for factors of production, adding to inflationary pressures[11]. Cumulative price increases would be curtailed because bank reserves would not sustain *ad infinitum* the public demand for gold, so that banks would eventually have to raise the money rate to the "natural level." The adjustment mechanism regains the automaticity of the commodity money system (Laidler 2004: 25). But the adjustment is not necessarily immediate: Wicksell noted that banks maintained excess reserves for substantial periods of time (Leijonhufvud 2007).

While Wicksell effectively sanctioned policy interventions to accelerate the adjustment, his account retained the quantity-theory concerns with inflation, a theoretical conceptualization which would later provide the cornerstone for New Keynesian monetary theories. Given the uncertainties surrounding the exact level of the natural rate, he advised a simple policy rule-immediate interest-rate adjustments in response to inflationary pressures:

> So long as the prices remain unaltered the banks' rate of interest is to remain unaltered. If prices rise, the interest rate is to be raised; and if prices fall, the interest rate is to be lowered; and the rate of interest is henceforth to be maintained at its new level until a further movement of prices calls for a further change in a direction or other. (Wicksell 1962: 189)

Wicksell's account reclaimed the theoretical relevance of the central bank and the banking system, recognizing that interest-rate decisions influence credit dynamics. The importance of the institutional characteristics of the banking system is twofold: first, it justifies the setting of a pure credit economy, and second, by delaying automatic adjustments, it justifies policy interventions. Further reflecting on the policy implications, Wicksell (1962: 191) noted an essential challenge to the applicability of his theory: the Gold Standard, which tailored policy decisions to external considerations rather than domestic price dynamics. This was not a shortcoming of the theory but evidence that the Gold Standard was no longer suitable for an increasingly interdependent world economy. He recommended a fundamental overhaul that replaced the obsolete arrangement with an international paper standard and institutionalized international cooperation between central banks to maintain the stability of prices.

These reflections would provide theoretical foundations for the Keynesian narratives of monetary activism.

2.1.2 Monetary policy and the Keynesian welfare state: The journey from the Treatise to the General Theory

The dominance of the Ricardian account as an interpretative framework cemented the idea of a policy process on automatic pilot with nothing to offer for political priorities or interest groups. Ricardian theories promised to wrestle control away from the Bank of England and to place it in the hands of the market. Nevertheless, in practice, monetary management bore little resemblance to the automatic adjustment mechanism. Rather than informing practice, the Ricardian policy models functioned as a legitimizing device to allow Bank of England autonomy in pursuing the interests of the financial sector (Bain and Howells 1999).

The interwar period put an end to the autonomous conduct of monetary policy, replacing it with increasing contestations as governments and politicians began to change their subdued acceptance of the Ricardian narrative (Elgie and Thomson 1998). This became fully apparent during the postwar reflections on the desirability to return to the Gold Standard. Whereas the financial community and the Bank of England hailed Britain's 1925 decision to unilaterally reinstate the Gold Standard at the pre-war parity as the cornerstone of return to stability, the contractionary consequences of an overvalued pound led government and academic concerns toward unemployment. While the Bank of England refused to accept any theoretical connection between its interest-rate policy and unemployment – a money-neutrality argument – politicians worried that the rising unemployment was undermining social cohesion (Chick 1983). Yet the effectiveness of political arguments was undermined by the lack of a theoretical framework that explained the relationship between interest rates and the internal economy, leaving a frustrated Winston Churchill to complain about his impotence in preventing several interest-rate increases (Elgie and Thompson 1998).

The increasing deterioration of internal economic conditions prompted the first public inquiry into monetary policy: the 1929 Macmillan Committee on Finance and Industry (Sayers 1976). The title itself questioned the money-neutrality assumptions underpinning monetary policy, a scepticism toward the Bank of England's position further strengthened by Keynes's appointment to the committee. Even if intended "to give the appearance, not the reality, of radical movement" (Skidelsky 2005: 419), Keynes's heterodox reading of unemployment, that the interest rate (rather than the real wage) was too high (Chick 1983), would leave a mark on the proceedings.

The final report was the result of an intense process of negotiation and compromise (Stamp 1931). While it avoided incriminating the Bank of England, it insisted that the depression was linked to monetary issues: the monetary system was found to have failed "to solve successfully a problem of unprecedented difficulty and complexity set it by a conjunction of highly intractable phenomena" (Macmillan Committee 1930: 93). To inflate the economy, the Macmillan Committee recommended discretionary monetary policy while maintaining the Gold Standard. The case for discretion first challenged the traditional story of automatic adjustment which, the Report warned, sidelined the connection between the Bank (of England) rate and domestic credit conditions. The central bank rate was thus rescued from the theoretical obscurity to which the Ricardian narrative had condemned it, "a delicate and beautiful instrument" of monetary policy that involved two conflicting policy objectives: the maintenance of the Gold Standard and internal lending. Still, the concerns with the Gold Standard prevailed: contractionary implications aside, the Report held that monetary policy was better suited to target external stability.

The Report hinted at the need for a new instrument of monetary policy: "the monetary authority is not as powerless as is sometimes supposed," a sentence widely attributed to Keynes (Stamp 1931). The answer, I suggest, can be found in the original source of most of the revolutionary ideas the Report contained, Keynes's *A Treatise on Money*.

Keynes's 1923 *A Tract on Monetary Reform* had already suggested institutional innovations that would have allowed central banks' interest rates to function outside the Gold Standard. While accepting the political necessity of the Gold Standard, Keynes suggested direct market interventions, through the sale or purchase of gold – an innovative policy he saw at work during his civil-service period in the India office. This would ensure the defence of the Gold Standard and allow the Bank of England to tailor its interest rate decisions, along Wicksellian lines, to influence credit dynamics and economic activity. The *Treatise* was intended to provide theoretical grounding for his early policy recommendations[12].

However, the *Treatise* developed a different policy narrative, a shift arising from Keynes's recognized flexibility in dealing with policy issues (Skidelsky 2005). It redefined policy room for manoeuver by framing OMOs as the instrument and bank reserves as the operational target of monetary policy, a strategic choice emerging from Keynes's participation in the Macmillan hearings.

OMOs had entered policy discourse as a discretionary policy instrument in the USA after the November 1919 crisis that saw massive hikes in interest rates to defend the Gold Standard. Bindseil (2004) explained it as a discursive device to shift away from responsibility for the contractionary impact of short-term interest-rate decisions[13]. In British policy practice, OMOs were nothing new[14] – a method of making the central bank rate effective in the money market to attract inflows of gold introduced in 1890. Nevertheless, Phillips's theoretical formulation of the money multiplier (1920) paved the way for a conceptual shift, from OMOs as passive instrument of monetary policy subordinated to interest-rate decisions to an active tool of credit control through control of bank reserve positions. This suited perfectly Keynes's attempt to move away from interest-rate accounts of policy discretion.

The money-multiplier story's appealing simplicity is, in a similar fashion to the Ricardian excess-money story, rooted in an automatic adjustment mechanism. The account went as follows: through OMOs, the central bank determined the desired level of bank reserves. If the policy intervention aimed to increase the money stock, the central bank would buy government securities and would pay for these by creating high-powered money. The effect on bank reserves depended on the counterpart to their purchase (the banks or the public). Only if they bought from banks were bank reserves affected directly and in full. Reserves would also be affected if the public deposited their proceeds, but not if they switched from treasury bills to corporate securities or goods. The excess reserves, that is, banks' current account holdings with the central bank over the required reserves, automatically set off an increased lending activity (i.e. the multiplier mechanism). The asset adjustment would "trigger liabilities adjustment, bringing the reserves to the required level and the money stock to the level desired by the policy intervention" (Gabor, 2008: 513).

Keynes thought to integrate this new adjustment mechanism with the Wicksellian theoretical framework. From the Wicksellian connection the *Treatise* retained the explanation of price level changes on account of the difference between the natural and the monetary rates of interest produced by activity in the credit market, and the emphasis on the importance of long-term rates for investment (Leijonhufvud 1981).

Keynes enlarged and modified the Wicksellian framework to support the essential policy recommendation of the Macmillan Report: the desirability of tailoring policy activism to internal considerations. The adjustment process is nevertheless quite different in the Keynesian narrative; OMOs are constructed as an instrument of a much more interventionist nature than the interest rate. Keynes (1930) first asked "how the quantity of money is related to reserve money," an enquiry into the stability of the money multiplier. For policy purposes and despite the inadequacy of the crude quantity theory of money, he maintained that: "the quantity of money remains [...] of exceptional practical significance because it is the most controllable factor" (Keynes 1930: 49).

The important question to address, he maintained, was the outcome of a reserve[15] injection through OMOs. To reframe policy through the multiplier, it was necessary to prove that banks would not hold excess reserves – if they did (for instance, during periods of high uncertainty), then the predictable relationship between reserve injections and bank deposits would break down[16]. Keynes discarded such a possibility because banks could exchange excess reserves for interest-yielding assets on the interbank market (an argument later marshalled against Friedman's money-multiplier story – see Goodhart 1994). However, the reconciliation of a money-multiplier framework with the operations of the interbank money market required various argumentative turns. In response to a reserves injection, banks turned to the interbank market[17] twice (see Figure 2.1): first to dispose of any excess reserves and second, once the stock of money was settled, to decide the composition of the asset side. To prove that the central bank, and not commercial banks, dictated reserve positions, the Keynesian narrative declared the first stage was "irrelevant": choice

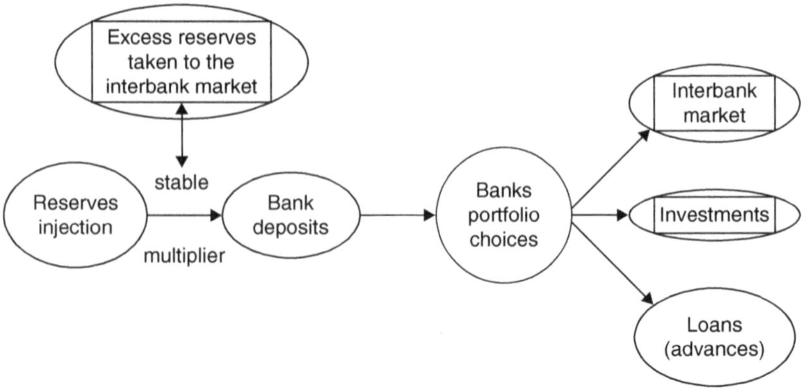

Figure 2.1 The money multiplier process in the *Treatise on Money*
Source: Produced by author from the *Treatise on Money* (Keynes, 1930).

was only exercised over the second stage and within the constraints of the reserves-determined bank deposits:

> what bankers are ordinarily deciding is, not how much they will lend in the aggregate – this is mainly settled for them by the state of their reserves – but in what forms they will lend – in what proportion they will divide their resources between the different kinds of investment which are open to them. (Keynes 1930: 67)

Portfolio preferences are then exercised between the interbank money market, investments, and loans (advances), in this order of liquidity, depending on expectations. While loans to customers (for working capital purposes) can fluctuate over time, in the aggregate credit activity is constrained by reserve positions according to the money multiplier causality.

Thus, Keynes suggested that an injection of reserves would set, via the money multiplier, credit and monetary expansion. Discretionary policy-making means, in fact, discretionary OMOs rather than discretionary interest-rate decisions. OMOs, Keynes held, granted the Bank of England an "absolute control over the creation of credit by the member banks" (1930: 225).

What accounts for this conceptual shift from the *Tract* to the *Treatise?* Keynes's advocacy of using Indian-style direct interventions on the gold market would have helped isolate interest-rate decisions from balance-of-payments considerations. And, indeed, he began the Macmillan hearings with a strong critique of the Bank of England for having neglected the contractionary consequences of imposing high rates to defend the Gold Standard. However, the Bank of England's response, seeking to avoid responsibility for the depression, forced Keynes to revise his narrative: bank officials denied the link between the bank rate and overall credit conditions, a revival of the Real Bills doctrine where credit is demand-driven (Sayers 1976; Skidelsky 2005). Because the Bank of England's position that "there is always the right amount of credit" ran contrary to the agenda for interest-rate manipulations, Keynes's recognized pragmatism led to a redefinition of monetary activism through OMOs.

Would OMOs work independently of the central bank rate? The traditional position held that liquidity-tightening OMOs would be offset through borrowing from the central bank's discount window (through discount houses) unless accompanied by a change in the central bank rate – indeed, Keynes accepted that the effectiveness of liquidity-draining operations in increasing money-market rates ultimately required the Bank of England to prevent access to the discount window by raising its discount rate (by then it was accepted that the central bank would accommodate demand for liquidity as a lender of last resort).

Put differently, Keynes was less interested in the consistency of the multiplier account than in the effects of a monetary stimulus through open-market policy. While insisting that liquidity injections would have a direct effect on bank reserves and credit without a sizable effect on market rates (rates would fall "later a little lower" if at all), the important effect lay elsewhere. The technique of implementation involving long-maturity gilts (bonds) would have a direct effect on long-term interest rates and investment activity, à la Wicksell.

Keynes understood that a critique of a dominant policy narrative is effective to the extent that it manages to construct its own story. Just as Ricardo had promised the critics of the Bank of England a world of automatic adjustments and equilibrium free of the "dangerous" intervention of the monetary authority, Keynes offered those sceptical of equilibrium a central bank that could engineer a successful postwar economic recovery. This required the development of an equally straightforward counter-narrative, and in this Keynes could not escape the simplistic nature of the narrative he was trying to displace. The Macmillan hearings made it clear that a narrative built around the central bank rate would not be powerful enough to change policy, as the bank officials' Real Bills doctrine would have caused lengthy controversies unsuited for his sense of urgency. In response, he proposed a policy innovation: OMOs to influence long-term interest rates rather than to make the Bank of England interest rate effective in the short-term money market, an account that required a money-multiplier framing. Even though in between the lines the *Treatise* recognized that OMOs cannot be separated from bank-rate decisions because of the operating principles of the call money market, the inconsistencies did not invalidate the key message: discretionary monetary management in the form of reserve injections would trigger increased investment activity, if not by increasing banks' willingness to lend, then by lowering long-term rates through the bank's participation on the bond market – a rationale emphasized by the Bank of England as the basis for its policy of quantitative easing during 2008–2009.

Indeed, in the *Treatise*, the signal of the divergence between the natural and the monetary rates of interest is a rise or fall in investment that would further trigger price adjustments (Leijonhufvud 1981). A monetary effect requires a monetary treatment; hence it is the role of the central bank to correct the market rate, by interventions at the long end of the market through an extraordinary dosage of open market purchases "to the point of satisfying to saturation the desire of the public to hold savings deposits" (Keynes 1930: 370). This amounted to an extreme intervention for extreme circumstances, best suited to bring long-rates down when the "bearishness of the public" was not very strong.

It is important to point out that the *Treatise* narrative assigns the central bank an essentially enabling role in a market-driven paradigm of economic management: its discretionary liquidity policies create the necessary conditions for the private sector (businesses) to resume investment and growth. The underlying policy principle, of governing "at a distance," would reappear in the 1980s shift to neoliberalism (Rose and Miller 1992).

2.1.3 The suspension of the Gold Standard and the General Theory

Keynes's rhetorical efforts to construct an alternative to the interest-rate policy under the constraints of the Gold Standard were neutralized by a deepening crisis in the world and British economies. The instability following the 1929 US stock-market crash increased the difficulties of maintaining the Gold Standard, which Britain abandoned in 1931, only six years after reinstating it. The *Treatise*'s policy proposals were translated into practice: the conversion of the 1917 5 percent war loan rate, commonly understood to have been an essential factor in maintaining interest rates on securities at high levels, marked the beginning of a period of cheap money policy (Sayers 1976).

The policy failed to produce the expected fall in long-term interest rates and recovery in investment. Keynes's next publication, the 1936 *The General Theory of Employment, Interest and Money*, signalled his scepticism that monetary policy could effectively respond to the extraordinary depression. The power of the Bear Army – the private sector's expectations acting to curtail credit and investment[18] – had to be confronted by a strong public-spending program. Fiscal policy thus became the instrument of short-term stabilization efforts.

The new focus of the *General Theory* on liquidity preference retained the Keynesian narrative of monetary policy articulated in the *Treatise*. OMOs remained the instrument for arriving at a "given" stock of money, through the money multiplier.

The apparent continuity understates the radical shift in the principles of economic management after World War II and the institutional changes in central banking it brought about. The 1944 White Paper translated Keynes's economic ideas into a public commitment to full employment. The Bank of England was nationalized soon after (1946), a move that testified to concerns that its preference for the Gold Standard was inimical to the policy priorities of a Keynesian agenda.

Whereas the central bank of the *Treatise* conducted discretionary OMOs to stimulate private investment, the golden period of the Keynesian state reconfigured practices of monetary management around the sustainability of public debt to underpin fiscal activism. Exchange rates were fixed under the Bretton Woods system, while the money-multiplier account lost policy relevance – as the 1959 Radcliffe report put it: "the control of money supply to be no more than an important facet of debt management" (in Kaldor 1982: 6). The external challenges of the "cheap money" policy were addressed by capital controls (promoted by Keynes in the Bretton Woods negotiations) as pressures for interest-rate equalization under free capital mobility ran antagonistic to public debt sustainability.

The Bank of England resented such a loss of autonomy, particularly because it had important consequences for the role of sterling (and the City of London) in the international monetary system. For the next thirty years, it would insist on incorporating external considerations into policy decisions, somewhat more successfully during Conservative governments, more inclined to accept rises in the interest rate. However, regardless of political persuasions, governments insisted on retaining control over monetary policy formulation (Elgie and Thomson 1999).

Ironically, the political success of Keynesian ideas in elevating the state to a central role in smoothing unemployment and business cycles created an inescapable policy dilemma. Negative economic outcomes could no longer be assigned to ill-functioning markets but were interpreted as the consequence of mistaken policy decisions. The attending legitimation crisis (Habermas 1973 in Krippner, 2007: 479) marked intense efforts to define an effective response to inflationary pressures throughout the 1960s and early 1970s. A shared reluctance to pressure trade unions into wage restraint reduced anti-inflationary policies to two possible avenues: either fiscal or monetary restraint to reduce aggregate demand. The choice was not easily resolved. Fiscal restraint questioned the commitments to full employment. Yet interest-rate decisions affected financial institutions rather than individual spending, so that the first-order effect of interest-rate rises could raise concerns for the solvency and viability of the financial sector (Kaldor 1982). Such a narrowing of policy options resulted in direct ceilings on private credit in order to offset inflationary pressures.

The limited success of credit controls was symptomatic of the larger loss in governments' ability to influence economic conditions in the context of the oil-price shock and the abandonment of the Bretton Woods system, accompanied by relaxing capital controls (Helleiner 1994). Rising unemployment aggravated the dilemmas: to preserve welfare capitalism, public discourses shied away from explaining inflation entirely through wage pressures or fiscal activism. Yet to assign monetary roots to inflation confronted politicians with irreconcilable priorities: the cure – an interest-rate hike – would further aggravate unemployment and reduce growth. Eventually, the 1977 sterling crisis, which required the IMF's intervention, saw the Labour government abdicating the common wisdom prevailing in academic circles (as, for instance, expressed by the Radcliffe Report), that the quantity of money – in whatever definition – had no policy relevance. The adoption of monetary growth targets shifted policy debates toward monetarism and its protests against the failures of state-run capitalism.

For many, the crisis of welfare capitalism should have triggered a detailed reflection on the dichotomous portrayal of Keynesianism as a coherent victory of the state over the market (Eatwell 1982). Whereas Keynesianism did succeed in validating the idea that the state could be actively involved in economic management, its application in Britain (less so in Continental Europe) was governed by the principle that economic management had to ultimately place economic decisions in the realm of the private firm. Yet the subsequent policy discussions reappropriated the state–market dichotomy, only to assert this time the primacy of the market and to plead for deregulation in a tragic restoration of the pre-Keynesian status quo (Chick 1983). Of the various economic ideas articulating the "new" ideology, commonly identified as neoliberalism, monetarism and Milton Friedman were initially pivotal in shaping policy debates on macroeconomic management (see Mirowski and Plehwe [2009] for an overview of what they term the "neoliberal thought collective" to capture the increasing influence of neoliberalism in various fields of economic theory).

2.2 Neoliberalism, financialization and central banks

As the combination of high and rising inflation with high and rising unemployment during the 1970s was narrated as a crisis of the Keynesian state, monetarist warnings of the dangers associated with discretionary monetary policy subordinated to fiscal priorities gained influence. The monetarist articulation of the "economic problem" arising from the state's incapacity to perform as an efficient economic actor fitted well with the right's political diagnostic and offered a blueprint for reforming a state overloaded and overburdened by the hegemony of Keynesianism and corporatism (Hay 2004). The solution appeared simple: predicate economic policy on monetarist foundations, allow markets to get prices right, and roll back the institutions of social protection, as socially optimal outcomes could only be delivered by the market. Indeed, with neoliberalism came an epistemological shift toward a new metric of measurement: the efficiency of the market (Lemke 2001). Efficiency would not only apply to economic activity but also other forms of human action and institutions, instating the market as "a kind of permanent economic tribunal" (Foucault 1978, in Lemke 2001).

Yet it would be a mistake to treat neoliberalism as a static or monolithic project (Mirowski and Plehwe 2009). Instead, Peck and Tickell (2002) identified three historical shifts. What began as a philosophical moment of the early 1970 (a proto-neoliberalism) in the Chicago School of free-market economics was transformed by the Reagan and Thatcher governments (and various dictatorships in Latin America and Asia) into a specific economic-political project seeking to roll back the Keynesian state. From this normative stage, neoliberalism increasingly crystallized in a roll-out (Peck and Tickell 2002) or normalized and necessitarian stage during the 1990s, when it spread quickly from Western countries to the developing world (Hay 2004). These shifts occurred against neoliberalism's resilience and impressive capacity to redefine itself, a resilience which Bourdieu (1998) assigned to its successful alignment with the dominant configurations of political-economic power.

Critical analysis changed to reflect these stages: neoliberalism has been increasingly understood as the transformation rather than the end of politics (Foucault in Lemke 2000: 11). Thus, the understanding of neoliberalism evolved from "monetarism, supply side economics and minimal government" (Plehwe 2009) to a more nuanced representation that emphasizes the construction of neoliberalized modes of (self-)governance and regulatory relations characterized by a logic of re-regulation rather than deregulation (Peck and Tickell 2002). The emphasis on re-regulation allows for diverse and heterogeneous instances, accepting that the degree to which ideological commitments to free markets translate into practice depends on the particularities of national configurations of power and politics.

Monetary-policy discourses broadly echoed these stages, a consequence of the key role central banking occupies in neoliberal agendas of economic management (Krippner 2007). Monetary-policy discourse shifted from the monetarist insistence that discretionary policy obstructed the market's ability to automatically adjust (a roll-back account) to the Wicksellian vision of a central bank instrumental in overcoming the "market rigidities" delaying adjustment – a roll-out moment where (inflation-targeting) policy is important to *support* the market if adequate mechanisms of accountability are in place.

2.2.1 Monetarism and roll-back neoliberalism

Monetarism sought a radical redefinition of the Keynesian approach to economic management, ranging from policy priorities to the hierarchy of policies necessary to achieve these, the instruments and transmission mechanism (Hall 1989). Monetarism premises an economic system in equilibrium. It assigns monetary origins to both inflation and output fluctuations (Laidler 1991). In a Ricardian fashion, maintaining money at a neutral level by constraining the discretionary power of the monetary authority would limit the possibility of major disturbances. Thus, inflation replaces unemployment as policy objective, and monetary policy becomes the primary tool for stabilization. Drawing on the Ricardian equivalence – the theoretical proposition that rational consumers adjust current spending patterns to take into account future tax increases necessary to finance deficit spending, thus offsetting the effects of fiscal activism – monetarism insisted that expansionary fiscal policy, rather than producing the Keynesian crowding-in effects, was inefficient at best and inflationary at worst (see Table 2.1).

Table 2.1 Paradigms of economic management

		Keynesian	Monetarist	Inflation-targeting
Policy goal		Unemployment	Inflation	
Priorities of the policy mix		Fiscal policy	Monetary policy	
Fiscal policy		Crowding in (Keynesian multiplier)	Inefficient: Ricardian equivalence	
Inflation		Cost-driven: mark-up theory of pricing	Aggregate demand pressures: excess money	
Monetary policy		Key priority: public debt dynamics	Money supply growth target	Policy rule: interest-rate manipulation to achieve the inflation target. Output gap concerns. (Output gap monetarism.)
Exchange-rate policy		Fixed exchange rates under Bretton Woods, capital controls	Exchange rate flexibility and full capital account convertibility	
Transmission mechanism for monetary policy	**Instrument**	OMOs (and low base rate)	OMOs	OMOs and standing facilities
	Operational target	Relative sovereign yields	Base money	Short-term money market interest rate
	Intermediary target		Money supply	Aggregate demand (long-term interest rates)
Policy practice		Interest-rate changes made effective through OMOs		

Furthermore, Friedman dismissed the Keynesian concerns about the speculative behaviour of uncontrolled financial markets. Speculation is to be applauded because it functions to stabilize markets: speculators will arbitrage price differentials back to fundamentals (Friedman 1953). To foster this essential role of intermediating economic efficiency, the Keynesian range of repressive instruments (for instance credit ceilings) have to be replaced by full-blown liberalization of the domestic financial system and of international capital flows.

The monetarist narrative of inflation further reformulated the quantity theory of money in terms of a stable demand for money built around Friedman's empirical observation (1956) that monetary processes in the United States supported a consistent relationship between the changes in money supply and money income. With output determined by productivity and individual preferences, it implied that the quantity of money moved in tandem with prices (Laidler 1991).

While a stable demand for money per se could not logically establish a causal relationship from the quantity of money to money-income (Laidler 1991), the neutral money assumption dictated the direction of causality: a central bank fully in command of the money stock determines price dynamics. Once inflation was framed as a problem of discretionary monetary management, the adjustment process echoed the Ricardian excess money narrative. Any excess expansion in the supply of money over the level of desired balances would create additional purchasing power and set off an inflationary process so that the curtailment of inflation necessitates the curtailment of money supply growth.

Defining policy through the neutral-money assumptions changed the representation of the central bank, now a key initiator of monetary change through its decisions to alter reserve positions (Chick 2005), and provided an array of policy instruments defined through a money-multiplier framework. Indeed, a strict consistency with monetarist principles required that the OMOs alone be used to achieve the operational target – bank reserves, and further movements in the money stock (Bindseil 2004). While the monetarist experiments of the early 1980s created a definitional fuzziness in terms of operational targets, Milton Friedman clearly argued that the case for monetarism had to be made by distinguishing between interest rates and base money (bank reserves). The case for targeting bank reserves was not simply a strategic choice, as in the Keynesian story, of which instruments and targets would be politically feasible to advocate, but claimed strong theoretical foundations (Friedman 1968)[19].

Interest rates made a poor target, Friedman explained in his 1968 address to the American Economic Association, "The Role of Monetary Policy". Whereas Keynes's concerns with the time lag involved in bringing down long rates prompted a shift to fiscal activism supported by monetary policies focused on public debt sustainability (Leijonhufvud 1981), Friedman argued that the low interest-rate elasticity of investment and consumption made any policy concerns with interest-rate dynamics difficult to justify. As an example he focused on OMOs that injected reserves and triggered a monetary expansion through the money-multiplier effect, a narrative line similar to Keynes's *Treatise*. Downward pressure on interest rates does not arise, as Keynes argued in the *Treatise*, through operations at the long end of the market but through a downward-sloping liquidity-preference schedule: people can be induced to hold a larger quantity of money only by bidding down interest rates. However, for the same liquidity-preference considerations, the increased spending (excess purchasing power over the real balances desired) would see rising income and a rising liquidity-preference schedule pushing rates back up toward the initial level within "something less than a year." Whereas Keynes admitted that OMOs could not be considered in isolation from their effect on short-term interbank interest rates, Friedman paid little attention to institutional details – an omission necessary to his rejection of interest-rate management.

The criteria used to construct the case against an interest-rate policy produced an account of "good" monetary policy: first and foremost "to prevent itself from being a major source of economic disturbance" (Friedman 1968: 13). This offers a clear articulation of the neoliberal program for institutional change of the central bank: an autonomy from political pressures that allows it to pursue the only objective relevant to optimal market functioning – preventing inflation from disturbing price signals. Policy discretion is only sanctioned in the extreme case where the disturbance is "a clear and present danger"; otherwise a money-growth rule would act as a built-in stabilizer of inflationary expectations:

> My own prescription is still that the monetary authority go all the way in avoiding [...] swings by adopting publicly the policy of achieving a steady rate of growth in a specified monetary total [...] a rate that would achieve rough stability in the level of prices of final products, which I have estimated would call for something like a 3 to 5 percent per year growth in currency plus all commercial bank deposits. (Friedman 1968: 16)

The neoliberal redefinition of policy practices further requires the abandonment of two traditional instruments for managing interbank market liquidity (the reserve requirements or discount window lending [through the standing facilities]), because their discretionary nature would endanger the operation of the automatic mechanism:

> The elimination of discounting and of variable reserve requirements would leave open market operations as the instrument of monetary policy proper. This is by all odds the most efficient instrument and has few of the defects of the other [...] The amounts of purchases and hence the amount of high-powered money to be created thereby determined precisely [...] and render the connection between Federal Reserve action and the changes in the money supply more direct and more predictable and eliminate extraneous influences on reserve policy. (Friedman 1960: 50–51)

Practices of monetary management

Friedman's unabated insistence that excessive money creation accounted for inflationary processes was eventually rewarded: policy in the USA and UK shifted to quantitative targeting to address the inflationary spiral of the 1970s. Monetarist thinking at the Federal Reserve had been in place since 1970, when M1 (i.e. the currency plus non-interest- bearing demand deposits held by the public) was established as an intermediate target, while in UK the 1976 Labour Government flirted with money growth targets in the aftermath of the sterling crisis (Goodhart 1994). Still, interest-rate manipulation remained central to achieving the quantitative target.

The election victory of the Conservative Party in UK and the appointment of a hawkish new governor of the Federal Reserve, Paul Volker, in 1979 marked the beginning of a three-year period of "high-water-mark monetarism" in both the UK and the USA (Goodhart 1989). While both the US Federal Reserve and the Bank of England committed to money supply targets (M1 in the USA, M3 in the UK, i.e. private and sectors' sterling and non-sterling deposits held with the UK banking sector), the choice of operational target differed. Volker opted for the full monetarist package, shifting the operational target to base money (nonborrowed reserve targets derived from the three-month M1 growth rate) while the Bank of England retained its practice of manipulating money-market rates.

What explains the different specification of the money supply target? Defining money only as means of exchange, neutral for the "real economy," has a bearing on the choice of relevant monetary aggregates. As only the narrow money (M1) confers direct purchasing power that induce spending increases and the attending inflationary pressures, for monetarist purposes M1 is the appropriate monetary target. In turn, the UK decision to target the broad money supply reflected the Radcliffe view that purchasing power had to be considered through a broader definition of liquidity (Kaldor 1982), an argument supported by the monetarist methodological claim that "anything goes" as long as it has predictive power (Ouanes and Takur 1997).

The outcome of monetarist experiments disappointed the believers. To start with, it was accepted that a shift to reserve targeting would be accompanied by substantial short-term interest-rate volatility. Indeed, as Keynes (1930) detailed in his *Treatise*, the effectiveness of the money multiplier (underlying monetarist accounts) crucially depends on the banks' liquidity positions on the interbank market – an inherently unstable market (Bagehot, 1876). Reserve injections through OMOs create, in the first instance, excess reserves that earn no or, at best, below-market interest rates. Profit maximization prompts banks with excess reserves to turn to the interbank money market for alternative placements with higher yields rather than to engage in time-consuming searches for credit-worthy borrowers (Gabor 2008). Only during times of high uncertainty might banks prefer to remain liquid and to park excess reserves at the central bank's overnight deposit facility (as indeed happened during 2008–2009 in UK and elsewhere). Similarly, banks that need to supplement their reserves to the required level will rather pay punitive rates on the money market than cancel loans (Bindseil 2004). Autonomous liquidity factors (cash in circulation, the treasury's deposits with the central bank) further trigger unpredictable changes in banks' liquidity positions. Thus, targeting bank reserves is inevitably accompanied by short-term money-market volatility – and, in fact, for many, the anti-inflationary credentials of the central bank would be truly tested by their willingness to accept high and volatile real interest rates. However, the volatility in long-term interest rates and monetary targets posed a different set of challenges (Anderson and Enzler 1987).

In the USA, the wholesale adoption of monetarist principles became difficult to reconcile with the dynamics of the targeted money supply. The Fed faced, in Goodhart's apt description, a problem of interpretation: while prices entered a downward trend, M1 continued to grow (Goodhart 1989: 303). The strict monetarist interpretation assigned such an outcome to the incapacity of the central bank to enforce the money growth rule, embedding a paradoxical reading of monetary policy stances: the empirical correlation between high interest rates and high money growth signalled an unduly relaxed policy stance, requiring further deflationary measures. It followed that an expansionary, rather than tight, monetary policy contributed to Volcker's success in establishing his anti-inflationary credentials by 1982, when in fact the high interest rates accompanying the shift to reserve targeting were credited to have triggered a global shift to deflationary conditions and the debt crisis for developing countries (Goodhart 1994), a point to be explored later. The inconsistencies of the account and the practical failure to produce the monetarist causal relationships despite several changes to the operating procedure saw the Fed quietly returning to manipulating money-market rates, prompting reflections that the monetarist experiments amounted to a simple rhetorical exercise designed to protect the Fed from the public disagreement with the contractionary implications of high interest rates (Bindseil 2004).

The British experience with monetary targeting offers interesting insights into how political forces contribute to translating neoliberal agendas into practice. Thatcher's age of austerity began in 1979 with the pledge that monetarism would be paramount to restoring competent economic policy-making – identifying monetary policy as the neoliberal policy par excellence (Krippner 2007). To the government's dismay, the M3 target spiralled out of control despite high interest rates (kept at around 16 percent) for the first eighteen months of the new policy framework (Elgie and Thomson 1999).

Because the UK shied away from outright targeting of bank reserves, the overshooting of the M3 target turned the attention to the sources of growth in broad money, analytically captured through the flow-of-funds approach. The focus on the balance sheet of the banking system, it was argued, would allow the central bank to identify which of the three key items of the asset side (net foreign assets, credit to government and credit to private sector) was most likely to trigger growth on the liability side (the money supply). As with the quantity of money, monetarist discourses transformed an accounting identity into a behavioural relationship, concluding that the government's borrowing requirements were too large (Goodhart 1994). The account went as follows: under flexible exchange rates, money-supply growth is driven by either credit to the private sector or by government borrowing. The first could not be directly inflationary, since it would potentially contribute to output increases (Nicholas 2003). On the contrary, the public sector's borrowing requirement triggered inflationary expansions in the money supply and put upward pressure on interest rates and effectively crowded out the private sector (Lawson 1980). The policy implication of this framing condoned the neoliberal arguments for downsizing government: the public-sector borrowing requirements were too large, a message that justified fiscal tightening decisions despite scant empirical evidence of a strong relationship between public borrowing and interest rates or monetary aggregate growth (Dwyer 1985). Through a series of argumentative twists without firm theoretical grounding, inflation was declared the ugly creature of irresponsible politics, in spite of the fact that irresponsible (i.e. democratic) politics had been around for centuries while peacetime inflation was a unique characteristic of the 1970s and 1980s (Blinder 1998).

Yet the articulation of the neoliberal insistence that rules-based policies depoliticized economic management functioned to hide deeply discretionary practices. As high interest rates and a liberalized foreign-exchange-rate market produced sharp appreciations of the pound, the loss of competitiveness inflicted enough political damage for Thatcher to refuse to allow the Bank of England to further manipulate interest rates in order to contain the M3 growth. For a period during the 1980s there was no public announcement of an official interest rate, on the alleged grounds that this would allow interest rates to be more "market-determined" (Gowland 1984: 195–196). Thatcher's own chancellor decried the politicization of interest-rate decisions driven by the Thatcher's recognition that interest-rate hikes made for unpopular decisions, especially for that crucial electoral group, mortgage holders (Elgie and Thomson 1998). Instead, she pushed for curtailing government spending. Having elevated monetary policy to the centre stage, the Thatcher government instead used fiscal contractions to pursue anti-inflationary commitments.

To understand the marked divergence between discourse and practice, critical accounts pointed to both theoretical and political economy considerations. In theoretical terms, post-Keynesians questioned the proposition that the money supply could be controlled by central banks (Kaldor 1982; Moore 1988; Dow 1996). Internal debates on the precise working of the transmission mechanism aside, post-Keynesians challenged the assumptions underlying of exogenous control of the money supply (control of bank reserves and a stable money multiplier). In fact, institutional innovations at different stages in the development of the banking sector endogenized the supply of money (Chick 1986, 2005). The systemic implications of the trust-based nature of money required central banks to act as lender of last resort to maintain confidence. Financial innovation, either through increasingly liquid interbank markets or liability management practices, rendered attempts to specify any particular money target irrelevant as the attributes of money (particularly liquidity) were extended to new types of assets (Goodhart 1994). Furthermore, even if the central bank overlooked financial stability concerns and refused to provide emergency liquidity, the lack of empirical backing for the assumption of a stable (and predictable) demand for money invalidated the monetarist causality.

Thus, monetarist experiments were further described as a "convenient, pragmatic and largely "presentational" device, behind which to conduct a familiar Keynesian deflation of the economy, without having the inconvenience of having to specify the likely real output and employment consequences" (Thompson 1986: 30). In other words, the neoliberal reformulation of policy paradigms entailed typical Keynesian methods of demand management but tailored to different policy priorities – curtailing effective demand through overvalued exchange rates, wage cuts, and a ferocious fiscal squeeze in the pursuit of low inflation (Kaldor 1982).

The highly discretionary nature of policy practice appeared to validate monetarist arguments that the politicization of the implementation process, rather than the underlying theoretical apparatus, were to blame for the unpredictable trajectories in monetary targets (with few exceptions, central banks across the world consistently missed targets; see Goodhart 1994). However, policy failures did not immediately translate into a loss of political legitimacy – even if it became increasingly accepted that monetarism was hardly equipped to describe central banking practices, the ideological appeal of its policy propositions saw the consolidation of the idea that "real" policy autonomy could only be secured through radical institutional change: formal independence for the central bank (Fischer 1994). And indeed, within a relatively short period, it became common wisdom that central bank independence offered the optimal method to enshrine the mandate of pursuing price stability, an institutional change embraced equally by developed and developing countries.

The answer to the puzzle that governments in developing countries willingly surrendered policy autonomy rested in the changing nature of their relationship with international finance (Carruthers et al. 2001). The optimistic developmentalism of the Keynesian agenda had prompted heavy borrowing from abroad to finance productive investment, a development strategy that became very costly once the rise of monetarism in developed countries brought sky-rocketing interest rates and a debt crisis. In the context of an increasing exposure to balance-of-payment crisis and volatile capital flows, central bank independence was intended as a signal of credibility to international investors. Vulnerability to international financial markets further opened up developing countries to the increasing hegemony of neoliberalism in international development discourse, which, the next chapter will show, was essential in the process of transforming post-socialist economic relations. The institution in charge of mediating the relationship between debtor states and the international financial market, the IMF, deployed monetarist narratives to identify two further key elements in constructing credibility: fiscal tightening and greater exchange-rate flexibility. Indeed, for developing countries, the imperative for macroeconomic management in the neoliberal era became the management of foreign investor expectations.

While monetarism turned out to be of little consequence for modifying policy practices, its consolidation as foundational monetary theory has to be understood through the consolidation, normalization, and institutionalization of neoliberalism (Hay 2004). The increasing hegemony of neoliberalism toward the end of the 1980s permeated international development interventions: monetarist narratives were parlayed into IMF's technocratic discourses, part of what became known as the "Washington Consensus" (Peck and Tickell 2002). A package of standardized policy measures underlying international development interventions, the Washington Consensus aimed at establishing the fundamental principle of the neoliberal economic doctrine: getting prices right to ensure an efficient allocation of resources. Subsequently, the "division of labour" in international development assigned stabilization to the IMF, while the World Bank, along with various regional organizations, focused on structural change through privatization and liberalization (Onis and Senses 2005).

The ascendance of macroeconomic stability on the IMF's policy agenda instated Chicago School monetarism as policy discourse and changed policy practice. Financial programming, informed by monetarist discourses, became the standard analytical framework (Mussa and Savastano 1999). Monetarist normativity translated identities into causal relationships that explained balance-of-payment problems and inflation through excess demand generated by fiscal misbehaviour so that macroeconomic stability became a question of enforcing macroeconomic austerity (Killick 1995). While conditionality sought to explicitly curtail government's interventions in economic policy formulation, Wood's study of the political economy of IMF operations

(2006) identified three key factors that shape the IMF's policies: US mercantilism, institutional politics, and the nature of the relationship with borrowing countries. Whereas the first two refer to factors internal to the IMF's political economy, its relationship with borrowing countries is shaped by the national political landscape, requiring the IMF to negotiate and establish alliances with policy actors that yield influence over policy agendas.

The definition of the policy problem through a narrative that privileged monetary policy in tackling the crisis served to construct the central bank as a point of entry for neoliberalizing economic management. Indeed, while governments might cooperate with the IMF because it provides legitimacy to unpopular measures, it is the "technocratic" elite of the central bank that shares most affinities with the "technocratic" rationale of stabilization packages – upholding the IMF's motto that "rational" policies will prevail where they can be formulated without the intervention of politics (Woods 2006). The emergence of central bank independence as the main institutional feature of the neoliberal conceptualization of economic stability marked a move in this direction: embedding "rational" economic policy into "depoliticized" economic expertise.

The key role that central banks play in processes of neoliberalization and the reshaping of central bank practices through the imperative of credibility contributes to institutional changes that further "denationalized," in Sassen's sense, the conduct of monetary policy, instead embedding it into complex networks of global governance. A further step in this direction would be taken by the widespread adoption of inflation-targeting regimes during the 1990s.

Indeed, if central banking was the most politically contested policy space during Keynesianism, and the target of depoliticizing discourses throughout the heyday of monetarism, by the early 1990s a paradoxical picture was emerging. Whereas governments willingly abdicated control over monetary policy, the now-independent central banks could offer little theoretical grounding for the widespread practice of manipulating short-term interest rates. The real business cycle models à la Lucas and Sargent (1978) dominating macroeconomic theory concluded that under rational expectations the effectiveness of monetary policy depended on unexpected actions. Furthermore, the turn to rational expectations raised a serious challenge for policy-makers. Lucas's famous critique (1976) argued that the large-scale econometric models deployed in policy-making were mistaken in assuming policy-invariant coefficients to describe policy-specific historical relationships.

On the other hand, endogenous money theories, despite presenting a closer picture of central banking practices, could not displace rational-expectations monetary models. Portrayed as too scholastic or philosophical, mainstream economists dismissed post-Keynesianism as being of little relevance for theoretical developments in monetary economics (Gale 1982: 183). Instead, a New Keynesian "paradigm" of inflation-targeting emerged, re-establishing, its advocates argued, the relevance of monetary theory for monetary policy (Walsh 2006).

This triumphalist message can be read differently if the dynamic character of neoliberalism is taken into account. The 1990s witnessed a softening of the free-market rhetoric toward a more nuanced representation of the relationship between states and markets. The early dichotomy of roll-out neoliberalism made room for an increasing acceptance of market failures and rigidities that called for corrective policy interventions and institutions supportive of equilibrium dynamics (Fine 2001). From this perspective, the widespread shift to inflation-targeting functioned to re-establish the functionality of the central bank in a changing neoliberal political economy increasingly redefined through processes of financialization, defined by Epstein (2002: 1) as "the increasing importance of financial markets, financial motives, financial institutions and financial elites in the operation of the economy and its governing institutions, both at national and international levels."

2.2.2 Roll-out neoliberalism, financialization and inflation targeting

The New Keynesian economics informing strategies of inflation-targeting articulate and further develop Kurt Wicksell's analytical insights. Inflation-targeting requires central banks to formally announce a target for inflation and a policy rule that explains how the policy instrument, usually the interest rate, would be adjusted in a manner consistent with achieving that target over a certain time frame (Walsh 2006). As its economic theory builds upon forward-looking individual decisions made under rational expectations, policy credibility depends on the ability of the central bank to anchor inflationary expectations through a systematic commitment to low inflation (Woodford 2003).

The theoretical grounding of inflation-targeting regimes offers many points of continuity with monetarism, described as the "new facade of neoliberal conditionality" (Epstein and Yeldan 2006) or "output gap monetarism" (Congdon 2007). Both monetarism and New Consensus economics identify monetary policy as key to controlling aggregate demand-driven inflation and emphasize the importance of a verifiable commitment to price stability (Woodford 2007). Both view low inflation rates as crucial for prices to function as signals for resource-allocation decisions.

The policy narrative underlying New Keynesianism runs as follows. Under perfectly flexible wages and prices, economic activity would be at a natural level and prices on a trend consistent with it. Aggregate demand or cost-push shocks produce a deviation of output from its potential or change marginal costs (without affecting the underlying equilibrium). Because not all firms adjust prices instantly, an inflation gap emerges[20]. Thus, market imperfections – price rigidity in this case – requires corrective interventions: the central bank will change short-term interest rates in response to deviations from the target and thus close the output gap. Similar to monetarism, New Keynesian economics retains long-term money neutrality (even if policy discussions mostly focus on the short term). Fiscal expansions have inflationary effects with little impact on output because of the Ricardian equivalence. High inflation, but not aggregate demand dynamics, change productivity and thus the potential level of output (Fontana and Palacio Vera 2004).

The central bank is essential in closing the output gap through deliberate interest-rate decisions (rather than the automatic adjustment in monetarism) because there is no underlying market mechanism that brings the economy to its "equilibrium" (Sawyer 2009). In turn, there is no significant role assigned to monetary aggregates, at least until the 2008 return to quantitative easing[21] (Issing 2006). Instead, the transmission mechanism assumes that short-term interest rates change the system of incentives by affecting, in a predictable manner, long-term interest rates relevant for decisions of consumption and investment. Policy decisions propagate smoothly, as the New Keynesian framework does not consider the possibility of money-market disequilibrium – the "expectations theory of the term structure" ensures a strict correspondence between short- and long-term interest rates (Blinder 1998). Concerns with financial stability are not necessary as long as monetary policy decisions are successful in maintaining low price inflation. Under assumptions of complete markets, no detailed analytical attention to financial market characteristics is necessary (Bernanke and Gertler 2001).

Since inflationary expectations and the future path of the interest rate are central to the price-setting mechanism, monetary policy must credibly establish an anchor for inflation[22]. Because agents are assumed to factor inconsistent policies into their behaviour, anchoring expectations is an essential mediator of the adjustment process. As a two-step process, it involves a discursive construction of credibility and a systematic rule that private agents understand. It requires the central bank to shape market expectations about the future path of its instrument and assigns transparency in communicating the policy rule a central role in the new policy framework.

Thus, inflation-targeting promised to address the increasing policy anxieties toward exchange-rate management in the context of liberalized capital accounts and volatile capital flows: credible and transparent policy guarantee safe integration into global financial markets and allow markets to set exchange rates according to comparative advantage (de la Torre et al. 2007).

Thus, inflation-targeting appeared to solve the neoliberal dilemma described by Krippner (2007): it offered a set of institutional innovations that enlist markets in the policy process without relinquishing central banks' control – "getting the market to do" central bank's job. Policy actions are then interpreted as the result of "market intentions" captured by the central banks through sophisticated modelling techniques. Yet the consolidation of inflation-targeting as hegemonic policy narrative cannot be simply explained through its success in solving the dilemma of how to construct a boundary, or, perhaps better put, a relationship, between the state and the market consistent with neoliberal discourses. Taking Krippner's argument that the move to transparency prompts central banks to "act less, and markets more, in setting the interest rate" (2007: 506) – to its logical conclusion, the link between inflation-targeting and financialization must be explicitly considered.

Quantitative measures of financialized globalization provide an indirect indication of the importance of central banking practices. Financial deregulation and flexible exchange-rate regimes brought new opportunities for gains from speculation. Initially applauded as instruments for protection against risk, financial markets quickly discovered the vast profit potential from using derivatives to trade (speculate on) risk: by June 2008, the total notional amount of derivative instruments reached US$684 trillion, over twelve times the world GDP and a fourfold increase over the previous ten years (BIS 2008). Deregulation opened up spaces for speculative gains from betting on volatility in interest rates and exchange rates: two-thirds of derivative instruments involved interest-rate contracts. With leveraging increasingly dominating practices in international financial markets and thus requiring predictable interest-rate movements, the New Keynesian return to short-term interest rates as policy instrument and the transparency in communicating interest-rate decisions had more functionality than the interest-rate volatility associated with monetarist experiments. The puzzle that New Keynesians identified in the policy rule – that central banks preferred to adjust interest rates gradually rather than take the aggressive stance prescribed by the theory when inflation shoots above the target (Clarida et al. 1999) – in fact captures the pressures for stability embedded in the proposition of "working with the market."

Political economists have long recognized that behind the superficial depoliticization of policy decisions neoliberalism has sought to take central banking back to the pre-Keynesian status quo of a "privatized" monetary policy where policy decisions are tailored to the interests of increasingly powerful financial markets, regrettably with considerably less theoretical opposition than during the heyday of the Gold Standard (Bain and Howells 1999). Yet, with a few notable exceptions, the literature on financialization has shied from exploring the relevance and implications of the global shift to inflation-targeting. Initially, analytical attention focused on qualitative shifts in the relationship between financial markets and large nonfinancial corporations, restructured through what Crotty (2003) termed "impatient" finance that abandoned its commitments to long-term financing of productive activity. In this area, the Western focus was expanded with Demir's (2009) study of Argentina, Turkey and Mexico's experience with financial liberalization, driving firms to change investment behaviour from long-term investments geared to the expansion of productive capacities to short-term, speculative investment. Then Hardie and Howarth (2009: 1018) emphasized the "increasing exposure to, and trading of, risk" to analyze the financialization of European banks that turned to investment banking, prioritizing "new market portfolio" instead of their more traditional "credit portfolio" activities. Langley (2007) described the production of "financialized subjects" through the Foucauldian notion of governamentality. D'Arista (2005) and Epstein (2005) further drew attention to the financialization of macroeconomic policy and the role played by the international monetary system. Palley (2007) identified three interdependent areas where the changes induced by financialization have become increasingly visible: the behaviour of nonfinancial corporations, financial markets, and economic policies.

Palley (2007), and in greater detail Epstein (2002), described the financialization of economic policy in terms of class conflict. In this account, the neoliberal intervention in the conflict over resources sees the shifting of power over economic decisions from labour (under Keynesianism) to rentiers who benefit from the monetarist (and then inflation-targeting) return to high interest rates. Epstein further acknowledged that the Keynesian dichotomy between finance and industrial capital loses analytical validity: the financialization of corporate behaviour destroys the old distinction as nonfinancial corporations become increasingly guided by rentier interests. The new category now covers central banks, which becomes a "rentier" central bank. The merging of interests driving industrial and financial capital change the priorities underlying practices of central banking: as leveraged financial practices translate into generalized asset bubbles, the new political economy of finance requires *low* interest rates to contain the risks of bubbles bursting. An interesting indication of this can be found in the academic debates on the inclusion of asset prices in the policy rule of the inflation-targeting central bank. Friedman's assured argument that speculation functions to bring markets back to "fundamentals" has been replaced by institutional anxieties that asset bubbles can spillover into the "real" (read productive) economy. The argument that won served well the concerns of the financial sector – along Alan Greenspan's proposition that it would be easier to clean up after a bubble bursts than to attempt to prevent it. Bernanke and Gertler (2001) developed the best-known theoretical legitimization, widely accepted until the 2007–2009 crisis. This rejected the possibility of tailoring interest-rate decisions to asset bubbles, on both ideological (markets should be allowed to freely allocate capital), policy (interest-rate decisions do respond to the effects of the asset bubbles on output and prices), and pragmatic grounds (misalignments are difficult to identify)[23].

In sum, Epstein's conceptualization raises several interesting questions. First, it is clear that closer analytical attention must be paid to the link between central banking and strategies of funding leveraged activity, as financial interests would require *low* interest rates in a funding currency to exploit *high* returns in domestic asset markets or other high-yielding currencies. It then becomes important to distinguish differences in the political operation of inflation-targeting between developed and developing countries, their different role in, and exposure to, global liquidity cycles. Furthermore, if institutions are instrumental in the creation of markets (Carruthers et al. 2001), as roll-out neoliberalism implies, is it not problematic to assume, as Epstein does, that central banks offer no resistance to rentier interests? Can financialization be read as a mechanic process of inscribing rentier interests in the central bank behaviour?

Table 2.2 The National Bank of Romania from a post Niebylian perspective

Periods	Theoretical foundations	Policy narrative	Practices of monetary management
Normative (roll-back) neoliberalism (1990–1996) *The central bank key to redefining the relationship between state-owned production and state-owned banks along "impatient finance" lines.*	**Monetarism (four IMF stabilization packages)** 1. Contractionary broad money growth targets. 2. Flexible exchange rates central to market-determined competitiveness.	**The gradualist years – "rational" policies vs. "bad" politics of implementation** 1. Excess liquidity produced by monetization of soft-budget constraints feeding inflationary pressures. 2. Relative PPP approach to rationalize exchange rate devaluation.	**Expanding policy repertoires under conflicting demands:** 1. Liquidity shortages through credit ceilings, then restricted access to the discount window and prohibitively high discount rates. 2. Directed credit to priority sectors at *ex-ante* positive real interest rates. 3. Switching from attempts to stabilize exchange rates given the high pass-through to complying with IMF demands for flexibility.

Normalized (roll-out) neoliberalism (1997–2008) *Central bank key to reconstituting policy fields (and markets) through a logic of financialization.*	**1997–2005 Partly liberalized capital account**	**Monetarism** 1. Reserve money targeting. 2. Exchange rate as nominal anchor, central to fast disinflation.	**1997–1999 Austerity and crisis** 1. Aggregate demand contraction. 2. Separating economics from politics: money market financing of budget deficits.	**Sterilized currency interventions produce a structural excess of liquidity on the money market.** Sterilizations not monetary targeting *stricto sensu* but as vehicle for attracting speculative capital channelled through the banking sector, and engineering exchange rate appreciations.	1. Asymmetric distribution of excess liquidity. 2. Liquidity tightening through foreign currency sales, increasing reserve requirements and limited lender-of-last-resort financing. 1+2 => crisis opening up banking sector to foreign ownership and financialization.
			2000–2005 recovery and growth Encouraging sustainable real appreciations to ensure disinflation, under a tight control of liquidity.		1. Expanding structural excess of liquidity. 2. Limited policy repertoire (reserve requirements) to tackle the financialization of the banking sector (asset bubbles) and growing current account deficits.
	2005–2008 Fully liberalized capital account	**Inflation-targeting** 1. Commitment to inflation target. 2. Short-term interest rate central to aggregate demand control. 3. Flexible exchange-rate regime.	**Internal and external credibility** 1. Output gap and broad monetary conditions. 2. Adequate liquidity management to redefine policy instrument as cost and signal for spending decisions.	1. Currency interventions formally abandoned. 2. After failed attempts to divorce practice from speculative capital, sterilizations resumed without eliminating excess interbank liquidity. 3. Policy rate little relevant for spending, instead tailored to stabilizing currency dynamics dominated by non-resident carry-trades. 4. Currency appreciations tying financial stability into transnational actors' choices as growing borrowing from mother banks/companies increased exposure to short-term, foreign-currency liabilities. 5. Limited crisis options: reluctance to stabilize interbank rates during the October 2008 speculative attack as extra liquidity feeding speculative pressures on currency markets.	

2.3 Conclusion

This chapter examined the two broad shifts in paradigms of central banking throughout the 20th century to set the stage for understanding what the central bank does when the formerly planned state "retreats" from the markets. Indeed, there is a historical dimension to the policy choices in post-socialist Eastern Europe: had change occurred in the 1960s or 1970s, policy priorities would have been different. Through a historical coincidence, the dismantling of the Eastern European socialist system began as neoliberalism consolidated its hegemonic position in global agencies and discourses. A discursive system that instituted the market as the "tribunal" against which all economic (as well as social) activities must be judged, neoliberalism insisted at the time that markets can only allocate resources efficiently if the government disappears from economic domains. Drawing on critical conceptualizations of neoliberalism in its shifting forms, the chapter questioned its ideological separation between states and markets that positions the central bank at the frontier between the two. Central banks do not vanish from monetary policy processes, as the rhetoric of free markets triumphantly suggests, as much as they did not disappear from Keynesian strategies of aggregate demand management. In fact, the experience of both the USA and the UK suggests that under monetarist rhetoric hid Keynesian policy measures, only geared toward different policy objectives. The Keynesian concern with public debt sustainability that guided central bank interventions on money markets was replaced with concerted efforts at reducing inflation rates through a combination of high interest rates, fiscal contractions, and overvalued exchange rates. Once monetarism permeated the IMF's interventions, the economic problem in developing countries affected by the debt crisis was redefined through the monetarist account of excessive money creation driven by irresponsible politics. In a world of liberalized capital inflows, reassuring foreign investors became the new mission of independent central banks. Similarly, the inflation-targeting central bank became essential to practices of leveraged investment and the shift to "impatient finance."

To understand how central banks contribute to neoliberalization, both in its roll-back and roll-out stages, the next chapters turn to the nexus of ideology and practice in post-socialist Romania. To guide the reader, a schematic representation of the post-Niebylian approach to central banking in Romania can be found in Table 2.2.

Part II

Central Banking and Financialization in Central and Eastern Europe: A Romanian Account

3
The "Gradualist" Years, 1990–1996

The fall of socialism left Eastern Europe keen to embrace the Western norms of a liberal democracy and a market economy, the opposite of the plan and the monopoly of the Communist Party (Pop 2006). The mood was confident, as were the promises: a quick transition to a market paradise of consumer well-being and efficient production. Riding the wave of optimism that the development gap could be bridged quickly, the free-market advocates presented system-wide change as a fundamentally simple process if policies were consistent with market efficiency assumptions. The challenge was fundamentally political, requiring an irreversible decision to separate the economic sphere from government interference and to replace the failed central planning mechanism.

International institutions, including the IMF, the World Bank and the European Bank for Reconstruction and Development (EBRD), played a critical, threefold role in this process (Zecchini 1995). They catalyzed financial support from multilateral sources, provided economic policy advice, and ensured that this advice was complied with. For a substantial time, however, the IMF had a more immediate and relevant presence because multilateral assistance insisted on its approval of a country's economic strategy (Portes 1994), so that deviation from IMF policy advice has been the exception rather than the rule (Sachs 1996).

The most scathing appraisal of the Romanian economic strategy up to 1997 appeared in that year's IMF country report (IMF 1997a). At the time, Romania's unenviable record showed four successive SBAs cancelled a few months after signing, a signal of the national hesitations to implement market reforms. Negotiations with the IMF started in late 1990, and the first SBA was signed in April 1991, followed by a second SBA in May 1992, a third in May 1994, and an extension of the May 1994 one signed in December 1995.

By IMF standards (indeed, by any standards), the 1990 to 1996 period were lost years: a series of failed stabilization attempts punctuated by temporary revivals, inflation rates substantially higher than other formerly planned economies, and large external imbalances that systematically depleted foreign reserves and threatened a balance-of-payment crisis. This, the IMF held, was not a problem of policy design but of policy implementation. Whereas the SBA negotiations committed national authorities to a series of policy measures that would have ensured a quick and painless transformation, the intervention of politics at the implementation stage reproduced the imbalances inherited from Communism. State-owned industrial interests emerged as a powerful political force that resisted restructuring and transformed the "rational economic policy" advice into a gradualist approach to reform. The 1997 report identified two policy domains where vested interest captured policy implementation. Both exchange-rate and monetary policy acquired a quasi-fiscal objective that further fed the excess demand inherited from the years of central planning, resulting in inflation and in balance-of-payment problems.

This narrative of the period, which the National Bank of Romania repeatedly endorsed and reproduced (NBR, 1997a; 1998a), conceptualized economic policy as a solution to prevailing economic problems (Hall 1986) and portrayed the IMF and the NBR as technocratic institutions whose success in promoting "appropriate" stabilization policies was always short-lived against the government's preference for promoting employment. Getting prices right, the IMF held, raised two immediate policy concerns: to identify what would obstruct price adjustment, and, once these obstacles were removed, how to ensure that prices continued to convey market signals. Once prices were liberalized, the challenge remained that state-owned companies, unbounded by profit considerations, would undermine the efforts to correct price distortions by perpetuating the excess demand. The IMF prescribed monetary restraint.

However, a cursory look at the theoretical origins of the excess demand narrative challenges this unproblematic representation of the policy problem and its solutions. The narrative blended concepts from two competing approaches to the economics of socialism engaged into an intense debate during the 1980s, a debate yet to be resolved at the time when socialism collapsed in CEE. The most contentious point of the debate was the existence of chronic excess aggregate demand (Kemme 1989). Yet, when the IMF arrived on the policy scene in formerly planned economies, it declared excess demand as the immediate stabilization problem (Wolf 1990; IMF et al. 1991), replacing the nationally defined priority of industrial upgrading outlined by the Romanian Commission for Transition in early 1990 (Government Commission 1990).

Against this context, this chapter asks why and how did the excess-demand account come to dominate policy thinking, linking it to the politics of international development interventions. It treats policy narratives as instruments in ideological struggles because they offer control over the interpretation of events and thus allow a set of interests to be translated into policy models (Mosse 2005) in a monetary policy space structured as a contested terrain (Epstein 1992). Furthermore, even if the policy innovations did seek to (re)produce and continuously legitimize the neoliberal approach to reform, the effects were not purely ideological. The excess-demand narrative set in motion the financialization of the banking sector.

To analyze these effects, the chapter will first explore the historical context of Romanian socialist planning. It maps how the IMF discourse produced Romania as an object of intervention and explores the shifts that the IMF's presence produced in the politics of policy-making. It further asks how policy discourse rationalized repeated SBA failures and the changes in central bank practices these brought about.

3.1 A (very brief) history of Romanian socialism

At the time of the fall of the Communist Block in the early 1990s, Romania was a particular case of a planned economy. Its peculiarity derived from specific historical and geographical circumstances: once the Soviet Union ended the short occupation after World War II, the country went from being just another soviet satellite in the first two decades to taking a more nationalistic, self-sustainable approach that sought independence from external influence.

The ambiguous position of the country in World War[24] II weighed heavily on postwar settlements Romania had to pay the Soviet Union war compensations[25], and after the Yalta Treaty in 1945 it was assigned to the Soviet sphere of influence. The Soviet-backed Romanian Communist Party seized power in 1945 and set out to construct a centrally planned economy.

The 1950s and 1960s: The socialist industrialization model

During this period, the country underwent the standard industrialization strategy characteristic to planned economies, aimed at creating an industrial structure advanced enough to manufacture means of production (implying a pronounced bias toward capital-goods production).

Across the socialist bloc, the case for central planning claimed superiority on grounds of economic efficiency rather than ideology. Since technological change was the driving force of capitalism, it inevitably required concentration to achieve economies of scale and scope (Persky 1991). Innovations occur in monopolistic or oligopolistic capitalist production, rather than small companies operating in atomistic markets because technological change requires commitments of time and capital (Galbraith 1967). Given the inherent instability of capitalist production, state monopolies, carefully guided by central planners, could successfully replace the large-scale production characteristic to capitalist monopoly structures.

Socialist planning sought to blend economies of scale with high specialization in the production of capital goods. The basic socialist model of production envisaged large, vertically integrated firms, each operating under monopoly or oligopoly conditions and producing a narrow set of intermediary inputs. Except for a few resource-intensive countries, domestically produced raw inputs were reserved for internal use. Furthermore, international trade within the Communist Block was based on production requirements rather than on considerations of competitiveness (Winiecki 1988).

The typical planned financial sector consisted of a central bank, a few specialized credit institutions that channelled credit from the central bank to different sectors of the economy, and a savings bank that attracted deposits from the population but that did not engage in credit operations (Amsden et al. 1994). The organization of the financial sector institutionalized two distinct monetary circuits, for enterprises and for households, to counteract the inherently destabilizing role Marx identified for money in capitalism (Ellman 1989). Thus, enterprise financial flows were endogenized through the central plan to eliminate the volatility of uncoordinated, profit-driven production. As central planners dictated economic decisions, prices played no role in the allocation of resources. Determined as mark-up on labour and input costs, they were strictly controlled by central planners and occasionally adjusted to reflect changes in costs. In the productive sector circuit, bank deposits were adjusted to physical flows (settling inter-enterprise transactions) but not for payment of personal income: money functioned as a unit of account (Dow et al. 2008). Credit activity was subordinated to the requirements of the physical plan (Sundararajan 1990), financing inter-enterprise transactions according to output targets. Further, this implied that SOEs were highly dependent on bank credit for financing working-capital requirements (Dow et al. 2008). The volume of currency (cash money) was determined by wage payments established through the central plan, to be either spent on consumer goods and services or saved. The only domestic financial assets were bank deposits and currency, while access to foreign-exchange holdings would be restricted for companies and forbidden for individuals (Demekas and Khan 1991).

The 1970s: The golden years of national sovereignty

The dynamics of industrialization then changed when Khrushchev shifted the Soviet discourse from "simultaneous transition" to socialism to specialization within the Soviet trading bloc, the Council for Mutual Economic Assistance (CMEA). This established the Soviet Union as key producer of heavy industry, while the Eastern European bloc would focus on supplying consumer goods and primary products (Spulber and Gehrels 1958).

Romanian leaders objected to a division of labour that positioned the country as a producer of primary goods[26] and light industry After the 1964 "Declaration" stressing Romanian sovereignty, Nicolae Ceauşescu's election marked the beginning of a new vision for national development: an industrial economy producing capital goods, an approach stressing the interdependency between industrial development and national sovereignty (Linden 1986).

Consequently, Romania redefined itself as a "socialist developing country" in 1972, seeking preferential treatment both from its more developed socialist neighbours and from non-socialist organizations such as the European Economic Community. It was the first CMEA country to join the General Agreement on Tariffs and Trade in 1971, and the IMF and the World Bank in 1972, to receive generalized trade preferences from the European Economic Area and to allow Western companies to operate joint ventures within its borders. Simultaneously, it resisted the CMEA 1971 "comprehensive program" which delegated planning authority to a supra-national level, rejecting the idea of a dominant "leading centre" of the Communist world. It instead centralized economic activity and established a five-year horizon to the economic development strategy.

The orientation of Romanian foreign trade reflected foreign policy shifts. By 1974, the country was trading more with capitalist states than with the Soviet bloc. Essential to the industrialization strategy, investment grew at a rapid pace, most concentrated in industry, transport and communication, with little attention paid to agriculture. Economic growth was the fastest in the region. The rapid expansion was mainly financed from domestic resources, by heavily drawing labour from the agricultural sector[27] and by restricting consumption. Machinery and raw-material imports, the bulk of imports from capitalist countries, were financed by oil and gas exports.

The apparent success in self-sufficient industrialization had important repercussions. While both capitalist and Soviet countries struggled against recessionary pressures during the later 1970s, Romania followed unabated with its rapid investment strategy, particularly in energy-intensive industries in steel, chemicals, and petrochemical refining. However, the quest for heavy industrialization proved elusive. The investment in oil refineries turned out to be a particularly unfortunate choice, as refining capacity increased while domestic oil production peaked. The ensuing oil imports reflected in rising current-account imbalances, mainly financed by foreign loans, leaving the country exposed to the international debt pressures of the 1980s.

The 1980s: Structural adjustments

Recognizing that its external debt position required international support, Romania signed a three-year agreement with the IMF in 1981 that lasted until 1984. The key objective of the program was to improve economic efficiency – a challenge which Ceauşescu had already sought to address by the introduction of the New Economic and Financial Mechanism in 1979. While the Central Plan retained control over economic activity, a series of measures sought to give more autonomy and responsibility to state-owned companies. Production would be guided by value-added targets rather than physical quantities, to avoid the overstating of production or the stock-building the government introduced forward contracting between enterprises (seeking to match demand with supply). The IMF-sponsored program attempted to make enterprises less dependent on the state budget for investment financing, to be replaced with bank credit or profits. The IMF obtained that interest rates on investment credit be raised in 1983 to improve the efficiency of capital allocation. The program unified the various exchange rates applied to different trade transactions and depreciated the currency against the US dollar. The system of subsidies for exports and imports – known as the price equalization fund – was changed to ensure greater sensitivity to world prices, taxing exporters out of profits if the export prices received were not competitive (Demekas and Khan 1991).

Whereas the IMF later challenged the effectiveness of these measures, it was Ceauşescu's decision not to renew the program after the initial term finished. In fact, the irony remains that Ceauşescu saw through the completion of a three-year agreement, far more successful than the successive post-socialist governments. The reason to refuse further IMF support were immediately clear. Afraid that the IMF's conditionality would soften his grip on power, as was all too clearly happening in Poland, Ceauşescu embarked on a nationally owned "structural adjustment" plan seeking to repay the external debt and to curtail the country's dependency on external creditors. The emphasis shifted from fast capital accumulation to campaigns for efficiency, frugality, and personal sacrifice.

SOEs bore the brunt of the adjustment. Official figures show that industrial production decreased by an average of 1.5 percent throughout the last five years of Communism, a larger contraction when taking into account tendencies to overstate production (Daianu 1994). Indeed, the emphasis on self-financing reduced budgetary outlays for investment (on which a capital charge was levied), and interest-rate hikes on bank credit during the IMF program had already affected industrial production. Now, imports of intermediary inputs essential for production were curtailed to redirect foreign currency to debt payments. While some of the measures agreed with the IMF were relaxed[28], the emphasis on debt repayment continued to affect capital investment. Indeed, toward the end of the 1980s, unrealistic plan targets, on which the tax liabilities were derived, resulted in heavy taxation. Attempts to rein in credit demand for bank credit saw the expansion of the interfirm credit market, similar to various other planned economies. By the end of 1989, IMF (1991) estimated inter-enterprise credits at around 40 percent of GDP, a level close to more "reformed" planned economies – around 48 percent of GDP for Poland, 43 percent for Yugoslavia, and around 40 percent for China (Calvo and Corricelli 1992).

Ceauşescu's structural-adjustment program did achieve what it set out to do: the previous trade deficits were transformed into trade surpluses, and the outstanding foreign debt was reduced from around US$ 7 bn in 1985 to US$170 million in 1989, at the expense of a serious contractionary blow that reduced consumption and capital investment. Thus, the fall of the Berlin Wall found in Romania a social climate favourable to unrest and public protest. The December 1989 regime change resulted in the public execution of the Ceauşescu couple, one of the bloodiest of the 1980s "revolutions" in Eastern Europe. A singularly Stalinist political regime ended in a singularly bloody upheaval.

The two structural adjustment programs eroded the viability of the industrial sector and the credibility of its management. It left post-socialist policy-makers with difficult decisions about how to proceed with industrial reform. Two competing accounts emerged after 1990. One viewed the industrial sector as too obsolete, concentrated and energy-intensive to warrant anything other than an immediate exposure to the full discipline of the market – a sort of economic Darwinism of the survival of the fittest. Market pressures would be instrumental in replacing large-scale enterprises with flexible small and medium-sized private companies. According to Daianu [1998], in 1989 a small number of enterprises with over 3,000 employees provided more than 50 percent of total industrial output whereas firms with fewer than 500 workers employed only 4 percent of the labour force and 6 percent of output. The second account recognized the importance of introducing market mechanisms in the state-owned productive sector, guided by a well-designed industrial policy seeking to restore the competitiveness of the manufacturing sector (Government Commission 1990). This optimistic view was embedded in the nationally defined strategy of the Commission for Transition established in May 1990. Its importance in informing policy decisions was short-lived: the onset of negotiations with the IMF toward the end of 1990 changed the dominant view of the industrial sector toward the pessimistic account.

3.2 Competing views of the post-communist macroeconomic problem: Industrial restructuring versus excess demand

To understand the struggle over policy priorities it is important to take into account the constraints on autonomous policy decisions. Initial conditions appeared favourable for Romania. The only positive outcome of Ceauşescu's push for external debt repayment was that, unlike its neighbours, Romania started its transformation process with no foreign debt. Despite such a positive outlook, the country found it impossible to secure external loans from private sources. The IMF approval of SBAs, usually perceived in international markets as a guarantee of credible policies, made little difference. The central bank managed to secure a US$60 million international private loan only in 1993. For most of the period, international organizations remained Romania's main source of foreign capital[29], thus increasing the leverage of international policy advice.

International official lending functioned more like a lifeline. The NBR continuously struggled to improve its foreign (convertible) currency reserves throughout the first four years, despite the successive

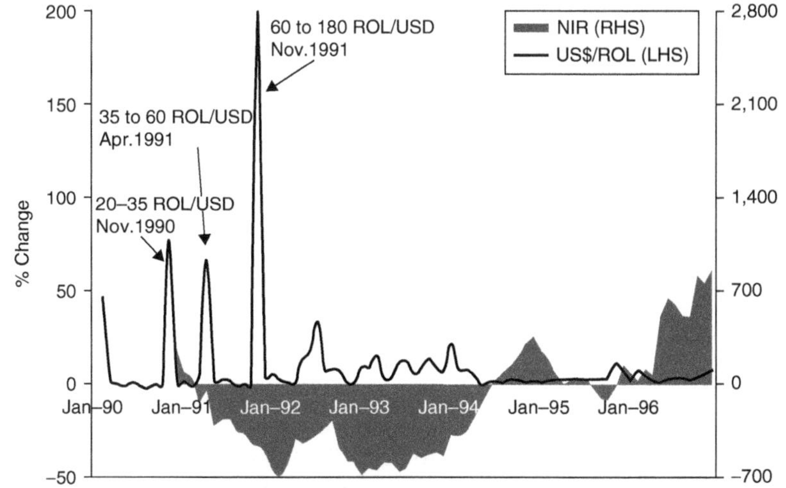

Figure 3.1 Exchange rate (ROL/US$) and foreign reserves (US$ billions), Romania, 1990–1996

Source: Computed from the Statistical section of *the National Bank of Romania Annual Report 1995* and *2000*.

devaluations advised by the IMF as a method for restoring competitiveness and international reserves (see Figure 3.1). The foreign reserve position gradually strengthened during 1994 and then reversed during 1995 as both the trade and the current-account deficit widened. The reserves position improved again in 1996, boosted by short-term borrowing.

Such a volatile pattern made the exchange rate the most politically disputed policy arena. Indeed, despite devaluations and periods of exchange-rate flexibility, Romania maintained a trade and current-account deficit throughout its post-socialist history, failing to bring about the structural change necessary to replace the import-dependence of industrial production with an export-led growth model.

3.2.1 The national priority: Industrial upgrading

One of the immediate priorities of the provisional government after the disappearance of the tightly controlled system of resource allocation was to define a policy agenda for reform. The Commission for Transition drew on a wide participation of various social actors in society (economists, governmental bodies, industry, trade unions, and international organizations), seeking to mark an epistemological shift from the central-planning years and to render policy deliberations participatory and consensual.

The report advanced an economic reform strategy that crucially premised industrial development as the basis for a rapid catch-up with capitalist economies (Government Commission 1990). It recognized that state intervention was required to support capital investments in order to rebuild the technological capabilities of the Romanian industry, particularly since the last years of socialism had been so detrimental to industrial production[30]. Second-order priorities included the traditional Washington Consensus measures of price, trade, and capital-account liberalization, to be spread over a period of two to three years. The report rejected across-the-board price liberalization, as the monopoly/oligopoly structures prevailing in the Romanian economy warranted price controls while a more competitive setting emerged. It further identified a set of key intermediate and final products that would remain under administrative control, reflecting the industrial policy concerns of the report[31].

The report conceptualized a financial system subordinated to restructuring the productive sector. While it recognized the need to improve enterprises' financial discipline, the report contained an endogenous money argument: the money supply was to be managed in line with the requirements of the productive sector, prioritizing its technological upgrading. The central bank would channel credit through commercial banks, who would be assigned a more active role in setting interest rates. Simultaneously, the legal framework would be modified to allow and indeed encourage the entry of private, foreign or nationally owned commercial banks. The report further discussed the conditions and time frame for introducing exchange-rate convertibility[32], and recommended a devaluation to bring the exchange rate to a more realistic level. It set 1992 as the earliest date for introducing full convertibility, conditional on the existence of foreign reserves and of mechanisms to defend the national currency from excessive fluctuations.

This careful approach to exchange rate liberalization signalled structuralist concerns with the link between costs of production and exchange rates (Taylor 1983). In developing countries where intermediary imports were substantially used in the export sector and where the country could not substantially influence its terms of trade, exchange-rate volatility would affect production costs and reduce profitability. Domestic currency overvaluation might be necessary to support a policy of capital accumulation (Katseli 1983).

However, domestic and international developments produced a dramatic reformulation of reform priorities by November 1990. Internally, politics was increasingly polarized between the Frontul Salvării Naţionale (FSN), a party positioning itself on the left of the ideological spectrum, and the formerly outlawed "historical parties" of the right. This polarization had immediate consequences for the program of economic reform. During the summer of 1990, violent confrontations between the newly elected government headed by the FSN and opposition forces[33] reinforced the perceptions of a volatile political climate Furthermore, it appeared to confirm the antidemocratic, neo-Communist credentials of the governing party and instituted the historical parties as "true" democrats, with the corresponding different representations of political will to reform. While the FSN was generally accused of colluding with conservative industrial interests associated with the dominance of large, state-owned monopolies in the industrial sector, the international media and international organizations identified the "true" democrats as the "true" reformers, better positioned to create capitalism (Pop 2006).

Economic problems added to this sense of political instability. The delays in creating viable alternatives for allocating resources to SOEs following the collapse of the State Planning Committee saw industrial production quickly contracting. The crisis in the Middle East, Romania's main source of imports for the energy-intensive productive sector, pushed up oil prices and led to the freezing of Romanian assets in the region[34]. Together with a policy of favouring imports of consumer goods to satisfy some of the pent-up demand, these events concurred to produce a sharp deterioration in the foreign trade balance. In the absence of international private loans, the central bank's foreign reserves were diminishing at such a rapid pace that the government had little choice but to seek assistance from the international organization in charge of balance-of-payments problems: the IMF.

3.2.2 The IMF's view of post-socialist stabilization: The excess demand problem and the disequilibrium vs. shortage debates

The analytical core of the IMF's stabilization plans, consolidated during its Latin American engagement in the 1980s, identified excess demand produced by excessive money creation as the source of external imbalances. Imprudent macroeconomic policies thus affected countries' ability to access international financing markets and to close the "financing gap" (between foreign currency reserves and current-account deficits). The standard format for assistance, an SBA, established a money-supply growth rate consistent with the desired level of inflation and foreign-reserves accumulation intended to restore international credibility.

The typical monetarist flow of funds or monetary base approach described in the previous chapter would be employed to establish ceilings on domestic credit (or central bank credit) complemented with a floor on international reserve. The SBAs reproduced the monetarist message that fiscal spending had to be reined in by instituting quantitative performance criteria to ensure government compliance. A money-neutrality approach underlined the monetarist expectation that credit constraints would have few negative consequences for output.

The standard stabilization plan entailed two further concerns with exchange-rate management: the immediate policy response to balance of payments crisis and the optimal regime choice for avoiding future imbalances. During the 1980s, the IMF tended to favour exchange-rate flexibility, legitimized through equilibrium discourses. It however accepted that particular circumstances, such as the Latin American inflationary episodes, warranted the use of the exchange rate as a nominal anchor to add credibility to an anti-inflationary stance (Edwards 1994). Whatever the policy regime choice, the IMF interpreted a balance-of-payment crisis as a sign of exchange-rate misalignment and invariably recommended devaluation. This was expected to increase competitiveness by moving the real exchange rate closer to its equilibrium level. To ensure that the nominal devaluations would "stick" in real terms, the IMF resorted to the open economy monetarism – the monetary approach to the balance of payments, a theory that constructed external imbalances as monetary problems. An extension of the traditional purchasing power parity (PPP), the monetary approach explained nominal exchange-rate dynamics through excess money-supply growth (under a constant equilibrium real exchange rate). It linked the effectiveness of nominal devaluations to a tight monetary policy aimed at keeping monetary aggregates and thus prices in check (MacDonald 2000).

In Eastern Europe, the IMF faced the challenge of translating its economics of crisis designed for (developing) capitalist economies to a system where money and prices played a marginal role at best. The IMF had already been present in the region during its structural-adjustment program with Poland and Romania in the early 1980s. It interpreted the failure of Poland's experiments with limited marketization as a clear indication that the macroeconomic implications of central planning could not be neglected (Wolf 1990). Its policy advocacy in Eastern Europe in general, and Romania in particular, blended its standard approach to macroeconomic stabilization with a radical set of policies destined to free the economy from planned control.

Whereas the Romanian authorities emphasized the importance of industrial restructuring, the IMF's definition of the transition problem focused on the key neoliberal message: the necessity to get prices right in order to allow free markets to allocate resources efficiently, a principle which the quantity-driven logic of socialism violated. Two features of the planned system contributed to the existence of a large pent-up demand that threatened to transform the one-off surge in prices triggered by across-the-board price liberalization into an inflationary spiral: the monetary overhang and the soft budget constraint (IMF et al. 1991; Winiecki 1993).

The money supply exceeded what would be demanded if existing prices were market-clearing because of the monetary overhang prevailing in individual economies, a by-product of chronic shortages and rationing (Lin and Osband 1992). The SOE behaviour represented the other source of concern: while standard stabilization policies premised profit-maximizing firms, the soft-budget constraints pervasive in planned production implied government-backed "soft" credits would further feed aggregate demand and reproduce allocative inefficiencies (Lane 1991; Fischer and Gelb 1991). To contain inflationary pressures, monetary and fiscal restraint would accompany price liberalization (Wolf 1990; IMF et al. 1991; Bruno 1992).

The IMF's definition of the policy problem drew on a long debate between two competing approaches to the economics of socialism: the shortage and the disequilibrium schools.

The disequilibrium – shortage controversies

The debate originally arose from academic concerns with the possibility that central planning offered a model of economic organization better suited to avoid the instability of capitalist production all too visible during the 1970s episodes of high and volatile inflation. While it was commonly agreed that the socialist insistence on capital accumulation did result in queues and shortages associated with excess demand (and inflation), Western economics dominated by Walrasian models with instantly adjusting prices could not provide an analytical framework to explore these. Eventually, the disequilibrium models developed by Barro and Grossman (1971) allowed for temporal rigidities that could capture the across-the-board price controls prevailing in planned economies, and by the late 1970s disequilibrium models were applied to explore the economics of planning (Portes 1986; Portes and Winter 1977).

The translation of disequilibrium analysis to planned economies required two controversial assumptions that triggered a long controversy with a competing approach: the shortage school (Van Brabant 1991). Because the analytical framework treated disequilibrium as a temporary state of a system otherwise governed by equilibrium laws, disequilibrium models assumed planners made occasional, rather than systematic, mistakes correctible in the new planning period. Second, in the two agents (households and planners), two markets (labour and consumer goods) setting, the errors in planning manifested only through excess demand on the consumer markets – either directly through demand for consumer goods or indirectly through wage payments in excess of the planned (and actual) consumer goods output (Portes 1986). The models assigned no analytical relevance to the potential contribution of enterprise demand for intermediary inputs.

The definition of the Soviet economy as a wage-led system and the premise of "passive" enterprise money implied that monetary imbalances would only manifest in the household circuit, assumptions key to the later design of the IMF's stabilization plans for formerly planned economies. Quantity rationing in the consumer market demand forced households to save (and eventually to substitute leisure for consumption), leading to "rising excess liquid balances in the hands of the population with respect to what they would wish to hold if markets cleared at official prices" (Nuti 1986: 38). In the absence of financial markets and instruments, the wealth overhang would in fact materialize into a monetary overhang – purchasing power in excess of the total supply of goods and services (Cottarelli and Blejer 1992).

Disequilibrium analysis thus offered a theoretical basis for suspicions that planned economies were better at hiding, rather than avoiding, inflationary pressures. Empirical investigations, however, suggested that various planned economies had experienced both excess demand and excess supply (Portes et al. 1987). In other words, central planning had no systematic tendency toward excess demand and repressed inflation.

Such conclusions were met with harsh criticism. Janos Kornai, an economist exiled from native Hungary, accused disequilibrium analysts of attempting to fit models developed for capitalist economies to a context they knew little about. Even a mild understanding of how Soviet production worked in practice would have led analysts to accept that pervasive shortages and not erratic planners' mistakes prevailed (Kornai 1982; Kemme 1989).

Disequilibrium models made a fundamental error in assuming that firms operated according to neoclassical assumptions of profit maximization, substituting the market with the plan in a general equilibrium setting. Yet political decisions and bargaining with central planners rather than price determines the allocation of resources, so that the system of incentives produces a *soft budget constraint:* socialist firms are not constrained into efficiency by competitive conditions because central planners encourage firms to produce above plan targets (Kornai 1982). Managers become valued for their ability to provide innovative solutions to shortages and for their success in negotiating long-term investment from central planners.

Thus, it is not planners' mistakes but enterprise behaviour that defines the imbalances of socialist planning. Rather than temporary deviations from equilibrium, the soft-budget constraint produces *perpetual* excess demand and shortages because enterprises' race for resources always pushes wage plans above targets. The shortage account did not spare planners either: errors in planning contributed to an output of consumer goods systematically lower than the plan (Winiecki 1985). The combined effect of the soft-budget constraint and planning inefficiencies clearly undermined the disequilibrium assumption that the system could generate aggregate excess supply or demand. In fact, Kornai held (1982) that shortages and slack at enterprise level rendered the use of "Western" aggregate variables – including repressed inflation – meaningless.

Beyond fundamental disagreements, the two competing approaches rejected the claim that repressed inflation characterized planned economies, one by empirical testing of "formal" models and the other on conceptual grounds. Then the planned system collapsed in 1990, the IMF entered policy arenas, and any traces of the intense debate were erased from its policy narrative. Instead, the IMF identified three structural features of a generic Centrally Planned Economy (CPE) that defined the post-plan macroeconomic problem:

1. the monetary overhang (of the disequilibrium school);
2. the soft budget constraint (of the shortage school);
3. pervasive exchange rate controls (Wolf 1990).

The Fund refused to treat these concepts as irreconcilable because both could be framed into a monetarist narrative of excess demand that legitimized the standard stabilization interventions.

To posit excess demand as the macroeconomic challenge, the IMF's narrative integrated the disequilibrium treatment of money strictly in relationship with consumer markets and the shortage treatment of the productive sector. Thus the IMF attributed excess household liquidity to imbalances at the micro level, even in the absence of aggregate excess demand à la Portes (Wolf 1990). Glossing over conceptual inconsistencies, the IMF approximated the monetary overhang through the quantity theory of money. In a monetarist fashion, it imposed behavioural characteristics to the identity and concluded from comparisons between actual and (estimated) equilibrium money-to-GDP ratios that most centrally planned economies faced similar excess demand pressures: around 40–50 percent of liquid balances were involuntarily held (Nordhaus 1990; IMF et al. 1991; IMF 1992).

3.2.3 The IMF's redefinition of the policy problem: Translating the shortage–disequilibrium debate to the macroeconomics of stabilization

The IMF's entry on the Romanian policy scene redefined the policy "problem" and its attending measures. Demekas and Khan[35] (1991), two IMF staff involved in the design of the stabilization agreement, commended the national pedigree of the May 1990 strategy but traced the origin of the ongoing balance-of-payments crisis to its approach to policy reforms. The May 1990 strategy had fundamentally underestimated the "degree of price distortion and the disequilibrium between aggregate demand and supply inherent in the existing monetary overhang and its inflationary potential" (Demekas and Khan 1991: 16). Consequently, it failed to appreciate the "true" extent of the necessary structural reforms and envisaged unrealistic policy measures given the existing monetary overhang. The "timid" price liberalization timetable would maintain price distortions and harm ambitious privatization plans while reducing the capacity to attract foreign direct investment. Furthermore, the social protection scheme would undermine stabilization efforts by generating additional demand, adding to the monetary overhang. To ensure SOEs increasingly responded to price signals, the IMF advised devaluations and exchange-rate flexibility complemented by trade and foreign-exchange market liberalization (Wolf 1990).

Thus, macroeconomic stabilization, and no longer industrial competitiveness, was identified as the essential policy priority. Framing the policy problem in terms of excess aggregate demand thus reconstituted policy discourse along monetarist lines: "Correcting relative prices and eliminating the monetary overhang in an orderly way are pre-requisites for achieving the other objectives of economic reform" (Wolf 1990: 19). Policy measures were predicated on two assumptions: that excess liquidity existed and would be spent, and, further, that a monetary policy designed according to monetarist principles could spontaneously invalidate the traditional cost mark-up pricing and replace it with the neoclassical marginal pricing strategy (Allen and Haas 2001). Indeed, one of the IMF's pressing concerns in Eastern Europe referred to the national policy-makers' reluctance to embrace monetarism and its view of price determination. Allen and Hass (2001: 11), both working for the IMF in the early years of "transition," described the challenges facing IMF representatives in negotiations with national authorities:

> There were few monetarists in transitional economies, at least in the beginning [...] The idea that prices were related to money was often not intuitive. Rather, the price formation process was viewed as a complex process that involved many technical elements and many factors outside the authorities' control, especially external factors. In fact, tight monetary policy was precisely designed to make the traditional cost-plus-mark up pricing policy impossible. This meant that the same situation IMF economists would see as inflationary would often be viewed as too tight a monetary policy setting by the local authorities. They frequently argued that the "monetary coefficient" (that is, the reciprocal of velocity) was too low, and the level of activity required more – not less – money to support it [...] there was always a local variant of the real bills doctrine – namely, credit expansion is not inflationary if it is issued for productive purposes, typically construction or agriculture.

Three related analytical angles derived from the shortage–disequilibrium debates underlined the economics of the quote (and of the IMF programs):

1. an aggregate demand explanation of inflation arising from the conceptualization, in both disequilibrium and shortage approaches, of inflationary pressures strictly in relationship to households demand in consumer markets;
2. cost-push pressures associated exclusively with wages, traced again to the disequilibrium treatment of the generic CPE as wage-led;
3. an emphasis on the need to curtail liquidity through contractionary monetary targets, arising from the normative implications of the soft-budget constraint.

Whereas the IMF insisted on an account of inflationary pressures from forced savings to demand pressures and then prices, the socialist mark-up pricing strategy placed cost-push pressures at the core of inflationary pressures in the productive sector. Concerns with preserving economies of scale created a productive sector dominated by highly specialized and vertically integrated firms, dominated by monopolies in Romania more than most other socialist countries. Increases in production costs would not be contained to one enterprise in the chain but spread quickly. The puzzling concern with "external factors" that the IMF dismissed reflected national authorities' understanding of complex industrial characteristics. To minimize waste, socialist production used all raw materials available domestically and imported the rest, so that there was little scope for substituting intermediary inputs. Devaluation strategies in the absence of price controls for intermediary imports would quickly translate in cost-push pressures and set in motion an inflationary spiral. Price stability required a stable exchange rate.

Had policy discourse encompassed a wider conceptualization of cost-push pressures in the context of vertically integrated, monopolistic productive structures, the strategy toward price and exchange-rate liberalization would have necessarily required a "gradual" approach, as the May 1990 Commission suggested. Without even reframing the policy problem along some state developmentalist line, to achieve the declared IMF objectives of containing inflationary pressures and reducing external imbalances would have warranted a complex "multifaceted price system," setting different prices and rationing in certain markets (Zhukov and Vorobyov 1991) rather than across-the-board liberalization and active currency management (Amsden et al. 1994).

Thus the treatment of cost pressures and exchange rates (devaluations combined with a flexible exchange-rate regime) that, as I later show, exacerbated inflationary pressures, was not a consequence of the IMF's ignorance (or misunderstanding) of the socialist economies, as many have chosen to understand it (Winiecki 1993). In fact, the IMF had firsthand experience with supply bottlenecks in Latin America. As (neo)structuralist critiques pointed out, devaluations and exchange-rate flexibility typically favoured in monetarist narratives would set off inflationary spirals in economic systems where mark-up pricing prevailed (Taylor 1988: 148–149). Later IMF research indeed recognized that its policy advice in Latin America had been successful where it recommended the deployment of the exchange rate as a nominal anchor, whereas monetarist targets for credit growth coupled with exchange-rate flexibility failed to arrest the growth in either money supply or inflation (Schadler 1995). The IMF, however, refused to learn from its Latin American experience that pegged exchange rates provided a less contractionary approach to stabilize high inflation (Sachs 1996), instead pushing for "shock therapy": price liberalizations, currency devaluations, and floating exchange rates. It rejected calls for endorsing currency stabilization plans that allowed Poland to stabilize its exchange rate and prices after the initial shock therapy (Bofinger 1996). Instead, it assured national authorities that market processes would ensure a faster, more effective method of bringing exchange rates to equilibrium levels, particularly given the difficulties a managed exchange rate raised. Establishing a parity to defend made little sense not solely because of it was virtually impossible to estimate equilibrium levels where economic processes had been little marketized, but also because it would have required international reserves that formerly planned economies simply did not have, and the IMF would not provide.

The incorporation of the disequilibrium emphasis on labour as the main input in the production process grounded a restrictive incomes policy (wage cuts). Maintaining nominal wage growth lower than the rate of change in prices would achieve a double effect: reduce demand while simultaneously keeping enterprise costs under control. The IMF expected income policies to work as in its previous programs with Israel in 1985 and Mexico 1989 (Winiecki 1993). Such optimism fundamentally ignored the socialist approach to establishing workers' wages. Free social services (education, housing, health) were not included in wage plans while capital intensive production techniques implied that wage costs amounted to a relatively small proportion of production costs – ranging from 10 to 25 percent across the CEE region (Amsden et al. 1994). Including these structural characteristics would have undermined the IMF estimates of excessive household liquidity underlying its insistence on monetary tightening and would have raised doubts about the effectiveness of income policies in keeping production costs under control.

The soft-budget constraint became the metric for formulating macroeconomic policy. Where national authorities would have preferred to extend credit to production and thus mediate an industrial recovery after the break-up of both the Central Plan and traditional trade linkages, the IMF reorientated policy discussions to aggregate demand dynamics and tight credit policies to harden enterprises' budget constraints. Policy advice envisaged the creation of a two-tier banking system that separated the central bank and commercial banks. Private ownership, it was held, either through privatization or through greenfield investments, would contribute to the elimination of soft-budget constraints and gradually ensure the financial deepening characteristic of market economies (Ruziev and Ghosh 2008). However, the time frame necessary to institutionalize a market-driven bank behaviour and the pressures faced by SOEs raised doubts about the reliability of credit assessments based on past performance (Bevan et al. 1996). Influential neoliberal policy advisers went so far as to suggest temporarily prohibiting bank lending to SOEs, confining them to self-financing and non-bank capital markets (McKinnon 1991: 118).

The recourse to the simplified narrative of the monetary overhang *cum* soft-budget constraint allowed the IMF to discourage "gradualist" measures that would undermine its radical marketization strategy. The intention was clear: to reconstitute the economic space through a neoliberal vision of competitive markets, small-scale production and marginal pricing strategies.

Consequently, the IMF's presence on the Romanian policy scene redefined the policy problem in line with its preferred policy narrative, and its conditionality changed the politics of the policy process. Since monetary policy was identified as the fundamental anchor in all four stabilization episodes, policy discourse assigned the central bank an instrumental role in establishing and policing neoliberal rules of economic management. The design of the SBA played an important role, seeking to restrict room for manoeuvre and to institute a careful and detailed monitoring mechanism that maintained policy within its "rational" boundaries. The mechanics of the program sought to mobilize policy shifts before the official signing and then to closely monitor compliance. The SBA process first set a list of prior actions upon which agreement of the IMF Executive Board is conditional. The official agreement would be signed upon the satisfactory undertaking of the prior actions. This further specified the quarterly quantitative performance criteria, structured through a monetarist discourse that identified the central bank as the key institution in the enforcement strategy. Depending on the particular context of the program, negotiations would identify other quantitative benchmarks which were deemed important for stabilization. Third, the SBA envisaged a mid-term review where policy slippages that could potentially threaten compliance were identified and targets updated according to the developments in monitored indicators. The performance criteria would function as a straitjacket, dividing the loan into four equal tranches that can be drawn if the criteria are met.

The following sections turn to the exchange-rate and monetary policy narratives and their deployment in policy practice.

3.3 The 1991 stand-by arrangement

The 1991 SBA was the outcome of a process entirely consistent with a *modus operandi* perfected since the Chilean experiment of the Pinochet regime's Chicago boys (Klein 2007). It used the political and economic crisis unfolding in the second part of 1990 to push forward a package of policy measures that would have found little support under democratic conditions. The Prime Minister addressed the Parliament in October requesting exceptional powers to implement what Demekas and Khan (1991) termed a "substantially more realistic" approach to reform, defined by the prior actions requested by the IMF to sign the SBA. Invoking extraordinary politics, the government refused to submit the package for discussion or approval in the Parliament and instead pushed the reforms through an emergency ordinance. A series of measures targeting price and trade liberalization were implemented in November 1990, responding to the prior actions required for the SBA approval. The timetable for price liberalization deserves particular attention, as it became an important discursive operation for explaining policy failures or unexpected outcomes of the stabilization process.

3.3.1 Price liberalization

There are different, and at times contradictory, accounts of the timetable of liberalization. These share the claim that a gradual, politicized timetable reproduced the "rigidities" of the planned system by distorting the signalling role of prices and wider market mechanisms.

The strategy toward prices (liberalization) was first discussed in the May 1990 report. The report rejected a sudden liberalization, suggesting that the monopoly/oligopoly structures prevailing in the Romanian economy warranted price controls in certain sectors until a more competitive setting emerged. However, the turn to a neoliberal economic agenda in the second half of 1990 redefined price reform, seeking to eliminate the early industrial "bias." Three successive rounds of price liberalization, in November 1990, April 1991, and July 1991 left only 14 categories of consumer goods critical for social reasons under an administered regime[36]. Price controls on strategic intermediate imports were quietly abandoned a few months after their institutionalization, prompting the IMF to commend Romania on the speed of its price liberalization, as "in only eight months Romania went from a system of complete price controls to one that compares favourably with many market economies" (Demekas and Khan 1991: 21).

This pace of price reform has not been recognized in gradualist accounts. On the contrary, these picture price liberalization as a long and cumbersome process (IMF 1996; OECD 1998; Dragulin and Radulescu 1999), with harmful consequences for the establishment of much-needed allocative efficiency[37] (NBR, 1992a).

To maintain a gradualist representation, the discussion was framed around administrative control of consumer prices. Indeed, by 1993, prices of around 50 percent of the consumer basket were controlled, a share reduced, through successive liberalization rounds, to 15 percent in 2000 (Budina et al. 2002). While indeed the weight of administered prices in the consumer basket has been higher than in other Eastern European countries, in practice successive governments retained far less control over administered prices than is commonly recognized. Under the provisions of the successive SBAs, administered prices were periodically adjusted in line with exchange-rate devaluations and generally absorbed devaluations with a lag no longer than four months (see Figure 3.2). This inscribed administered prices a trend similar to those determined "freely."

Articulating gradualism around consumer prices had two effects. It first structured discussions around the speed of consumer price liberalization, thus removing from the policy discussions the very issue

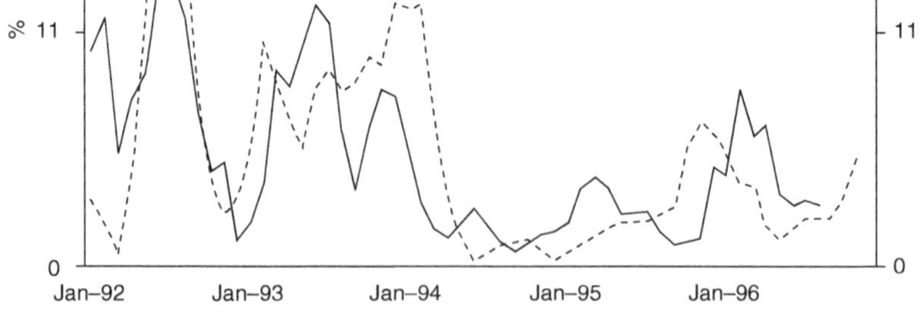

Figure 3.2 Exchange rate and administered prices index (four-month lag), Romania, 1992–1996

Source: Computed from the Statistical section of *the National Bank of Romania Annual Report 1997* for exchange rate data and Budina et al. (2002) for administered price index data.

that the 1990 Commission Report emphasized: that the structure of the Romanian economy required a careful consideration of whether and when to liberalize, particularly for intermediary inputs and raw materials unavailable domestically.

It further suggested that gradualism functioned to protect SOEs from the disciplining hand of the market by "distorting" price signals, when by July 1991 only certain consumer prices were controlled. SOEs received little if any direct subsidy through price controls. Furthermore, since energy imports formed the bulk of intermediary imports due to the high energy intensity of industrial production, energy pricing was identified as essential to both restructuring and tackling widening external imbalances. The government committed, at the IMF's specific request, to maintain domestic prices of crude petroleum and related products at or above international market levels and to adjust them monthly in line with exchange-rate movements. Retail prices would be adjusted to fully reflect costs and to allow for a profit margin. Thus, by February 1991, domestic energy prices (at official exchange rates) were above international market levels (IMF 1991a). Moreover, cross-subsidization from industrial consumers to households was a current practice until energy-sector liberalization began in 2001 (IMF 2001).

In other words, while policy discourse insisted on the distortions to allocative efficiencies engendered by price controls, price liberalization left SOEs unable to protect strategic cost factors (such as the price of energy) from international volatility – a widespread practice among capitalist multinationals (Galbraith 1967). Their ability to pass rising costs to consumers was further constrained in consumer-goods sectors targeted by administrative price control. Monetary policy then joined the neoliberal attack on state-owned production.

3.3.2 Tackling "excess demand"

The April 1991 SBA articulated the policy problem according to the IMF's policy priorities. It identified the monetary overhang as the main "problem" for stabilization. Indeed, while national authorities in the CEE region generally supported a real bills doctrine (Allen and Haas 2001), the IMF's monetarist discourse linked prices to money and inflationary pressures to excess demand arising from the monetary overhang rather than cost factors and recommended a tight monetary policy to ensure the adequate absorption of the monetary overhang through price liberalization.

Consistent with the neoclassical flow-of-funds approach that locates the source of inflationary pressures in excessive bank liabilities (here the monetary overhang), the first stabilization plan aimed to reduce the inflation rate to a 15 percent annualized rate for December 1991, for which it envisaged an annual 15 percent target in broad money growth and 26 percent in credit to the nongovernment (i.e. productive) sector growth. The logic of the programme was purely monetarist. It assumed a constant velocity of circulation, no short-term impact on output, and a one-for-one relationship between broad-money supply growth and price increases. Furthermore, the IMF estimated that up to 50 percent of the money stock was involuntarily held at the end of 1990 by comparing the income velocity of money at that time with the 1970s' and early 1980s' averages (Demekas and Khan 1991). Given the size of the monetary overhang, the combined impact of price liberalization and the attending exchange-rate devaluation was expected to push inflation levels to about 100 percent year on year, a one-off corrective episode (IMF 1991a).

Moreover, it was widely agreed that exchange-rate devaluations combined with a freely floating exchange-rate regime were required to correct the socialist legacy of substantial misalignment (Demekas and Khan 1991; NBR, 1992a), particularly since the differential to the level on the newly created foreign-exchange market signalled that official exchange rates were well overvalued[38]. The NBR (1993b) subscribed to this equilibrium discourse: even at a risk of a trade-off between external stability and inflation, the politicization of exchange-rate decisions inherent to a pegged regime would prevent the necessary adjustments to equilibrium and reproduce external imbalances. The use of the exchange rate as a nominal anchor to stabilize inflationary dynamics would appreciate the real exchange rate, divorcing its dynamics from its fundamental determinants and eventually forcing large devaluations.

Relative PPP normativity guided the magnitude of the adjustments: devaluations would offset the price increases associated with price liberalizations so that real depreciation would move the exchange rate closer to its equilibrium level. Perversely, the phasing of price liberalizations legitimated repeated "corrective" devaluations[39], so that within a year of the first SBA, the nominal exchange rate against the US dollar weakened by around 900 percent (see Figure 3.1).

The monetary program aimed at transferring money holdings from the household sector, where most of the monetary overhang was assumed to be located, to the enterprise sector. The data appeared to support this policy proposition. At the end of 1990, time deposits amounted to 60 percent of broad money stock, of which 84 percent were household ROL[40] savings. The ratio of cash to broad money (19 percent) was similar to former centrally planned economies at the time (Ruziev and Ghosh 2008). Enterprise deposits amounted to only 16 percent of total deposits, a consequence of the Ceauşescu-era policy of limiting access to bank credit for working capital purposes only, as capital investment would be financed from retained earnings.

In other words, the IMF held, a tight credit policy would not affect output but merely redistribute excess money. Price liberalization and exchange-rate devaluation would absorb excess monetary holding without creating liquidity shortages for the state-owned productive sector. Further, the IMF stabilization plan explained (1991a: 46), the fall in real credit would be mitigated by the removal of existing restrictions on enterprise deposits in the banking system. Eliminating the segmentation between household and enterprise money, and thus the different degrees of liquidity and moneyness, would foster financial development[41].

The monetarist assumption of money neutrality failed to consider the possibility that households viewed money as a store of wealth. From this perspective, the broad money-to-GDP ratio, the variable commonly deployed to measure the monetary overhang, could not represent unspent purchasing power, particularly when considering that secondary (black) markets provided alternative spending opportunities (Alexeev 1988) or that households chose to maintain higher voluntary savings to maintain available purchasing power for acquiring consumable goods entering the markets in a random fashion (Cottarelli and Blejer 1992). A second important policy implication arises from the Keynesian link between money and uncertainty (Dow 2004). With little confidence in expectations, money would be demanded and held as an asset to deal with fundamental (unquantifiable) uncertainty. Thus, placing household monetary holdings in a Keynesian narrative changes policy implications as households confronted with the extreme uncertainty of a collapsed political and economic system would have demanded precautionary balances rather than disposed of the extra purchasing power. If uncertainty, rather than pent-up demand, guided households' economic behaviour then attempts to redistribute liquidity would have perverse effects, creating instead liquidity shortages.

Indeed, the outcome of the IMF's advice followed closely the above scenario. Faithful to its SBA commitments, the NBR proceeded to tighten credit at the beginning of 1991. With no indirect instruments to influence credit decisions (bank reserves in the multiplier account), it established bank-by-bank credit ceilings. This created a severe liquidity shortage: while credit to nongovernment (largely to SOEs) kept pace with the IMF benchmark target, expanding by around 30 percent from April to December 1991, inter-enterprise arrears quadrupled throughout the same period, from ROL480 million to ROL1.7 billion (see Figure 3.3). Industrial production contracted by more than 25

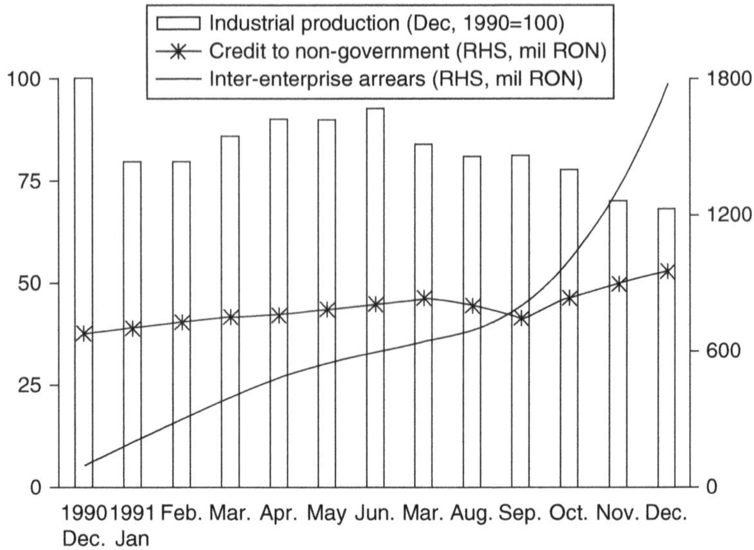

Figure 3.3 Credit, arrears and industrial production, Romania, 1991
Source: Data from Demekas and Khan, 1991.

percent. Romanian developments confirmed a well-documented tendency of the IMF's stabilization programs to produce liquidity crunches (Schadler 1995). Indeed, IMF stabilization programs in other formerly planned economies produced similar outcomes. Calvo and Coricelli (1992) documented the 1990 stabilization strategy in Poland, where the price liberalization provoked a supply shock that combined with the credit ceilings (justified similarly by a focus on household liquidity) led to a severe liquidity shortage in the enterprise sector. Behind the Polish stagflation (a collapse in industrial production and high inflation rates) were credit-crunched rather than demand-side factors.

The credit crunch resulted from the combination of higher working capital needs (driven by price liberalization and exchange rate devaluations) and tight monetary policy. Credit rationing in productive system linked through vertical integration resulted in arrears that post-Keynesians would recognize as the transition equivalent of a money-endogenizing process.

The monetary-policy prescriptions sought to redefine the relationship between finance and production, ignoring the role of money as a vital institution of capitalism (Dillard 1980). Ironically, the IMF program extended Ceauşescu's attempts to prevent SOEs' access to bank loans for financing investment to now curtail access to credit for financing working-capital requirements. Whereas Ceauşescu insisted on financing from retained earnings as a method of increasing the sustainability of state-owned production, the post-Plan demand collapse triggered by the loss of export markets and trade liberalization left SOEs with the exotic advice to turn to market-driven sources of financing such as issues or long-term debt instrument issues (McKinnon 1991) – useless given the embryonic nature of the Romanian financial system of the time.

Such a contractionary macroeconomic programme could not be upheld for very long. After the government had ignored trade unions' increasingly vocal contestations of the economic strategy, at the end of September 1991 several trainloads of miners descended on the capital[42]. Following several days of protest, the Prime Minister was forced to resign. A new government of "apolitical technocrats" vowed to continue with (neoliberal) economic reform.

It soon became apparent that social unrest was only a manifestation of the upheaval the country was experiencing. From the "jobs for everyone" socialist doctrine, unemployment increased quickly to around 7.7 percent by the end of 1991, worsened by severe wage cuts. The difficulties in accessing international financial markets curtailed available hard currency for essential imports of raw materials and energy, further affecting industrial production. The SOEs were asked to surrender all export earnings, a highly controversial measure in place until May 1992. Furthermore, price developments challenged the monetarist logic: while broad money increased by 19 percent up to October 1991, consumer price inflation reached 156 percent (producer price inflation by 103 percent), clearly tracking exchange-rate devaluations.

By December 1991, the government recognized the obvious danger of economic collapse if contractionary monetary policies were to be further pursued. Indeed, the attempts to institutionalize "market relationships" produced a severe (financial) payments blockage: arrears reached 40 percent of enterprises' turnover (World Bank 1992) as unpaid firms were unable to pay in turn. While the government advocated a selective bailout, the Parliament passed legislation for a Global Compensation Scheme (GCS), a one-off credit injection that would clear arrears across the board. Rather than a "gift" to enterprises as most analyses claimed (NBR, 1992a), the GCS was designed on a commercial basis. It required collateral (government guarantees or debtors' assets of six-month maturity or less), while the interest rates it charged reflected the prohibitive credit conditions in the economy (at around 70 percent).

However, the credit injection breached the SBA performance criteria on credit to productive sector. The monetization of inter-enterprise arrears brought the actual figure five times above its target[43]. In response, the IMF suspended the program, portraying the GCS as a politicized solution subordinated to industrial interests (IMF 1991b). In fact, the IMF casting of tight monetary policy as "apolitical" instead functioned to eliminate any critical reflections of the economics of stabilization predicated on the assumption of excess liquidity, although the magnitude of the deviation from target suggested a massive liquidity crunch. Instead, the IMF attributed inter-enterprise arrears to weak financial discipline caused by the soft-budget constraint. Consistent with this explanation of crisis, the NBR took measures to minimize the net GCS liquidity effects. It enforced credit repayments before maturity and introduced reserve requirements on bank liabilities so that the liquidity injection was largely sterilized in the first months of 1992 (IMF 1992a). Credit contracted in both nominal and real terms (see Figure 3.4), again starving the system of liquidity.

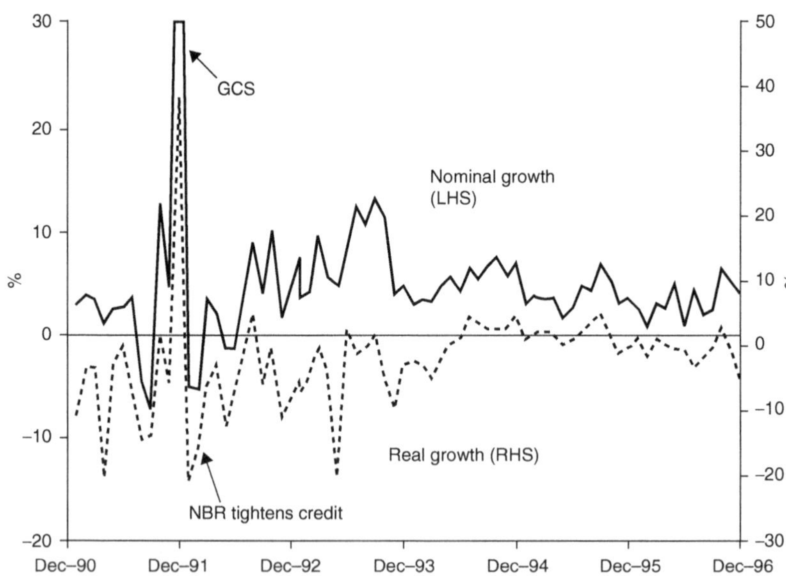

Figure 3.4 Non-government credit dynamics, Romania, 1990–1997

Source: Data from the Statistical section of *the National Bank of Romania Annual Reports 1995* and *2000*.

It is important to note that throughout both 1990 and 1991 there was no domestic debt because of budget surpluses. The central bank did not directly monetize government debt as in the monetarist/IMF explanation of inflationary pressures. In fact, the Treasury's positive balance with the central bank rendered it a net creditor to the banking sector (NBR, 1998). Since fiscal policy could not directly account for the rampant inflation, the IMF turned to monetary and exchange-rate policies, which, it held, acquired a quasi-fiscal character because of the government's attempts to support the state-owned industrial sector (IMF 1997a).

3.4 Expanding the policy repertoire: The 1992 stand-by arrangement

Negotiations for a second SBA resumed immediately. A new set of policy commitments was agreed by May 1992, essentially recommitting the national authorities to the principles of the first stabilization plan. In the letter of intent, the Romanian authorities pointed out that external shocks had worsened an already difficult economic environment and that further discipline was required to tackle the crisis. While income policies had remained consistent with the SBA prescriptions (real wages had declined by 22 percent since November 1990), further monetary tightening would signal commitment to economic restructuring and help reconstruct policy credibility after the GCS episode. The authorities also acknowledged that exchange-rate policy practice during February–May 1992 had deviated from its discourse of flexibility. It portrayed the episode as a temporary measure to contain wage demands and again vowed to entrust the exchange rate to the market's self-regulating forces.

The new SBA identified the soft-budget constraint as the main policy challenge. Indeed, the IMF (1992a: 55) drew a valuable lesson from the GCS episode: price stabilization was conditional on micro-restructuring efforts to enforce hard-budget constraints[44], so that "to obtain the desired reduction of inflation, stringent credit policies are needed". The second stabilization plan set an 88-percent money-growth target and a 70-percent limit on cumulative changes in bank credit. The difference of magnitude between the money-growth targets in the two stabilization programs reflected a more pessimistic outlook for inflation and the alleged absorption of the monetary overhang. The 15 percent broad-money growth established in the first SBA premised a monetary overhang that would allow the absorption of price jumps without additional monetary growth. The substantial overshooting in consumer price inflation (223 percent, compared with a target of 120 percent) implied that, whatever the magnitude of the monetary overhang, such substantial price inflation had absorbed it.

The range of policy instruments had to be expanded to legitimize the monetarist narrative of excess liquidity. A new round of credit ceilings could have hardly mobilized political support given the 1991 debacle. In response, the central bank turned to interest rates and indirect policy instruments (required reserves and the refinancing facility) to ensure monetary restraint. The 1992 SBA demanded a substantial increase in interest rates; the NBR (1992a) agreed that this would signal the end of abundant credit at negative real-interest rates as if credit decisions in 1991 had not been entirely determined by credit ceilings[45]. Instead, the emergence of the interest rate as a "viable" policy instrument sought to give the appearance that market mechanisms, rather than policy-makers, were behind highly contractionary policies – a rhetorical move successfully adopted by Volker during the 1980s monetarist experiments in the USA. The NBR raised its refinancing rate at 80 percent in May 1992 in the pursuit of positive real values. While in policy practice the institutionalization of the interest rate as policy instrument is conditional on its effectiveness for controlling aggregate demand, neither the IMF nor the central bank considered it necessary to investigate the functioning of the transmission mechanism.

The new monetary tightening programme again produced unexpected results. The IMF's October 1992 SBA review noted with dismay that enterprises' demand for credit was growing at an unexpectedly slow pace. Some of the subdued demand for credit was partly explained as a substitution to cheaper arrears, but, even so, the increase in total credit including arrears reached only half of the programmed level (IMF 1992b: 15). Indeed, for most of 1992, nongovernment credit grew at a slow pace in nominal terms and contracted in real terms (see Figure 3.4), which the central bank interpreted as evidence that the credit growth targets were too generous.

Rather than being driven by lower financing needs, the willingness to lend and borrow responded to the combination of the highly uncertain climate and the central bank's non-accommodative stance. The productive sector found it increasingly difficult to raise long-term finance: the share of short-term credit in total nongovernment credit rose to above 80 percent by the end of 1991, where it remained for the rest of the period (see Figure 3.5). As finance turned impatient, the first

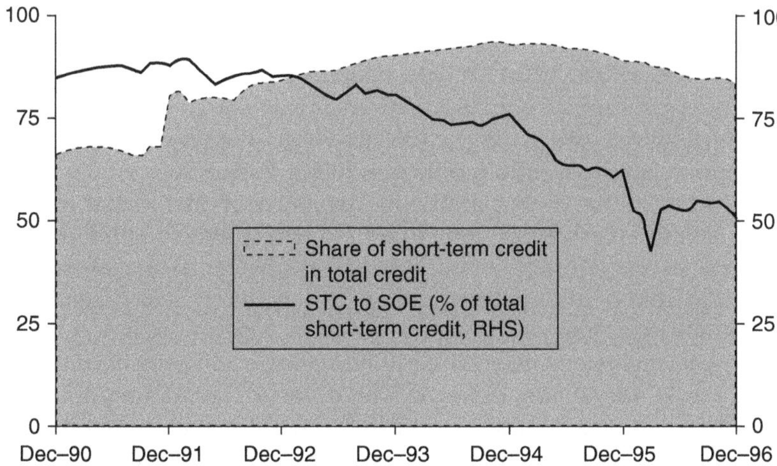

Figure 3.5 Term structure of non-government credit, 1990–96, Romania

Source: Computed from the Statistical section of *the National Bank of Romania Annual Reports 1995* and 2000.

round effects were felt by SOEs: up to 1994, their share in total short-term credit remained above 80 percent.

The central bank faced a new conundrum. If the SBA monetary targets were too generous, how come Romania was experiencing, in the words of the NBR director of monetary policy (Radulescu 1993), the third payments blockage in so many years and rampant inflation by the end of 1992, along with a 13 percent GDP contraction and a 22 percent contraction in industrial output?

Even though the typical neoliberal response attributed the economic chaos to political interference that perpetuated financial indiscipline, the government was forced out of office in September 1992 on the grounds of an overblown predisposition towards "shock therapy" rather than lax policies (Pop 2006), a signal of economic debates intensifying in the political arena.

In the debate, the central bank took, without hesitation, an anti-government position. Its 1992 annual report clarified the policy "failure" as follows. Preferential credit, extended under governmental pressure, had produced an excess of liquidity in the system (Radulescu 1993) that further fed speculative pressures on the exchange rate, since the loss of the domestic currency's "moneyness" shifted portfolio preferences to foreign currency and complicated monetary control. Indeed, in early 1992, the government had decided to open two special credit lines for agriculture and energy producers[46], extended by a state-owned commercial bank[47] at subsidized rates Underlying this "nonmarket" measure was not an industrial revival strategy but rather an attempt to cover the large losses enterprises were incurring due to the asymmetry between administered prices (for food and household energy) and liberalized prices on inputs into production (NBR, 1995: 55).

Notwithstanding these claims, the dynamics of the central bank's credit facilities throughout 1992 and up to the middle of 1993 invalidated the excess liquidity account. Whereas preferential credit rose to over 80 percent of high-powered money, it was the *composition* and not the volume that changed. As Figure 3.6 shows, against mounting inflationary pressures (consumer price inflation rose to 200 percent in 1992), average daily refinancing from the NBR decreased in nominal terms[48]. To comply with the domestic credit (NDA) performance criterion, and in line with the excess liquidity discourse, the NBR significantly reduced

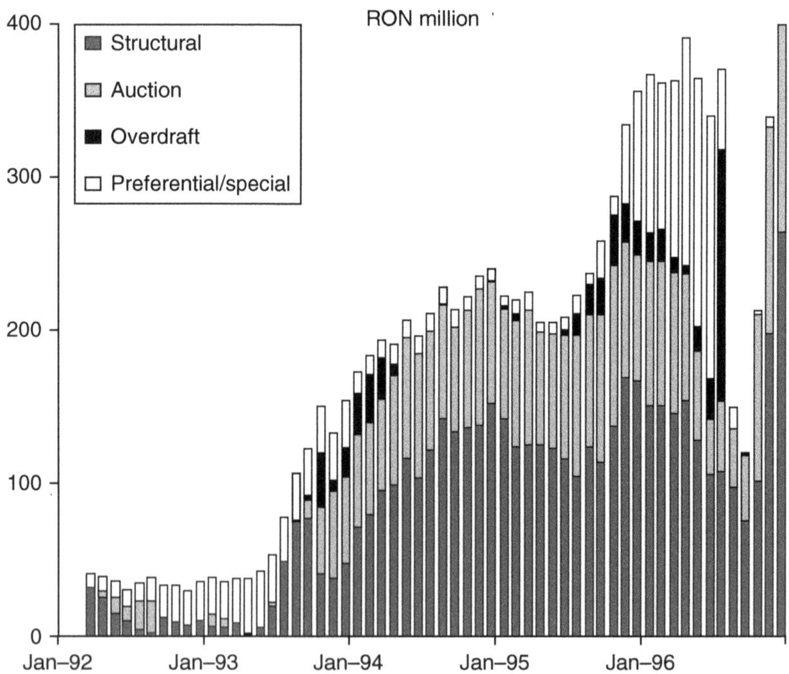

Figure 3.6 NBR's credit facilities (million RON), Romania, 1992–1996

Source: Computed from the Statistical sections of *the National Bank of Romania Annual Reports 1995* and *2000*.

access to the discount window (through either the structural or auction facilities) to offset the growth in preferential credit.

The industrial sector, supported by several government officials, mounted a substantial challenge to the excess-money narrative. It argued that the banks' credit decisions, rather than financial indiscipline, were posing unprecedented challenges to economy-wide payment operations, short of sabotage in the words of a Ministry of Industries official (Adevarul 1993a). Since the NBR had raised its refinancing rate and had imposed administrative measures that would approximate market outcomes – higher loan rates – state-owned banks had discovered their capitalist instincts and were damaging productive activity. The following quotation captures well the outrage:

> [We are] a state-owned enterprise that succeeded in both increasing production and mobilizing demand. Whatever we have achieved through restructuring production, banks are destroying, through extremely high interest rates and a very slow payment mechanism. We have ROL200 million with CEC[49], which requires thirty days for access. While the essence of restructuring, money, is at banks' discretion, there is a silent war going on. (Priescu 1993, author's translation)

The metaphor of the "war" deployed here to describe the relationship between production and finance hints to the onset of financialization in the banking sector: an economic system where the lending decisions no longer respond directly to the priorities of production. As the industrial sector became increasingly reluctant to borrow at prohibitive interest rates, banks purposefully delayed payment transfers (Adevarul 1993b; Priescu 1993b). Such reports further questioned the common wisdom describing banking development in transition as a slow process where state-owned banks, unaccustomed to market practices, functioned to validate the state's populist credit subsidies for its productive system. On the contrary, the excess demand narrative and the central bank's liquidity management effectively catalyzed the redefinition of state-owned banks as separate "entities" with competing interests.

The productive sector had a limited capacity to withstand such operational blockages. Without access to its bank deposits, financing options were narrowed to either accepting payment delays, with the attending slowdown in activity, or to playing into banks' game by contracting credit at penal rates. The first choice would result in arrears while the second implied either a contraction of profits or prices increases to reflect increasing costs. A temporary solution saw enterprises turning to large-value cash payments[50] which the NBR subsequently recognized as a consequence of banks' deliberate delays in settling interbank payments (NBR, 1993a). To circumvent banks' reluctance and to reduce the payment cycle, the NBR decided to create fixed-sum cheques, paid on sight. Furthermore, the government took additional measures to tackle the payments blockage. The four big state-owned banks were mandated to implement a subsidized three-month credit programme[51] that sought to alleviate the temporary liquidity problems among exporting SOEs with good economic performance.

The shifting relationship between production and finance opened up a new field of policy contestation: NBR's interest-rate policy. Policy argumentation framed interest-rate decisions through a discourse of financial liberalization (McKinnon 1973; Shaw 1973), in line with the IMF's own position. According to this, once the corrective component of inflation was absorbed, tackling structural inflationary pressures required the fast marketization of the two relevant financial variables: the exchange rate and the interest rate (NBR, 1992b). The primacy of market-driven financial intermediation built on the claim that saved resources would be better channelled into productive use, while simultaneously "discriminating" against investments with lower returns. The last point was of particular importance, for it implied that, under a liberalized financial sector, SOEs would no longer benefit from subsidized interest rates. Removing loan-rate ceilings would increase the average efficiency of investment and thus accelerate restructuring and the reorientation of resources toward more efficient activity. Furthermore, financial liberalization would positively influence growth as higher (deposit) real interest rates could mobilize savings at the expense of consumption and thus increase the productive capacity of a country.

However, the episode described above, where additional regulation was necessary for the banking sector to behave according to basic "market rules" (such as timely payments), questioned the optimistic promises financial liberalization discourses made to the productive sector. Against this background, the NBR proceeded to reconstruct the legitimacy of its interest-rate policy (NBR, 1993a). It dismissed the Keynesian argument that an increase in the marginal propensity to save reduces consumption, aggregate demand, the rate of profit, and therefore investment (Arestis and Caner 2004). The 1991 collapse in investment, it argued, when interest rates were highly negative in real terms, indicated that investment showed little sensitivity to interest rates – a weak argument when taking into account that credit ceilings had substantially reduced companies' access to financing. The NBR further maintained that Keynesian-informed interest-rate policy would undermine its emphasis on contracting excess demand. Besides, increases in real interest rates could not generate either cost-driven inflationary pressures or affect the rate of profit because interest payments represented a small share of enterprises' operating costs.

This last claim was quite controversial, particularly since under central planning enterprises were dependent on bank credit for financing working capital (Dow et al. 2008). Indeed, with interest rates hovering at around 80 percent throughout 1992, the Ministry of Industries (1993) estimated that interest-rate repayments rose to around 30 percent of enterprises' operating costs, significantly higher than the 5 percent produced by the NBR (1993a). Elsewhere, however NBR admitted that the lack of capitalization affecting the state-owned sector after the collapse of the planned economy implied that enterprises' own resources for working-capital needs amounted to 35 percent, compared to a necessary average of 80 percent (Radulescu 1995). The rest had to be covered through bank loans. If the Ministry of Industry's estimation was closer to the actual value, then high interest rates would be detrimental to capital investment, particularly where SOEs responded to payments blockage by reducing demand for credit[52].

While the NBR maintained liquidity management in line with the excess demand narrative, its exchange-rate policy again departed from the commitments to flexibility. Mounting inflationary pressures triggered interventions to reduce currency volatility after June 1992. These suggested a different impact of the 1992 SBA: inflationary pressures arising from massive exchange-rate devaluations[53] and financial blockages arising through a combination of banks' attempts to force SOEs to demanding expensive credit combined with NBR's policy of reducing access to its credit facilities.

The IMF refused to consider alternative explanations and instead cancelled the second SBA in April 1993. New negotiations began in July 1993. The central bank promised a fresh beginning (NBR, 1993a).

3.5 The dawn of a new era: The 1994 stand-by arrangement

Negotiations extended for nearly a year (the SBA was approved in May 1994), amidst a difficult economic environment. Inflation rates remained stubbornly high while industrial production was contracting at an alarming rate. Increasing policy contestations made the excess liquidity story difficult to defend, while simultaneously the central bank was abating from its commitments to exchange-rate flexibility.

The central bank produced two reports explaining monetary policy (NBR, 1992b) and exchange-rate policy (NBR, 1993b). The 1993 exchange-rate report combined competing claims. On the one hand, it insisted on the PPP causality from prices to nominal exchange rates[54], and deployed the monetary approach to the balance of payments to argue that, rather than devaluations feeding into price increases, excess liquidity caused inflation. On the other hand, the report recognized some pass-through from exchange rates to prices, positing a trade-off between competitiveness and price dynamics[55].

The report used a relative PPP approach to estimate the magnitude of misalignment (NBR, 1993b). It situated the equilibrium exchange rates at ROL/US$33 for 1990 and calculated subsequent equilibrium levels and deviations using the retail price difference between Romania and the USA. The approximation took no account of the comparability of price indices, the base-year equilibrium was derived on the questionable assumption that it would have equilibrated the external balance during the last years of Communism, and it subsequently produced highly volatile equilibrium levels for the 1991–1992 period. Essentially, the central bank assumed that the real equilibrium level remained constant throughout the period under analysis, a strong assumption given the significant structural changes in the economy. Furthermore, the report used two "common sense" signals of misalignment: the persistence of trade deficits despite successive devaluations and the differentials between the interbank/black-market levels and the official interest rate. It glossed over the possibility of either structural trade deficits arising from the permanent loss of export markets or the persistent foreign-reserves shortages that translated into interbank exchange-rate volatility.

In policy practice, this ambiguity translated into shifts between stabilizing the currency and withdrawing from the foreign exchange (currency) market. What explains the apparent inconsistency of exchange-rate decisions? Was it political interference into market processes, as the IMF alleged? While indeed currency market interventions did involve political decisions to sidestep commitments to equilibrium, the focus on politics again sidelines the economics underlying equilibrium discourses. Indeed, equilibrium-seeking devaluations have perverse effects in the presence of an exchange-rate pass-through. Where nominal devaluations were reflected in prices (with a lag), as Figure 3.7 suggests for both consumer and producer prices, then the PPP

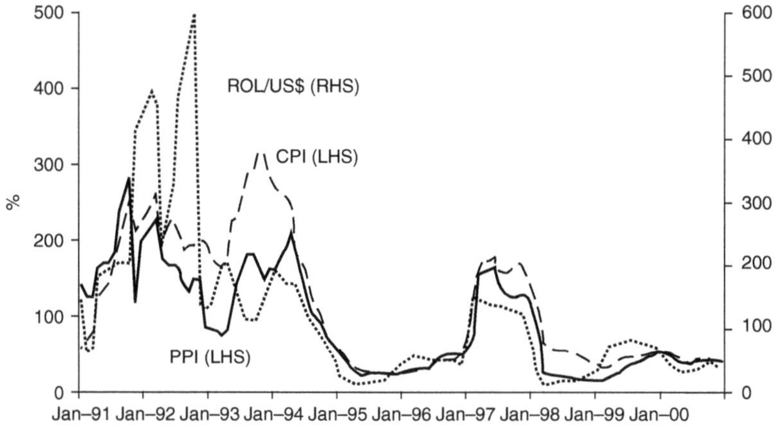

Figure 3.7 Price indices and exchange rate dynamics (percent change), year on year, Romania, 1991–2000

Source: Computed from the Statistical Section of *the National Bank of Romania Annual Report 1995* and *2000*.

discourse shaping policy practice produced inflationary spirals. In fact, relative PPP logic dictated that price liberalizations would be accompanied by devaluations to prevent the appreciation of the real exchange rate, but these would quickly push into increased prices, further requiring ex-post adjustments in exchange rates. Under these circumstances, commitment to market-determined exchange rates could not be upheld for too long unless policy-makers were prepared to accept the instability associated with highly volatile inflation rates. While currency interventions did require political validation, the PPP approach contributed significantly to exchange-rate volatility.

NBR's policy discourse reflected this dilemma. While it acknowledged that arresting the speed of devaluation did slow down price movements, the NBR (1994a: 10) rejected what it called the "disproportionate emphasis" on cost-push inflation. It discussed monetary policy options as a trade-off between aggregate demand and cost-push explanations of inflation and argued that an undue emphasis on the latter had two essential shortfalls. First, the conditions for employing the exchange rate as a nominal anchor were simply not in place (Radulescu 1993). The NBR lacked the foreign reserves for credibly defending an established target while the IMF refused to support such a policy strategy. Furthermore, the politicization of exchange-rate decisions disqualified it as a policy instrument. Inflation could not be tackled through exchange-rate policies because the *real* cause of inflation was the gradualism delaying micro-restructuring. Once prices were liberalized, the government's insistence on maintaining an overvalued currency constituted another instance of protectionism of the SOEs, an implicit and indirect subsidy of the imports of raw materials and intermediary imports that undermined the critical link between exchange rates and competitiveness and thus reproduced external trade disequilibria.

By insisting that exchange-rate management represented the best example of technocratic policy-making frustrated by government pressures, the NBR was aiming to both orchestrate policy consensus and to deny responsibility for currency volatility. This was a difficult operation, for various policy actors challenged its economics. Industrial interests, the "big winners" of the insistence on nominal stability, rejected the claim that the exchange-rate decisions were functioning to allow it to recover its export competitiveness (Adevarul 1994). Instead, erratic policy decisions harmed export activity. The 1991 decision to "confiscate" exporters' foreign exchange earnings, a measure commonly employed throughout Eastern Europe to offset the loss of foreign currency reserves, was a good example of the institutional disorder affecting industrial exporters. Production depended on imports of intermediary goods and raw-materials revenue so that the surrender mechanism left exporters dependent on the NBR or on the interbank market for mobilizing these resources. The active encouragement of consumer goods imports as an anti-inflationary measure, a feature present in IMF-supported stabilization plans (Amsden et al. 1994), saw industrial producers competing for scarce foreign resources with retail importers or having the option of a greatly depreciated exchange rate. Thus, rather than receiving a subsidy through appreciating real exchange rates, the lack of a well-functioning mechanism for redistributing foreign currency greatly limited the ability to produce and export and compelled SOEs to innovate payment procedures in order to avoid the retention mechanism. Equally controversial were devaluation decisions when placed in the context of enterprises' dependency on imports of intermediary goods (Oana 1993). In theory, competitive devaluations function by changing relative prices and shifting consumption from more expensive imports to locally produced goods, while simultaneously improving export competitiveness. However, a significant pass-through effect to production costs, caused by the absence of domestically produced intermediary substitutes, not only increased domestic prices but also diminished the scope for correcting the current-account imbalances and exchange-rate flexibility.

PPP-driven ex-post adjustments aimed at preserving competitiveness would produce persistent inflationary pressures (Coricelli et al. 2004).

The existence of such an effect was later acknowledged in IMF research (2001, 2003), which estimated a substantial pass-through from exchange rate to prices. Undoubtedly the magnitude was higher before 1997, as domestic production depended to a greater extent on intermediary imports. Thus the existence of a large pass-through limits the scope for exchange-rate flexibility. Indeed, the IMF's 2001 country report put it as follows: "the actual path of inflation was largely determined by policy decisions regarding the timing and magnitude of price liberalization and exchange rate" whereas "the role of money and credit growth has also been important, though harder to demonstrate empirically" (IMF 2001: 10). Six SBAs later, the IMF's relentless criticism of national policy-makers for failing to implement monetarist principles gave way to a cost-push explanation of inflationary pressures that acknowledged there was little empirical support for aggregate demand accounts.

Yet, in 1993, the central bank rejected the idea that cost-push considerations could guide its policy. This would amount, in its own words, to a negation of its very *raison d'être:* to control aggregate demand (NBR 1994a: 36). What emerges here is a dichotomized construction of policy choices: politicized exchange-rate management versus "objective" aggregate demand control, a signal of how powerful neoliberal discourses were in shaping Romanian policies. The neoliberal central bank must stay out of politics, even if it involves disregarding empirical evidence of the relationship between exchange rates and prices. Indeed, the first report where the central bank described in detail its approach to monetary policy failed to mention the exchange rate as a possible cause of inflation and instead insisted on the usual suspects: gradual price liberalization and excess liquidity driven by gradualism in micro restructuring (NBR 1992b).

Attempts to frame inflation through an excess liquidity narrative were difficult to maintain. During the 1993 discussions with the IMF, the negotiators on both sides recognized that Romania was confronted with a peculiar type of inflation, for neither arrears nor monetary aggregates (and credit behaviour) could explain inflationary pressures (Adevarul 1993b). Monetarist policy measures, such as restricting access to NBR's liquidity facilities, seemed to have little impact on prices. Furthermore, the shift in portfolio preferences further debilitated the scope for monetary control: by the end of 1993, foreign-exchange liabilities amounted to around 30 percent of broad money, also reflected in a substantially lower share of ROL long-term household deposits[56] (see Table 3.1). The cash to

Table 3.1 Broad money composition, Romania, 1990–1993

	% Cash	% Sight deposits	of which SOE	% Time deposits	of which household RON savings
1990	19	25	68	60	*84*
1991	18	52	*91*	34	*78*
1992	22	33	39	45	*49*
1993	23	26	34	50	*29*

Source: Computed form the National Bank of Romania Annual Report 1995 (p.62)

broad money ratio changed relatively little through the first four years of transition, a trend different from other formerly planned countries that witnessed a period of growing reliance on cash transactions (Ruziev and Ghosh 2008). With the exception of 1991, when the GCS monetization of inter-enterprise arrears increased end-of-year enterprises sight deposits, the overall broad-money supply composition changed little. However, SOEs share in total sight deposits declined substantially (from 70 percent in 1990 to around 34 percent in 1993), both because of an increasing importance of the private sector and banks' continued reluctance to finance state-owned production except at high interest rates.

In this increasingly complicated argumentative terrain, the NBR brought policy innovations that would justify its commitments to become a "neoliberal" central bank. To enforce this change, it proceeded to reinterpret its policy record up to 1993. Its concerted efforts to curb access to liquidity by any means possible, even at the expense of payment blockages, were now represented as unfortunate instances of policy relaxation. Indeed, the NBR argued, a new IMF agreement depended on its ability, government permitting, to make a break with its past accommodative stance (NBR 1994a). A new era of monetary restraint would be accompanied by structural reforms that recognized the fundamental role state-owned production played in delaying, or even obstructing, stabilization efforts (IMF 1994a). The 1993 NBR annual report (1995: 12) explained that the policy shift would be underpinned by four objectives, all constructed through an excess liquidity discourse. These sought to:

- eliminate the excess liquidity arising from the government's deposits with the commercial banks by transferring the consolidated treasury account into NBR management (as explained earlier, the government was a net creditor to the banking sector for several years);

- commit to avoid new preferential credit or the rollover of existing outstanding loans, with most directed credit phased out by the end of 1993;
- ensure tighter liquidity control to keep money supply growth on path and thus ensure compliance with future NDA targets;
- raise real interest rates to positive levels – the increase in the cost of liquidity was intended to work both as a signal of the anti-inflationary stance and to force commercial banks to mobilize alternative funding sources.

However, negotiations with the IMF had reached a stumbling block: full liberalization of exchange-rate transactions (including NR's interbank auctions). Eventually, the IMF accepted a gradual move but leveraged the "exchange-rate gradualism" to pressure authorities toward faster liberalization in other policy domains. The IMF's Executive Board recommendations stressed two policy actions in September 1993 that would be incorporated in the central bank's four-point action plan:

1. positive real interest rates (to complement a tighter control of the money supply);
2. the termination of concessional credit programs.

The IMF also requested the government to downsize the imports of primary commodities (especially energy) destined to act as buffer stocks and a faster closing down of inefficient SOEs.

The NBR responded to these demands with a fundamental overhaul of policy practice: the effective deployment of indirect instruments for a tighter liquidity control. It thus instituted reserve money as an operational target and instruments for forecasting liquidity requirements in August 1993. The new policy framework, it argued, would reinforce monetary control because of the central bank's monopoly position in supplying high-powered money, the "true" monetarist policy envisaged by Milton Friedman.

This monetarist rhetoric was, however, qualified by uncertainties in estimating the demand for money. Hence, the NBR maintained, an unusual mix of policy instruments was required to tackle inflationary pressures. The NBR would target both the interest rate and the (broad) money supply (NBR 1995: 190). Thus, efforts to distance policy-making from its previous "ambiguity" instead resulted in conceptual confusions as the simultaneous use of the two instruments is theoretically inconsistent. Instating high-powered money as an operational objective precludes any interventionist interest-rate policies. Instead, the market sets interest rates at a level consistent with the demand for broad money, given a certain level of broad money (Friedman 1968). For the central bank to retain exogenous control over reserve positions (an essential condition for the quantity-theory causality), the demand for money has to be independent of its supply. This independence works to set the interest rate.

Thus, the central bank publicly committed to a tight monetary policy. In practice it did the very opposite. It stepped up liquidity injections, with total refinancing increasing substantially after June 1993: daily average refinancing from the central bank doubled between July 1993 and April 1994 (see Figure 3.6). If liquidity operations were driven by forecasts in line with projected price increases, then the significant increase in average daily liquidity made available to the banking sector challenged the representation of the monetary stance as accommodating before July 1993 and tightening afterwards. Indeed, it would seem that up to 1993 the system suffered from a systematic shortage of liquidity rather than from an excess.

While the NBR appeared to have finally accepted that the system could not function without liquidity, it nevertheless sought to maintain policy tightness by raising its refinancing rates to historically high levels (see Figure 3.8).

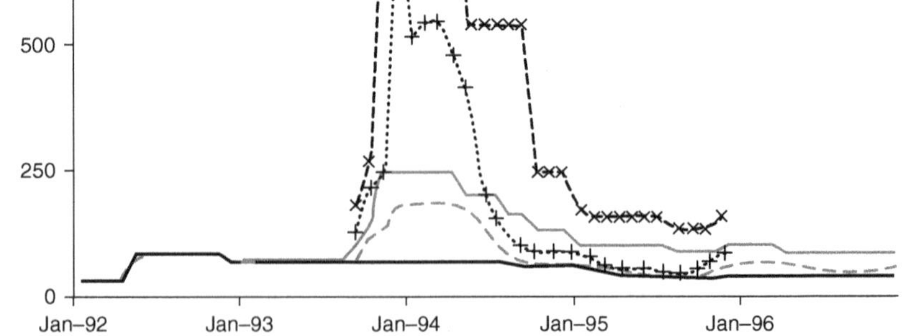

Figure 3.8 Interest rates on NBR credit lines (percent, annual), Romania, 1992–1996

Source: Computed from the Statistical Section of *the National Bank of Romania Annual Reports* 1995, 1999 and IMF, 1995a.

As explained earlier, the IMF had made the third SBA conditional on positive real interest rates (IMF 1995a). Previous attempts to impose real interest rates had been obstructed by failures to predict inflation rates: ex-post values moved real rates into negative territory. These failures reflected the challenges monetarism produced for either controlling or forecasting price developments. While exchange-rate volatility (and price liberalizations) drove price movements, and with little room for a longer, administratively induced, exchange-rate stability, forecasts tended to underestimate the magnitude of price inflation. Under these circumstances, the NBR could have either changed its approach to forecasting to explicitly account for exchange-rate dynamics or could have raised its interest rates enough to contain any unexpected price surges. The NBR chose the second option, raising interest rates to unprecedented levels.

Here a curious contradiction appears between IMF and NBR data, particularly since the central bank was the source of IMF statistics. In discussing the turn to tightening after mid-1993, the NBR (1994) published interest rates on refinancing operations were far lower than the IMF's. For instance, the NBR quoted a rise in overdraft (Lombard) rates at around 250 percent between November 1993 and April 1994, while the IMF (1995a) placed it at 860 percent for the same period (Figure 3.8). The same holds for the auction facility, where IMF figures show the rate rising to 800 percent in December 1993 then gradually decreasing to 159 percent in August 1994. Throughout this period, between 40 and 50 percent of total refinancing (see Figure 3.6) was granted through the auction and overdraft facilities. Furthermore, the NBR charged positive interest rates for the structural credit lines through which the government extended preferential credit to the agricultural and energy sectors, to avoid excessive interference with "market mechanisms" of allocating liquidity. It further maintained refinancing volumes at levels consistent with the quantitative targets for reserve money growth. In other words, the directed credit which the government intended to target priority sectors was neither creating excess liquidity nor providing an indirect subsidy through negative real interest rates.

The discrepancy in the reported figures has to be understood as an attempt to deflect criticism for it would have been difficult to defend such high interest rates in an environment where industrial interests accused the central bank and commercial banks of sabotaging productive activity. As in the US and UK monetarist experiments, behind the rhetoric of base money control, policy-makers deployed Keynesian measures: interest-rate manipulation seeking to make credit more expensive.

Following these policy measures, the third SBA was signed in May 1994. Reflecting lower inflation projections, it set lower broad-money growth targets and indicative targets for reserve money.[57] It further specified a quantitative benchmark for the stock of enterprise arrears, envisaging a gradual reduction toward the end of 1994. The national authorities renewed their commitment to exchange-rate flexibility and pledged to restrict currency market interventions to instances of substantial volatility. Interbank currency auction sessions were liberalized in April 1994, and a fully fledged currency market was fully operating from August 1994, replacing auctions with direct negotiations between dealers.[58] The income policy remained geared toward real wage cuts, setting a forward-looking indexation coefficient so that it only partly compensated for price increases. SOEs faced a punitive charge for excess wage increases (IMF 1994a).

The September SBA review (IMF 1994b) noted significant progress, with all quantitative criteria in line with projections, and recommended that Romania be allowed to make the second SBA purchase. Indeed, NBR (1995a: 15) identified 1994 as the best year in terms of the success of macroeconomic stabilization, "reflecting both authorities' learning curve and a better response of the productive sector to macro policy measures." It pointed to the substantial fall in the inflation rate (62 percent compared with 295 percent at the end of 1993), the pick-up in GDP growth (3.9 percent) and industrial production (3.3 percent annual growth). The improved export performance, on the back of increased stability in exchange rates, reduced the current-account deficit. Such positive developments were attributed to a better control of liquidity, when in fact data showed substantial reserve-money growth. Ironically, the 1994 success in slowing down the previously rampant inflation (from nearly 300 percent in 1993 to less than 65 percent a year later) went hand in hand with the monetization of government deficits. The breakdown of the contributions to the expansion in the money base over the period 1993–1996 shows that central-bank credit to the government was the driver of money base growth in 1994, in contrast to 1993 when the central bank's increased willingness to provide liquidity to the banking sector drove the growth in reserve money (see Table 3.2 and Figure 3.6).

Furthermore, despite extremely high refinancing interest rates throughout the first months of 1994, credit growth was for the first time positive in real terms since the 1991 GCS (see Figure 3.4). The NBR seemed more inclined to make liquidity available, even if at high prices, while money-supply developments invalidated the monetarist

Table 3.2 Contribution to changes in the high-powered money, Romania, 1993–1996

Year	Percentage change reserve base	Contribution to percentage increases in base money				Inflation rate (consumer price index)
		Net foreign assets	net credit		other net assets[59]	
			to government	to banks		
1993	115	63	56	95	–99	295.5
1994	151	–20	220	27	–77	61.7
1995	45	–29	39	40	–5	27.8
1996	68	–35	–102	114	91	56.9

Source: Author's computation, data from the Statistical Section of *the National Bank of Romania Annual Reports* 1995, 1999.

link between monetary aggregates and prices. The broad money supply grew at a similar pace in both 1993 and 1994 (around 135 percent) while inflation fell to 62 percent from 295 percent in 1993, confirming difficulties of forecasting money demand and thus employing a strict monetarist logic. It suggested that the inflationary implications of an increase in the demand for money were not always clear. If, for instance, broad money growth reflected a structural or portfolio shift in demand, driven by increase confidence in the domestic currency, its inflationary impact would be limited.

The honeymoon was again short-lived. By February 1995, the IMF's endorsement of the macroeconomic policy package disappeared. The SBA review concluded that Romania had failed to comply with the program's conditionality. The review (IMF 1995a) listed three main policy slippages:

1. accommodating policy practice which prioritized preferential credit to agriculture;
2. interference with the currency market (state-owned banks reportedly quoted overvalued rates and obstructed market clearance, producing expectations of future devaluations and a rapid extension in foreign currency credit for stockpiling intermediary inputs);
3. delays in enterprise reform that produced a fast increase in payment arrears.

However, the share or concessional loans to agriculture[60] in total financing did not change from the 37 percent registered in September 1994, when program continuation was approved. The IMF's decision to interrupt program relationships was most likely driven by the last two policy "slippages," both performance criteria.

During the same year, the central bank was faced for the first time with the prospect of bank failures (Pop 2006). Two private banks (Dacia Felix and Credit Bank) were provided with emergency liquidity to avoid systemic risks – as the country had no deposit-guarantee scheme and the two banks together held around 14 percent of household deposits. Despite the legal difficulties and political pressures the central bank had to overcome in order to declare the banks bankrupt, Pop (2006: 106) described the moment as an opportunity for the central bank to affirm the necessity of "greater market and regulatory discipline" and to tighten banking regulation. It also gave greater weight to arguments of the necessity to speed up the privatization of the state-owned banks: a law was drafted to detail the mechanism of privatization. It would only be passed two years later, in the great privatization push of the first openly "neoliberal" government.

By the end of 1994, foreign banks entered the Romanian banking system. Of a total of 26 banks, foreign banks operated through seven branches and participated in the capital of another ten. Yet activity remained concentrated in the hands of the state-owned sector: four large state-owned banks together extended 90 percent of private-sector loans and the large savings bank held the large majority of household savings (EIU 1996). The neoliberal pressure for privatization had been particularly inefficient in the banking sector so that the subsequent conditionality of both the World Bank and the IMF required the government to privatize at least two big banks.

3.6 A last attempt: The 1995 stand-by arrangement

In October–November 1995, Romania turned to the IMF once more as its foreign currency reserves were again contracting at an alarming pace (see Figure 3.1) and its plans to tap international markets depended on the IMF's seal of approval. The IMF (1995b) identified two policy problems undermining liquidity control: government-preferential credit policies and inter-enterprise arrears, substantially above the 1994 performance criteria targets.[61] A third "policy challenge" referred to the explosive increase in foreign currency loans, from 4 percent of total nongovernmental credit at the end of 1991 to 30 percent at the end of 1995. Predictably, the high interest rate policy saw demand for credit switching to foreign currency. The IMF's policy prescriptions did not go as far as the NBR's, who at one point contemplated the possibility of prohibiting foreign currency lending (but failed to mobilize enough political support). Since this would have interfered with market mechanisms, the IMF (1995b) instead recommended the typical regulatory measure for containing credit growth: increased reserve requirements. The NBR consequently raised the required reserve ratio on foreign currency deposits to 40 percent by the end of 1995. The IMF (1995b) recognized that the central bank had behaved according to its expected mandate. Domestic currency interest rates had remained positive in real terms on both refinancing credit and commercial bank loans throughout 1994 and 1995. What the monetary authorities faced now was a typical capitalist banking affliction: information problems. Since demand for credit had a low price elasticity, a combination of moral hazard and adverse selection was keeping problematic SOEs afloat. By now, structural reforms, and not macroeconomic policy per se, delayed stabilization.

Despite a dismal SBA record, the IMF did not, at any point, question the usefulness of its quantitative targets, even when the process of remonetization rendered the demand for money unstable. The fourth stabilization plan, signed in December 1995, set a 30 percent upper limit on broad money growth. Furthermore, interest rates on refinancing facilities were raised while the government committed to reduce preferential credit to the agricultural sector. The national authorities asked the IMF to consider the possibility that the exchange rate could receive "greater explicit emphasis" as nominal anchor (IMF 1995b). Again, the staff refused to support such a policy stance, arguing that the central bank lacked both foreign reserves and credibility in the light of previous unsuccessful attempts to stabilize currency-market volatility. Subsequently, the central bank vowed to refrain from further interference.

However, this last year of the "gradualist" period would prove particularly challenging for implementing monetarist policy measures. The government, attempting to shore up political support in an electoral year, instructed the NBR to provide concessional credit (Pop 2006). Preferential credit to agriculture rose to around 30 percent of total NBR refinancing credit in the first months of 1996. Under its monetarist impulse, the NBR sought to minimize access to other liquidity facilities while simultaneously raising the rate on its auction facility so that the net effect was a contraction in daily average liquidity released to banks (see Figure 3.6).

Thus, discourses at play suggested that Romania was again on the brink of a crisis. Indeed, a widening current-account deficit triggered faster exchange-rate depreciation in 1995, which the NBR failed to arrest. Inflation was again rising, driving ex-post real interest rates into negative territory. Monetarist discourses constructed this as an expansionary policy, although the central bank had tightened up liquidity to September 1996. New foreign currency regulation again broke IMF requirements: in early 1996 the central bank revoked all foreign banks' licenses, leaving only four state-owned banks to deal in the market.

The IMF suspended its fourth SBA in June 1996, four months before the general election. While the decision was explained by the breaching of the performance criteria on net bank credit to the government, the overall target on net central bank credit was well within limits (IMF 1996) and could thus not be inflationary. Nevertheless, the institution refused to contemplate a waiver, alleging that the NBR had lost control over reserve money, which indeed was above the indicative target in June 1996 because of the emergency liquidity provided to the two ailing private banks. Compliance with the IMF target would have required the NBR to refuse its lender-of-last resort function and to accept the systemic-risk implications of such a policy decision.

Was the IMF's decision the outcome of a quiet gamble for political change and a government of a more neoliberal disposition? In the election politics, the failure of the fourth attempt to comply with IMF conditionality was explained as another failure of nostalgic socialism. The alternative explanation, linking failure to the IMF's economics of stabilization, never gained much currency in public politics. Predictably, the right-wing "historical coalition" won the general election on a platform of change that promised a quick and painless shift in the road map to reform. Negotiations with the IMF resumed, setting the country on course for its fifth shock therapy in seven years, this time under the leadership of a political party with much greater appeal in neoliberal circles. The IMF's Managing Director visited Romania in December 1996 to salute the new momentum for reform.

3.7 A pause for reflection: The state-owned enterprises

The IMF's record of engagement in the Romanian policy space suggests that SOEs, rather than aggregate demand, were its main policy concern. Indeed, the ideological function of the excess aggregate demand account is revealed through its treatment of the productive sector. At play in the IMF's discourse was a sort of complicity between the exclusion of SOEs as economically viable and the wider systematic exclusion of supply-side discussions from the neoliberal discourse embedded in blueprint IMF stabilization packages and international economic advice to Eastern Europe.

The policy narrative constructed the stabilization problem as follows: SOEs were no longer productive units capable of generating economic growth but problematic entities whose functioning was governed by soft-budget constraints instead of market principles and so required restructuring. Restructuring, in the IMF's and NBR's discourse, required closures and privatization, while the unwillingness to restructure, validated through pervasive arrears, called for ever-tighter liquidity policies. In contrast, domestic industrial interests defined restructuring as a strategic intervention, through an industrial policy, that prioritized credit for capital formation and competitive exchange-rate management. In this framing, the systematic attempt to starve the system of liquidity underlying policy practice sought to transform liquidity problems into solvency problems and delayed restructuring. This homogeneous treatment of state-owned firms rendered them all susceptible to blockages in the payment system and ultimately required government-orchestrated rescue packages, such as the GCS.

Clearly governments could have contemplated restructuring through bankruptcies, as the IMF suggested. Political preferences influenced economic outcomes, and perhaps a coalition of "historical" parties would have been more prepared to uphold commitments to neoliberal prescriptions. However, such a claim, underlying the neoliberal argument that shock therapy could displace industrial interests and thus push a quick restructuring, glosses over substantial structural bottlenecks while simultaneously downplaying the extent to which "neocommunist" government did in fact implement contractionary measures.

Indeed, closing down SOEs implied massive unemployment when the emerging private sector was hardly generating significant employment opportunities. The temporary commitment to IMF targets tested the government's willingness to accept the political consequences of highly contractionary policies and found they were reluctant to do so for very long. But this reluctance was not entirely the outcome of political calculations and Communist reminiscing about the beauty of full employment. It partly reflected a stark consequence of the liquidity crunches and prohibitively high interest rates: a privately owned productive sector with little possibility of financing capital investment and thus operating mainly in the services sector. State-owned industrial production was the only source of much-needed export earnings.

During the planned economy, the manufacturing sector brought in most of the export revenue. Capital-intensive goods, destined for the

Soviet markets, such as chemicals and metal manufactures, formed the bulk of these exports. As the state-planned economy disintegrated, domestic companies were faced with several developments: the opening up of the domestic market to foreign competition, the disintegration of traditional export markets in the former Communist world, the disappearance of virtually all state support (that formerly provided inputs, distribution, and marketing networks), and the difficulties in raising capital from an increasingly impatient banking sector. Under these circumstances, exports and the industrial structure shifted away from the capital intensive goods (with complex processes in large-scale production) to labor-intensive goods (small-scale production requiring far less capital investment). Thus, textile exports moved from a mere 10 percent in 1989 to around 32 percent in 2000 whereas the worst decline was experienced by chemical products and metal manufactures exports (Table 3.3). Competitiveness shifted to low labour costs, a notoriously unstable source of revenue given the intense pressures from other developing countries in international markets.

Furthermore, the excess-demand narrative involved an attempt to redefine the organization of the productive system along competitive market lines, an economic engineering that the free-market discourse refused to acknowledge but inherently contained. For processes to function under the disciplining hand of the market, production required a radically different logic. However, as Karl Polanyi (1944) convincingly showed, markets do not emerge spontaneously but are human and contingent entities that have to be constructed. And this is what the IMF's discourse of stabilization and its structuring of the central bank sought: a radical engineering of the economic space to exclude state-owned monopolies and oligopolies. If power was to be exercised in the market, then it should be private rather than state-owned industrial interests attempting to influence policy-making.

Table 3.3 Romania, composition of exports, selected years (percentages)

	Agriculture	Manufacturing, selected items			
		Textiles	Chemical products	Metal manufactures	Basic metals
1989	1.6	10.2	28.6	35.4	13.4
1994	2.6	23.8	21	23.3	16.3
2000	2.7	32.1	14.1	27.9	11.7

Source: International Trade Statistics.

Thus, economic reform was shaped by an economic discourse that portrayed monopolies and oligopolies as unfortunate market structures that ought to be eliminated to achieve efficient market outcomes. However, the narrative that emphasized market efficiency generated through small-scale production in a competitive setting was built on a discourse disengaged from capitalist "realities": that capitalism engendered an inherent tendency to concentration and centralization. Hence, innovation, rather than price, underlined competitiveness (Schumpeter 1951), and the bulk of innovative activity is generated by large, oligopolistic firms (Baumol 2004). While free-market discourse vilified large-scale production for its power to obstruct the market, the greatest productivity was achieved precisely through technologically intensive processes that required increased commitments of both time and capital (Galbraith 1967).

The implication was that socialist and capitalist production shared a similar logic of planning despite the neoliberal ideological rejection of monopolization. Before the increasing financialization of large nonfinancial corporations (Crotty 2003), the capitalist industrial system fundamentally depended on firms' ability to circumvent the market (Galbraith 1967). While neoclassical economic discourse obscured the central role that technology played in industrial production, where production involved capital and technology, capitalist firms simply did not respond to spontaneously generated demand. The ubiquitous large-scale, technology-intensive, capitalist firm had to reduce uncertainty in order to be commercially viable. Planning became essential to business activity, for the market was too unreliable to generate spontaneously either sophisticated technological inputs or the appropriate consumer preferences. Thus, size allowed firms to address market uncertainties through one of the following mechanisms:

- Eliminating the market by vertical integration. This is aimed to control production chains and the price and supply of particularly important intermediary inputs who otherwise would be subjected to market volatility and threaten profits.
- Suppliers or buyers can control both prices and quantities by exercising market power (monopsony/monopoly).
- The market can be temporarily or indefinitely suspended when large firms mutually protect each other from price fluctuations by entering into contracts that specify both price and quantity for substantial periods of time.

Planning under socialism similarly sought to inscribe these principles in the logic of industrial production. Once the Central Plan disappeared, policy discourse constructed the state-owned sector exactly as Galbraith (1967: 138) described the neoclassical depiction of monopolies: "wasteful and inefficient in employing resources, exploitative in the price it charges, and challenging in its need for reform."

SBA policy prescriptions aimed to invalidate the mechanisms that large-scale production, be it under socialism or capitalism, deployed for circumventing the market. The soft-budget constraint was deployed to articulate the SOEs' problem as one of solvency rather than liquidity, lending support to the argument that the paternalistic hand of the state had to be replaced by the efficient hand of the market. The sole survival strategy had to be the ability to generate profit under competitive conditions.

SBA measures worked to systematically minimize SOEs' profitability by depriving them of means of protection against market uncertainties. Through IMF interventions, highly strategic cost factors (energy in particular and other intermediary imports) came to be dictated by international volatility and exchange-rate devaluations rather than strategic planning. SBA conditionality forced local energy prices for the productive sector above international market levels, and social concerns institutionalized cross-subsidization from industry to households. Compliance with this requirement was carefully monitored, and corrections of any deviations from commitments were regarded as a policy priority. Second, the scope for exercising market power was reduced through administrated prices: companies were often forced to absorb market-determined costs while facing price caps.

Furthermore, the central bank was instrumental in this neoliberal attack on state production. Monetary policy, consistent with an interpretation of money as a means of exchange de-linked from production, added the final nail in the coffin: credit crunches, or, when liquidity was made available, extremely high interest rates. Curtailing access to working capital accelerated the decapitalization of the productive sector and debilitated the essential driver of competitiveness in large-scale production: technological upgrading. The payments blockages and arrears also functioned to curtail the space for the third practice Galbraith described: temporary or indefinite suspension of the market through long-term contracts between large firms. With no means to distinguish between liquidity and solvency in such an environment, banks and firms became more reluctant to enter long-term commitments, and banks' balance sheets inevitably deteriorated.

Thus, restructuring according to the neoliberal road map created a perfect-storm scenario for industrial producers. Undoubtedly, industrial interests succeeded in exercising some degree of influence in economic policy decisions, as governments sought to alleviate liquidity shortages and to provide preferential credit. Even so, under conditionality pressures, preferential credit was granted at positive interest rates, requiring profit margins impossible to achieve in that particular economic context. That industrial interests were not quite so successful at capturing policy implementation is apparent from the collapse in industrial production, which, at the end of 1996, stood at around 55 percent of the level achieved in 1989 (by then already weakened by Ceauşescu's drive to repay foreign debt) and a contraction in capital investment that by the end of 1996 had failed to return to 1989 levels (see Figure 3.9). Thus, in Romania it was not "impatient finance" per se that saw a collapse in capital accumulation, neither financial liberalization per se that pushed firms into short-term speculative investments as described by Demir (2009) in Argentina, Turkey, and Mexico. Instead, the central bank's practices inflicted liquidity shortages and a general state of uncertainty in the banking sector, which at times went as far as to delay payments to encourage demand for expensive short-term credit. Long-term financing of capital accumulation was no longer an option.

Despite promises of a consumer paradise, the prolonged deindustrialization process had long-term economic and social consequences. The massive contractions in manufacturing not only "levelled" the field for international competitors (a process complimented by privatization

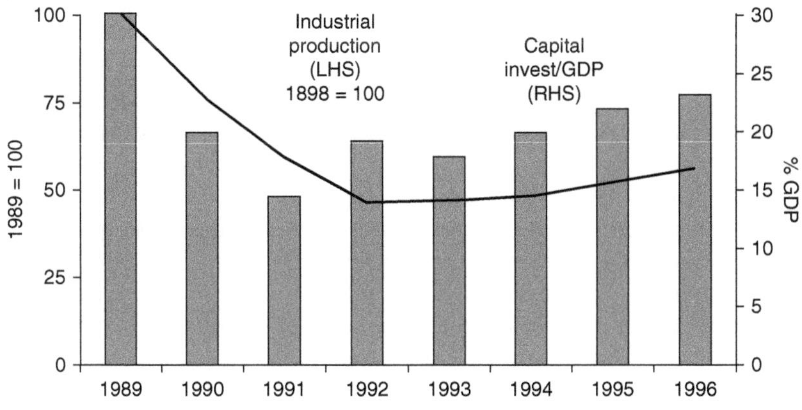

Figure 3.9 Industrial production (1989=100) and capital investment/GDP, Romania, 1989–1996

Source: Data from the Statistical section of *the National Bank of Romania Annual Report 1999.*

discourses) but also shifted competitiveness drivers from technology intensive processes to labour costs. It further resulted in massive social upheaval, at times reversing rural–urban migration patterns and increasing inequality to pre-World-War-II levels.

Had industrial interests shaped the policy agenda as the May 1990 Commission initially envisaged, the narrative of reform would have privileged industrial recovery as the main anchor for stabilization and prioritized manufacturing and capital accumulation as drivers of growth. Inflationary pressures, external instability, and competitiveness would have been better addressed by:

- a partial price liberalization allowing market mechanisms in the consumer sector and maintaining price controls for resources vital to production;
- a cost-push approach to inflationary pressures which fundamentally required managed exchange rates, an approach advocated by structuralist policy advice (Amsden et al. 1994);
- the provision of liquidity to the productive sector to offset temporarily the loss of revenue from collapsing export markets, complemented with a mechanism for inscribing a medium-term profitability logic into the behaviour of enterprises.

3.8 Conclusion

If the metric for IMF policy success is the institutionalization of central bank practices according to roll-back neoliberalism, then the IMF's record in Romania between 1990 and 1997 is one of success rather than failure. Its interpretation of the shortage–disequilibrium debate was harnessed to change the definition of the policy problem away from the initial concerns with industrial regeneration articulated in the national strategy of the 1990 Commission for Transition. In the IMF's account, Ceauşescu's Stalinist approach to central planning left the state-owned sector in such disarray that no other intervention than complete market discipline made economic sense. The IMF's monetarist discourse redefined the problem of transition as a problem of stabilization (first).

Notwithstanding discursive commitments, monetarism was "translated" in different degrees into policy practice. The central bank explained differences between policy commitments and practices through a discourse of gradualism constructed around price liberalization, foreign-exchange liberalization and restructuring of SOEs. The government's intervention in economic domains was held to reproduce inherited Communist rigidities and to create damaging obstacles to "rational economic policy." As the IMF argued, and the NBR concurred, both the exchange rate and monetary policy functioned with a quasi-fiscal objective, through administratively induced stability of the exchange rate and preferential credit to "strategic" sectors.

As various interests struggled over policy priorities, the SBA agreements established a temporary communion of interests between the central bank and the government. This dissolved, not because policy implementation was necessarily captured by state-owned industrial interests but because "reality" failed to produce the outcomes projected through monetarist discourses. Policy practice created liquidity shortages where policy discourse saw excess liquidity, produced repeated payment blockages where it was supposed to liberate a "repressed" financial system, contracted industrial production instead of producing growth, and fed exchange-rate devaluations into inflationary pressures.

The question of governments' lack of will to reform was more complex than either the central bank or the IMF recognized. While the NBR routinely deployed monetarist explanations of policy failures and continued with contractionary measures, governments eventually refused to do so. This was not nostalgia for full employment but rather reflected a stark political choice: governments, neoliberal credentials or not, will find it difficult to comply with the highly contractionary requirements the IMF imposes through its SBAs. The worldwide poor record of compliance with IMF conditionality testifies accordingly.

Nevertheless, the lack of foreign-currency reserves required Romania to continue its program relationship with the IMF. Every new stabilization plan brought policy innovations destined to make the economic system behave in line with monetarist premises. Remarkably, a discourse that cherishes the theoretical rigor underlying the perfect world of competitive markets made little attempt to ground policy decisions firmly in empirical evidence. Instead, it insisted on expanding the policy repertoire with little, if any (empirical) proof that those policy innovations were consistent with theoretical requirements. In one example, the volatility in the forecast demand for money was never accepted to undermine fundamentally the quantity theory framework. Interest rates were institutionalized as a policy instrument with little concern for a functioning transmission mechanism.

These audacious approximations required a continuous rewriting of the past. The technique was similar in every new stabilization plan: portray past monetary policy measures as accommodative and formulate the future through a commitment to eliminate excess demand.

For instance, policy argumentation surrounding the 1992 SBA deplored the previously expansive monetary policy measures, even though the NBR set to immediately sterilize the GSC credit injection. The turn to tightening in mid-1993, when high-powered money had been identified as the operational objective of monetary policy, saw a substantial increase in the liquidity made available to the banking sector compared to the previous period. In policy discourse, the episode was presented as a success in ensuring a tighter control of liquidity.

Throughout the period, the central bank marginalized, dismissed, and denied the link between exchange rates and cost pressures. Indeed, missing from its narrative was a critical interrogation of whether its focus on containing inflation was consistent with a "freely" determined exchange rate. Rather than contemplating critical interrogations of the economic theories underlying stabilization, the NBR sought to develop new practices for tightening its grip on liquidity. For instance, complying with the prior requirements of the second SBA, the NBR raised the interest rate on its refinancing facilities. While this introduced the interest rate into policy discussions through a financial liberalization discourse that required positive interest rates, it also increased the scope for policy contestations. Whereas policies directed at containing the supposed monetary overhang appeared to have few consequences for the productive sector, the detrimental impact high interest rates could have for investment were easier to challenge. Both government officials and the industrial sector voiced concerns about the contractionary policy stance – rightly so, for the monetary policy measures guided by the positive interest-rate discourse drove the NBR, in the absence of credible projections about future price rises, to hike interest rates on its two facilities to extremely high levels (according to the IMF, 800 percent in the last months of 1993). The tight liquidity measures laid the foundations for "impatient" finance. Even the state-owned banking sector increasingly turned to a predatory financing of productive activity, extracting high interest rates for short-term financing of working capital.

Monetarist approaches met with structural and institutional resistance, arising from socialist legacies and ongoing political struggles. At times, government pressures did push practices of monetary management outside neoliberal boundaries, particularly when the central bank was instructed to extend preferential credit. Yet a coherent industrial strategy that recognized the crucial role of the exchange rate and of a financial system orientated toward recapitalizing the productive system never emerged. Rather, policy discourse and practices throughout the period sought to subject large-scale state-owned industries to the disciplining hand of the market, when in fact business practices of large-scale capitalist production, as Galbraith documented, consisted of eliminating the market. Liquidity problems were transformed into solvency problems as policy systematically targeted every avenue available for protecting profits. The neoliberal structuring of the central bank achieved, in this respect, what it set out to do: it played an important role (along with neoliberal measures in other domains, such as price and trade liberalization) in the systematic, if not always coherent or consistent, reconfiguration of economic relations between state-owned production and the (largely state-owned) banking sector.

4
The Dawn of a New Era, 1997–2005

In public discourse, 1997 is identified as the crucial moment when politics finally got in tune with the economic reforms repeatedly demanded by the IMF (Pop 2006). Before 1997, the reconstruction of economic relations along market principles suffered from a mismatch between "good policies" agreed and negotiated with the IMF (in the first instance) and "vicious politics" that surrendered policy implementation to vested industrial interests. The political willingness to reform changed, however, with the election of a centre-right coalition with recognized neoliberal sympathies at the end of 1996. While subsequent policy measures triggered a three-year recession and a near default on foreign debt service, it is argued that such developments were the unavoidable consequences of seven years of delayed reforms and a singularly unfavourable Communist legacy (Daianu 1999; IMF 2001). The improved macroeconomic performance since 2000 was interpreted as a clear indication that commitment to reform, unwavering in the face of inevitable social and economic costs, would eventually clear the field for a dynamic and efficient privately owned economy. The year things turned around for Romania also cemented the reputation of the central bank governor – Mugur Isărescu – as an apolitical technocrat whose economic expertise could command broad political support for painful reforms. This reputation was not acquired while at the helm of the central bank but through his eleven-month period as Prime Minister of Romania (December 1999–November 2000) when he was credited for single-handedly steering the country out of three years of crisis and putting the country firmly on its path to EU membership (negotiations for EU accession formally started in February 2000).

Monetary-policy discourse broadly echoes this account. Independent monetary policy allowed the central bank to curtail inflation. Where slippages and the pace of disinflation were not consistent with the NBR's commitments, these were explained away by appealing to international shocks and domestic political imperatives. Indeed, the narrative goes, international volatility, particularly around the 1997 Asian and 1998 Russian crisis, together with requirements of the export sector, have at times imposed upon the NBR competing objectives: external or domestic stability. Notwithstanding these, monetary policy is acknowledged and applauded with very few exceptions as the instrumental factor in stabilizing the economy.

The emphasis on the "right" politics finally allowing the implementation of "right" policies operates on two levels. It links economic success to the effective separation of states and markets, with central banks as guardians of the border. Second, it downplays the fundamental changes in central bank practices brought by the 1997 IMF SBA. Since 1997, and against all previous discourses, the IMF sanctioned and legitimated a managed exchange rate while simultaneously pushing the government into the disciplining arms of the market: it demanded, and obtained, that budget deficit financing be contained to domestic or international money markets.

The two policy changes set the stage for the second stage of the neoliberal economic governance. From the early "destructive" emphasis on the incapacity of the state to generate efficient economic outcomes, an increasingly "constructive" phase would cement the growing importance of, and dependency on, speculative flows. As Western European banks became involved in the privatization of state-owned banks, the financialization of the banking sector gained pace and changed qualitatively. Whereas before 1997 excess demand narratives turned the state-owned banking sector to a form of "impatient" finance, practices of central banking after 1997 introduced "sterilization games" that rendered interbank operations and currency markets as the main source of profits for strategies of commercial banking orientated at the intermediation of capital inflows. During the 1997–2005 period, the monetarist narrative, rather than informing policy, functioned to legitimize the sterilization games. The central bank's practices increasingly faced the challenges of large capital inflows characteristic to other developing countries.

The chapter is structured as follows. It first explores the changes brought into the economic policy space by the 1997 SBA. It then describes the economic dynamics throughout the period to set the context for discussing monetary policy choices. The analysis then turns to the Romanian policy scene to explore how speculative capital, channelled through the banking sector, redefined the rules of the game for monetary policy practice by focusing on the central bank's management of liquidity.

4.1 The 1997 shock therapy

As explored in the previous chapter, the IMF's (1997a) appraisal of its record of engagement in Romania up to 1997 identified two "problematic" policy areas: monetary control and exchange-rate management, where implementation was captured by vested interest groups. The narrative of policy failures, grounded in excess-demand explanations of inflationary pressures, ran as follows: monetary-policy attempts to drain excess liquidity were systematically compromised by pressures for directed credit to agriculture and energy, while commitments to exchange-rate flexibility gave way to demands for an overvalued currency to support inefficient, energy-intensive production. Thus, the 1997 SBA established three "priority" areas that would address inconsistencies between policy and practice:

1. Refocus monetary policy by narrowing liquidity management to inflation control. The success of these efforts would be conditional on a commitment to reduce to a minimum subsidies for restructuring SOEs, and, where absolutely necessary (as closure would be, to some extent, inevitably constrained by social considerations), to include them directly in the budget.[62] In other words, all preferential credit would be switched from the central bank's to the government's balance sheet.
2. Allow the exchange rate to foster external equilibrium by refraining from any exchange-rate market intervention.[63] To emphasize the overall importance of this requirement for the stabilization plan, the IMF made every SBA purchase subject to an exchange-rate policy review and warned that any sign of exchange-market interference, or even a minor backtracking on the commitment to unburden the NBR, would be perceived as the beginning of a return to accommodating policies (IMF 1997a: 25).
3. Immediately undertake a comprehensive, upfront reform of the energy-intensive and agricultural sectors, building upon the authorities' willingness for reform. The 1997 SBA expanded structural conditionality to specify a detailed timetable for closing down "fundamentally unviable" SOEs.

The IMF program made the privatization of state-owned banks a key reform priority. This included the second largest bank, the Romanian Development Bank, and Banc Post (by November 1998). In addition Banca Agricola was to be restructured in order to clean its balance sheet from the bad loans extended to the agricultural sector under previous governments with a view to privatize it by the end of 1998. The program also demanded an audit of another state-owned bank, Bancorex, where suspicions of mismanagement were abundant.

Macroeconomic conditionality changed to establish high-powered money targets as the SBA quantitative performance criteria. Similar to previous programs, the 1997 SBA identified a considerable build-up of excess liquidity, the legacy of the 1996 political populism targeting the agricultural sector, as the main monetary policy challenge to be addressed. Simultaneously, the program specified a new round of price liberalization, hikes in prices remaining under administration, and an exchange-rate devaluation.

The three-month review (IMF 1997b) confirmed the centre-right government's commitments to the principles and policies embedded in the 1997 SBA. It further applauded the faster-than-expected fall in inflation, the improvement in international reserves position and substantial capital inflows. While it drew attention to delays in structural reform that threatened this improvement in monetary control, the overall assessment found the reform program on track.

The review recognized that national authorities had finally understood and wholeheartedly subscribed to the policy measures the IMF had long advocated. However, rather than "policy advice as usual," the 1997 SBA brought two policy changes that would fundamentally overhaul institutional practices. First, by August 1997, the NBR had institutionalized, and the IMF endorsed, the active use of the exchange rate as an anchor for stabilization. Against previous requirements of, and commitments to, flexibility, from this point onwards currency interventions would be systematically deployed in policy practice.[64] The threats of exchange-rate "politicization" that drove the IMF and NBR to reject suggestions of managed rates before 1997 disappeared from policy argumentation.

A second, complementary, "innovation" required the government to shift its financing to market-based instruments and to further "depoliticize" monetary policy. The IMF's wide experience with conditionality confirmed that governments seldom do what they are told. Nevertheless, if it was impossible to prevent the repetition of past mistakes, it was within reach to alter the outcomes of "unconstructive" policy choices. Thus, deliberate delays in structural reforms would no longer be monetized, with the attending increases in liquidity and overall "disequilibrium." Instead, politicized economic decisions would be subjected to the unforgiving discipline of the market: market financing of budget deficits required governments to convince markets, the ultimate instance, of their credibility.

Indeed, by June 1997, a primary dealer system was set in place for auctioning government securities, a prior SBA requirement that aimed at replacing the previous subscription method for government securities issuance with a market mechanism. The first T-bill auction took place in late April 1997, followed by a "smooth and competitive" working of the system (IMF 1997b). This opened up (substantial) profit opportunities for foreign capital: capital inflows for the first semester of 1997 amounted to US$1.8 billion as foreign investors took advantage of what the IMF termed exceptional yields: 400 percent return on three-month government paper. It also marked the beginning of a substantive change in money-market liquidity conditions: currency interventions, undertaken to limit the exchange-rate overvaluations, produced a structural excess of liquidity (NBR 1998a) characteristic to countries with large balance of payment surpluses, including those in Eastern Europe (Balogh 2009).

The formalization of high-powered-money targeting as the new policy strategy was essential to this shift, for it allowed the IMF to sanction exchange-rate management as long as the central bank isolated bank reserves (and thus monetary aggregates) from the liquidity impact of currency interventions. The central bank thus introduced sterilized currency interventions when academic circles were debating their role in the 1997 Asian crisis. Indeed, sterilizations of currency interventions have not been a localized, specific Romanian policy practice but a common policy response to capital inflows (Caballero and Krishnamurthy 2001). By the early 1990s, a flourishing literature discussed the effects of sterilizations under a fixed exchange-rate regime, as monetarist theories had prompted central banks in Latin America to sterilize capital inflows (Calvo et al. 1993). The traditional view at the time, derived from the standard Mundell–Fleming model (Mundell 1962), conceptualized the effectiveness of sterilization in close relationship to the degree of capital mobility. Under perfectly mobile capital and a fixed exchange rate, sterilizations are undone by the exploitation of arbitrage opportunities, an extension of the Ricardian narrative of automatic adjustments in an international context. Hence, discretionary attempts at either easing or tightening the policy stance are ineffective: the famous impossible trinity of a fixed exchange rate, autonomous monetary policy, and capital mobility. The uncovered interest-rate parity holds, and the domestic interest rate is entirely determined by international markets. The Mundell–Fleming theory thus sanctioned sterilizations as an instrument for protecting the money supply from the undesirable side effects of the managed exchange-rate regime, i.e. the monetary expansion triggered by currency interventions.

Calvo's (1991) influential challenge of this traditional understanding grounded an emerging consensus that sterilizations could be counterproductive. Under a stabilization program designed along traditional IMF targets of monetary growth, he argued, sterilizations involve an increase in domestic interest rates and nominal debt. Higher debt service levels threaten commitments to stabilization, as the government prefers to devalue/increase inflation in order to reduce the public debt burden. This critique was further substantiated in Calvo et al.'s (1993: 10) conclusion that sterilized inflows "perpetuate a high domestic-foreign interest rate differential and that gives rise to an increased fiscal burden." By the late 1990s, while theoretical developments saw Mundell–Fleming models replaced by inter-temporal approaches to balance of -payment analysis (Obstfeld 2001), common wisdom rejected the Mundell–Fleming analysis as a satisfactory framework for exploring policy responses to sustained capital inflows. Sterilizations were not only difficult to operate, particularly in illiquid markets characteristic of emerging economies, but could also prove self-defeating: an apparently successful operation could raise domestic interest rates and stimulate even greater capital inflows (Lee 1997), as the uncovered interest parity did not hold. The 1997 Asian crisis was a paradigmatic example: Montiel and Reinhart (1999) argued that domestic-policy responses to early capital inflows were responsible for the crisis, at a moment when conventional wisdom identified Latin America as the most likely next victim of "hot money" reversals. Sterilized interventions in Asia had altered the term composition, shortening the maturity of capital inflows while simultaneously increasing the volume. In other words, sterilizations increased exposure to short-term liabilities and vulnerability to reversals.

Notwithstanding Calvo's employment with the IMF at the time his two papers were published (as IMF staff papers), the IMF retained its standard monetarist approach and refused to contemplate capital controls or to change its insistence on capital account liberalization. Instead of undermining theories of financial liberalization, vulnerability to short-term flows was attributed to the choice of exchange-rate regimes. The IMF drew an important lesson from the Asian crisis: under liberalized capital flows, soft pegs and the attending sterilized interventions could no longer be defended as a viable policy option. Emerging markets would benefit from greater flexibility (Eichengreen 2006).

The changing politics of exchange-rate management produced a conundrum for developing countries: a discursive emphasis on flexibility along with an increased dependency on exchange-rate stability for containing inflationary pressures. Indeed, the neoliberal push for balance-of-payments liberalization strengthened the link between exchange rates and prices, for a larger share of imports in consumption (and sometimes production) increased the impact of exchange-rate movements on prices. It also expanded the scope for exchange-rate volatility, no longer solely a matter of vulnerability to terms-of-trade shocks but also to speculative flows (UNCTAD 2007). A market-determined currency exposed prices to exchange-rate volatility; however, currency management required substantial foreign reserves. I will show, in the next chapter, how inflation-targeting dovetailed perfectly with this dilemma: a credibility-enhancing regime that would stabilize prices while guaranteeing access to international finance.

The debate on sterilizations and exchange-rate regimes reverberated little on the Romanian policy scene. Despite its substantial involvement in designing and endorsing policy decisions, the IMF failed to issue one single warning of the destabilizing nature of sterilized currency interventions, let alone to explore alternative policy choices. Instead, it focused its attention on the speed of the disinflation process and on the ever-present concerns with the SOEs. The next sections will briefly describe overall developments in selected economic indicators, to then map the central bank's policy narratives and practices.

4.2 Macroeconomic trends

The 1997 SBA prescribed the usual medicine: tight credit policies, currency devaluation, price liberalizations, and a well-defined timetable for closing down or privatizing state-owned enterprises[65]. Further real wage cuts were implemented, without a corresponding increase in government spending, investment or net exports to offset its contractionary effect on aggregate demand (Kalecki 1971). The attack on "excess demand" contracted the economy by 4 percent on average throughout 1997–1999 (see Table 4.1), as did the previous IMF agreements. The industrial sector bore the brunt of the "adjustment," contracting at a staggering annual average of 7.7 percent. Romania went through

Table 4.1 Annual average growth rates (percent change), Romania, 1990–2005

	1990–1993	1994–1996	1997–1999	2000–2005
GDP	–6.45	4.97	–4	5.1
Industry	–10.55	5.30	–7.7	5.2

Source: Data from the Statistical Section of the *National Bank of Romania Annual Reports 1999* and *2005*.

a second transformational shock (Daianu 1999), an explanation that underplays the role of highly contractionary macroeconomic policies. Afterwards, economic growth resumed, reaching a 5.1 percent average annual growth rate.

The sectoral composition of GDP reflects the sectoral growth trends portrayed above: a move away from industry, whose share declines from 51.7 percent in 1990 to 24.6 percent in 2005, toward services. Agriculture's share increased in the early 1990s, to decline to less than 10 percent of GDP in 2005. The sectoral shift in income shares was not completely reflected in changes in employment composition, as the labour force shed from industry moved to the agricultural sector. From this perspective, the small increase in the income share of agriculture compared to the increase in the share of employment can be explained by low value-added agricultural production: the 1991 land reform[66] caused the dismantling of the large state-owned collective farms and a subsequent return to small-scale subsistence farming. Subsequently, the share of production retained within households increased significantly while simultaneously debilitating food security as it augmented the dependency on imports of food in the case of bad weather conditions.

Disinflation proceeded at a sluggish pace, in line with exchange-rate developments. The 1997 SBA imposed price liberalization, and devaluation pushed the consumer price inflation to around 150 percent (see Figure 4.1). Inflation slowed down in 1998, to increase again in 1999 when the NBR allowed the exchange rate to devalue by more than 60 percent in order to contract imports as sources of financing the external debt became scarce. Starting with 2000, price inflation entered a fast downward trend as exchange-rate volatility diminished. When the inflation-targeting regime was introduced in August 2005, inflationary pressures were contained to one-digit levels as the exchange rate appreciated in real (and often nominal terms) in the latter part of the period.

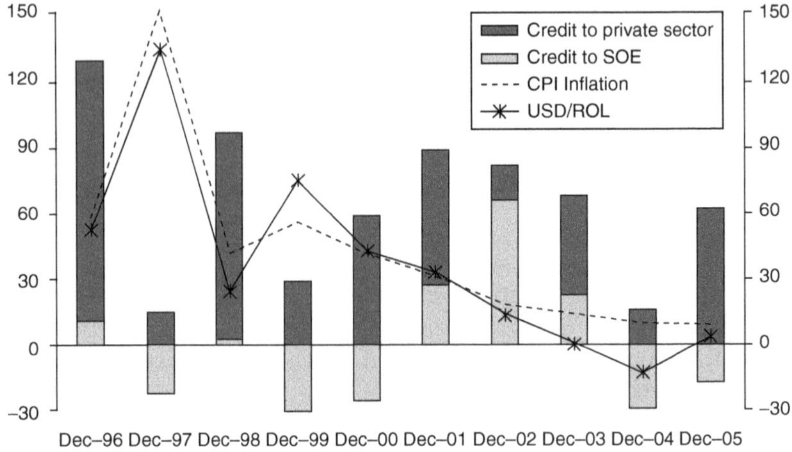

Figure 4.1 Growth rates, credit to private sector and SOE; exchange rates and consumer prices, Romania, 1997–2005

Source: Computed from the Statistical section of *the National Bank of Romania Annual Report 2000* and *2005*.

The SBA standard monetary tightening prescriptions saw a substantial reduction in willingness to lend. Credit to the private sector slimmed down, contracting in real terms in both 1997 and 1999, to gradually recover afterwards (see Figure 4.1). Reflecting a structural shift in the ownership of the productive sector and the neoliberal reluctance to finance state industries, credit to the state-owned productive sector was significantly worse affected: in four of the eight years of the period it decreased in nominal terms – by a staggering 21 percent in 1997 and 30 percent in 1999.

The drive to money-market financing saw domestic public debt increasing substantially throughout the period. With the introduction of treasury bills in 1993, domestic debt rose as a percentage of GDP and reached significant proportions after 1997 (see Figure 4.2). It peaked at over 12 percent of GDP in 1999, as Romania could not access foreign loans from either private or official sources, to reduce gradually afterwards. The structural composition changed after 1997, the first year that the short-term debt share increased above medium and long-term debt, a trend that was maintained afterwards (reaching almost 80 percent in 2003). The debt service reflects both the short-term nature and the penal rates at which the government was financing its deficit on domestic money markets: debt service increased to as much as 14 percent of

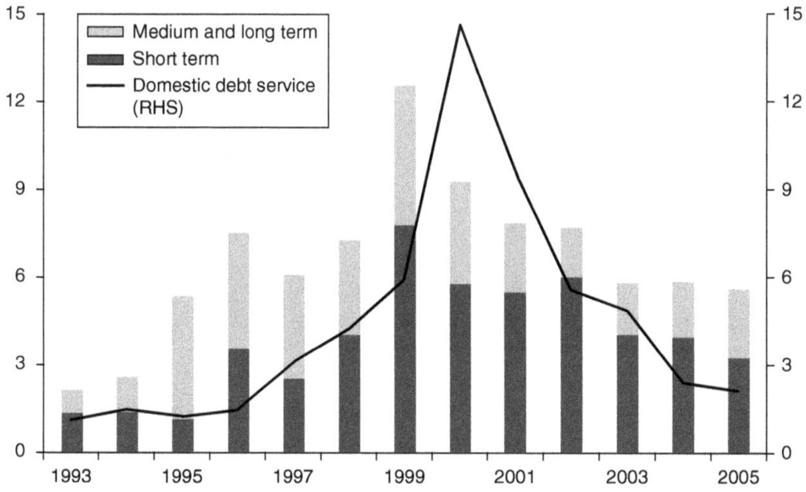

Figure 4.2 Public domestic debt, as percent of GDP, Romania, 1993–2005
Source: Computed from data from the Ministry of Finance.

GDP in 2000, higher than the outstanding stock at that time. As the government recovered its access to foreign markets, the terms at which it borrowed domestically improved markedly, with debt service declining to 2.1 percent of GDP in 2005.

The improved growth pattern after 2000 was accompanied by an increasing reliance on capital inflows to finance the structural current-account deficits. Indeed, none of the massive devaluations undertaken throughout the entire post-Communist period corrected Romania's net importer position. Since 2000, stimulated by exchange-rate appreciations, the current-account deficit entered again an expansionary trend, reaching above 8 percent of the GDP in 2005. While privatization-linked Foreign Direct Investment (FDI) and foreign remittances became increasingly important in financing the current-account deficit, debt-creating capital inflows played a key role in the expansion: external debt increased to 32 percent of GDP in 2005 (see Figure 4.3).

The vulnerability associated with reliance on international capital flows was never more obvious than in 1999. The second half of 1998 saw an emerging consensus that proclaimed an imminent default on Romania's foreign debt service (Isărescu 2008b). Ratings agencies[67] downgraded Romania's rating, questioning its ability to finance a foreign debt service double the amount of the NBR's foreign reserves[68], with payments concentrated in the first half of the year. The timing

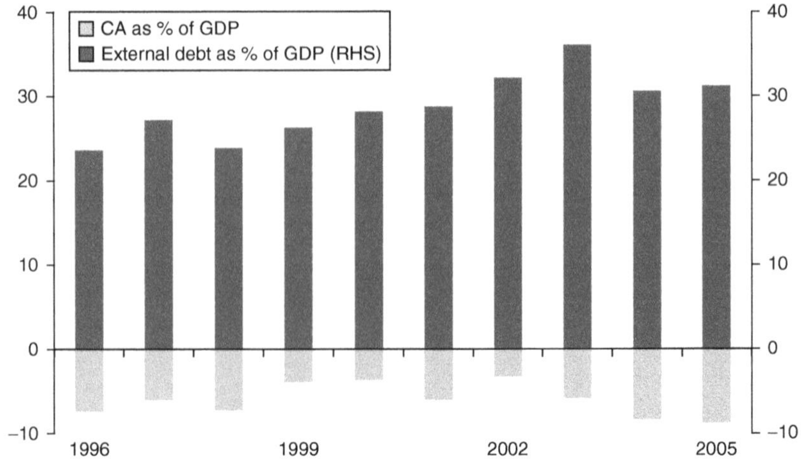

Figure 4.3 Current account and external debt, Romania, 1996–2005

Source: Computed from the Statistical Section of the *National Bank of Romania Annual Report 2006*.

of the foreign-debt service peak could not have been more unfortunate. The Asian and Russian crisis reduced the availability of lending to emerging countries, and the embargo imposed during the Yugoslav conflict affected Romanian exporters. Designation to participate in an IMF pilot program of burden-sharing further compounded the predicament, as balance-of-payments assistance was conditioned on securing privately contracted debt loans[69] (Pop 2006).

The IMF's policy shift came at a time of heightened political tensions on the Romanian scene. The political costs of the 1997 shock therapy increased the coalition tensions, pushing the long set of commitments inscribed in the IMF program behind schedule. The IMF cited delayed reforms, including the large privatization agenda for the banking sector, to suspend the 1997 SBA in February 1998. The Prime Minister resigned a month later. With access to international financial markets curtailed by the August 1998 Russian crisis, the government published an emergency anticrisis program in December 1998, which it hoped would help it regain the IMF's support (EIU 2000). This included commitments to fiscal tightening, closure of SOEs with losses and the privatization of two state banks. Indeed, by the end of the month, the controlling stake in the second largest bank, the Romanian Development Bank, had been sold to Société Générale of France[70].

Despite the acceleration in the privatization, the IMF refused to grant funds through a new SBA agreement unless access to private international financial markets was secured independently (NBR 1999a). This was a recipe for cornering countries into the highly predatory behaviour of speculative money markets which the IMF (2004) later recognized as thoroughly mistaken; it nearly cost Romania a default on its debt service. An unusual consensus was forged on the domestic-policy scene that the interests rates demanded on international financial markets were simply not acceptable. Instead, a highly contractionary set of policy measures succeeded in narrowing the trade deficit, bringing the current-account deficit to below 4 percent of GDP (see Figure 4.3). Romania made the May–June debt-service payments (around US$950 million) without IMF assistance, but at a very high political cost for the governing coalition: the contraction in real income saw wide industrial unrest and eventually led to the ousting of the prime minister. His successor, the central bank governor, Mugur Isărescu, was credited for pulling the country out of the crisis and onto a path of sustained growth.

Indeed, after 2000, Romania appeared very successful in harnessing financial globalization to speed up convergence with its neighbouring countries (Fabrizio et al. 2008). Policy credibility allowed it access international financial markets – since 2000, Romania accumulated large balance-of-payment surpluses, driven by both FDIs and foreign loans (see Figure 4.4). FDI has been mainly privatization-related, stemming from the constant pressure on the government to privatize, or rather to

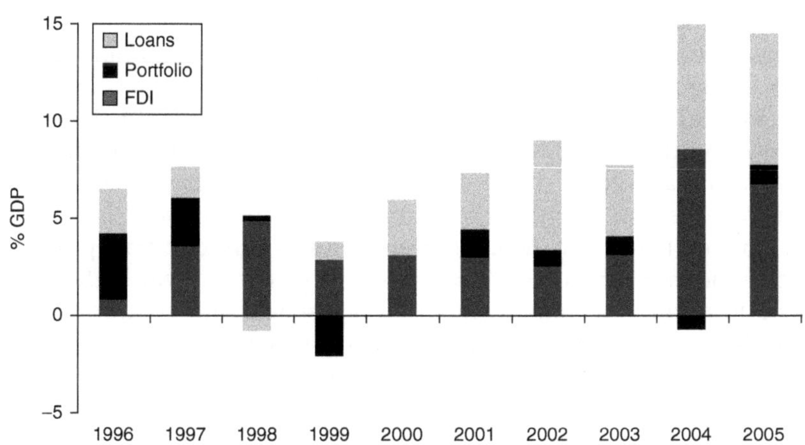

Figure 4.4 Capital account developments, percent GDP, Romania, 1996–2005
Source: Computed from *the National Bank of Romania Balance of Payment Reports* 2006 and Eurostat data.

fire-sell, assets, when it had little access to foreign borrowing. The year 1998 is a typical case, when the privatization of the telecommunications state-owned monopoly and a large state-owned bank accounted for the bulk of FDI inflows. The reliance on portfolio inflows, arising from international debt issuance (bonds or other financial instruments), throughout 1996 and 1997 produced a peak in debt service in 1999.

4.3 Policy narratives: Competing objectives

Once the IMF's 1997 SBA sanctioned currency interventions as legitimate if subordinated to the overall base-money targeting strategy[71], policy discourse acknowledged that the close relationship between exchange rates and inflation, driven by a substantial pass-through, rendered developments in the external position essential for its anti-inflationary strategy The NBR recognized a gap between its policy discourse and what it termed "eclectic" practices focused on exchange-rate control (Antohi et al. 2003). However, such eclecticism engendered competing policy objectives, internal vs. external stability, with the attending uncertainty and confusing signals to the economy.

Indeed, throughout this period, policy argumentation maintained the discursive ambiguity that characterized exchange-rate discussions during 1990–1997. Then, the NBR went to great lengths to justify its equilibrium discourse and to downplay the extent to which prices were responsive to exchange-rate movements. This time, the pass-through acknowledged, the ambiguity shifted to explaining exchange-rate decisions. The previous insistence on market-determined equilibrium levels was discarded by arguments that interventions no longer amounted to political interference, for the interbank currency market operated freely and the central bank intervened like any other trader (Daianu and Vranceanu 2001). The 1997 SBA altered the politics of exchange-rate management: previous central-bank interventions were "political" because exchange-rate dynamics were crucially linked to state production. The new government's commitment to reform, which the IMF held to signify a commitment to push through with contractionary policies regardless of the impact on state-owned production (a commitment previous governments were reluctant to maintain for very long), would increasingly sever this link.

This depoliticization of exchange-rate decisions nevertheless embedded an unavoidable contradiction: how to rationalize the central bank's systematic presence in the currency market against the neoliberal presentation as a regime of self-regulating markets. To negotiate this contradiction, the NBR explained its interventions either through a narrative of competitiveness or a monetarist discourse.

Exchange rate and competitiveness

The narrative of competitiveness gained importance during 1997, when the central bank engaged into (large) currency interventions to stem "unsustainable" appreciations associated with large capital inflows. Ever since, the gradual disinflation process has been explained as a "policy of encouraging moderate, sustainable real appreciations" (Popa 2004: 5), a policy stance constrained by the productivity pace in the exports sector (Vasilescu 2005). Indeed, the NBR (2002a) argued, the slow pace of export productivity growth forced it to strike a delicate balance between its inflation objective and the sustainability of the country's external position. It prompted policy interventions to slow down the pace of appreciation and, consequently, the pace of disinflation, in order to mitigate the negative impact on competitiveness.

The strategy of targeting real appreciations required balance-of-payment surpluses. The NBR's foreign reserves could only function in the short term as an instrument for manipulating currency movements. Capital account surpluses were required to offset structural deficits on the current account – as the SBAs greatly reduced the scope for an active industrial strategy, export-orientated production never emerged as a sustainable mechanism for redressing trade imbalances. Policy discourse thus encouraged FDI (to which the privatization of existing state assets would be a substantial contribution) and borrowing from abroad. The increased reliance on foreign capital had an added benefit: it would subject policy to the discipline of foreign "investment sentiment."

Furthermore, exchange-rate dynamics throughout the period suggest an increasing vulnerability to external volatility. Without access to foreign financing, the exchange rate fluctuated considerable (see Figure 4.5). The NBR intervened heavily during 1997–1999, first to contain strong appreciation pressures (throughout 1997) and then to contain depreciations triggered by substantial capital outflows. Riding on a tide of large foreign inflows, foreign reserves picked up after June 2000, with brief reversals[72]. The exchange-rate movements mark a substantial departure from the early patterns of volatility, with foreign inflows supportive of the NBR's policy of sustainable real appreciations. Critical voices questioned this stance, pointing to the increasing deterioration of the current-account position. A few economic analysts, Ilie Serbanescu having the highest public profile, questioned the "sustainability" of a

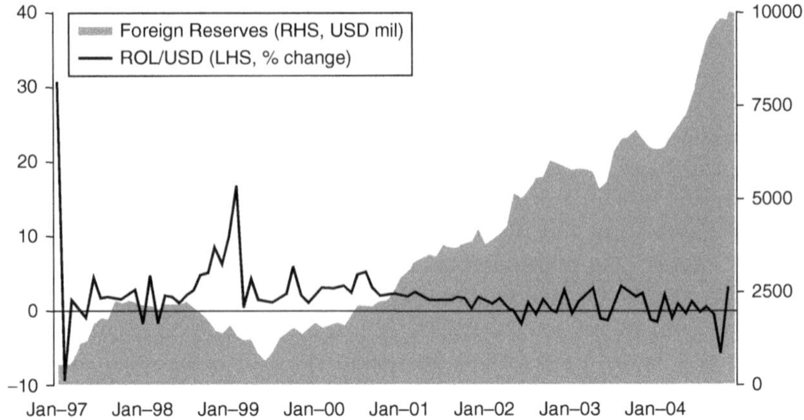

Figure 4.5 Exchange rate (ROL/US$, percent change) vs. and foreign reserves (USD mil), Romania, 1997–2005

Source: Computed from *the National Bank of Romania Balance of Payment Reports* (2000; 2006).

policy that relied on short-term, debt-creating capital inflows for producing stability (Paun 2004; Serbanescu 2005).

It was not entirely clear how a policy of real appreciation was beneficial to exporters, since strategies of export promotion usually entailed a competitive (read undervalued) exchange rate. The NBR rejected the criticism, arguing that without its currency interventions and an increasingly liberalized capital account exporters would have been worse off. Whereas the NBR constructed its currency interventions as an implicit subsidy for exporters, structural changes on the interbank currency market suggests exchange-rate movements increasingly divorced from export and growth performance. As in other developing countries with increasingly liberalized capital accounts, capital flows became the primary determinant of exchange-rate movements in most developing countries (Jalan 2003). While negotiations with the EU projected a sequencing of the capital account liberalization to end in 2004 (see Appendix I), by 1998 the Romanian currency market was replicating these neoliberal dynamics. Whereas historically, non-bank transactions dominated currency trading, in 1998 the interbank currency market outpaced non-bank transactions, a tendency maintained ever since (NBR 1999a). Volumes traded on the currency interbank market reached a monthly US$1 billion from August 1998, compared with US$500 million in non-bank transactions and against a US$2.6 billion trade deficit for the entire year.

The monetarist narrative

As discussed in the previous chapter, much of the NBR's argumentative efforts during 1990 to 1997 focused on legitimizing its excess liquidity narrative. After 1997, it faced a different challenge: how to reconcile its commitments to target bank reserves and to control aggregate demand with its exchange-rate strategy suggestive of cost-push drivers of inflation.

To resolve this contradiction, the central bank framed currency interventions in the context of its management of liquidity: exchange-rate dynamics conveyed important signals about liquidity positions in the money markets, of crucial importance for evaluating the monetary policy stance[73] (NBR 1998a). A depreciating exchange rate implied an excess demand for foreign currency arising from excess money-market liquidity that required sales of foreign currency to drain liquidity. On the contrary, interventions to counter appreciations increased money-market liquidity and required sterilizations in order to maintain reserve money within targets. This asymmetry was instrumental in consolidating speculative capital, primarily channelled through commercial banks, as the driving force for policy practice.

Indeed, the NBR's presence on the currency market was not akin to any other trader, for its participation affected the overall liquidity in the system. The next section explores in detail policy practice under a monetary-targeting regime with exchange-rate constraints.

4.4 Challenges to practice: Excess liquidity

The existence of structural excess liquidity belied the NBR's discursive anchoring of its policy successes in "tight monetary control"[74] (NBR 1998a). Under monetarist assumptions, excess reserves would increase credit activity and produce inflationary pressures. Commitment to price stability required the central bank to sterilize the liquidity effects of its currency activity and to maintain reserve positions within the targets established for money supply growth.

Currency interventions are reflected in the balance sheet of the central bank through the international reserves component. Pressures toward depreciation would trigger a sale of foreign currency, reducing money-market liquidity. The counterbalancing sterilization operation would require an increase in liquidity by increasing net domestic assets (either bank reserves or credit to the government) through OMOs. In the opposite case, if the central bank wished to contain excessive appreciations, it would pay for foreign currency by increasing domestic

Table 4.2 Sources of growth in the monetary base, 1995–2005

	Net Foreign Assets (percent)	Credit to Government (percent)	Credit to Banks (percent)	Other Net Assets (percent)	Refinancing from NBR (outstanding ROL bn.)
1997	108	25	–69	37	3367
1998	40	48	–16	28	3618
1999	82	52	–39	5	2433
2000	128	26	–44	–9	2296
2001	204	0	–79	–25	1148
2002	289	–9	–136	–44	0
2003	295	–12	–131	–52	0
2004	331	–37	–186	–18	0
2005	374	–23	–229	–17	0

Source: Computed from the Statistical Section of the *National Bank of Romania Annual Reports 1999* and *2005*.

liquidity, usually directly in the interbank market. The corresponding sterilization operation would require the central bank to reduce net domestic assets by reverse repos or other forms of liquidity mopping.

Since 1996, net foreign assets played an increasingly important role in reserve money growth (Table 4.2). With the monetization of government debt prohibited, the Treasury became a net lender to the central bank, implicitly assisting it with sterilization operations. The structural changes in the central bank's balance sheet brought up questions of how to manage money-market liquidity effectively. Exchange-rate stabilization tied money-market dynamics and the NBR's management of liquidity to currency markets. The central bank introduced new sterilization techniques, resorting to direct borrowing from the money markets (at maturities varying between two weeks to three months) and occasionally issuing own debt instruments because of the small portfolio of government securities and Treasury bills (Gabor 2008).

The table also suggests the magnitude of the structural excess of liquidity on the money market: beginning with 2002, the banking sector had no outstanding loans from the NBR. Instead, the central bank absorbed liquidity through the net-credit-to-banks position. The central bank's currency purchases became the main channel for injecting liquidity in the banking system. The year 2000 marked the beginning of a long period of "sterilization games," as Christiansen (2004) described commercial banks' behaviour in the Czech Republic during 1994 and 1995. Banks with access to international financial markets or borrowing from mother banks would channel capital inflows to engage in high yielding sterilization operations, changing the term structure of capital inflows toward short-term flows.

Such activities of short-term search for yield have been described as carry-trade activity. In the common form of carry trade, investors borrow and sell a low-yielding currency for buying and lending in a high-yielding one (UNCTAD 2007). With high leverage ratios, even small yield differentials can generate substantial returns. While there are a variety of ways to implement carry trades, each with different implications for market dynamics, the one predominant in emerging markets involves exchanging borrowed funds in the target currency in the spot market (Galati et al. 2007). These can be held until maturity in some short-term asset (bank deposit or government paper), or through derivative contracts, such as foreign-currency swaps. Banks participate in this process either as primary market intermediaries (providing loans in funding currency and deposits in target currency), as direct players through the proprietary trading desks or as counterparts in derivatives with carry-trade investors. It was no coincidence that banks' carry-trade activities as direct players gained momentum after 2000. Global liquidity conditions improved after the 1997–1999 crisis years, especially once Japan began implementing quantitative easing on a large scale from 2001 (until 2006). The yen became a key funding currency for global carry-trade activities (Nishigaki 2007), and against the uncovered interest-rate parity condition, commercial banks with access to international interbank markets began searching for attractive placement opportunities. Profits from yield differentials would be further increased by the appreciation of the target currency driven by higher demand (Cavallo 2006).

Thus, the shift to carry trade activity – eased by the entry of foreign banks on the Romanian policy scene, particularly after 1998 – triggered important changes in the distribution of liquidity on the wholesale interbank market. The liquidity effects of currency interventions did not affect all banks homogenously: because counterparty activities with the central bank on currency markets were mainly undertaken by banks who intermediated capital inflows (mainly foreign owned banks), the excess liquidity was asymmetrically distributed.

Throughout 1997 to 1999, the central bank combined changes in reserve requirements with currency-market interventions to mop up liquidity. The efforts to contain the current-account deficit saw hikes in required reserves combined with restricted access to the discount window (see Figure 4.6). However, actual reserve positions consistently differed from the required levels during the one-month averaging period

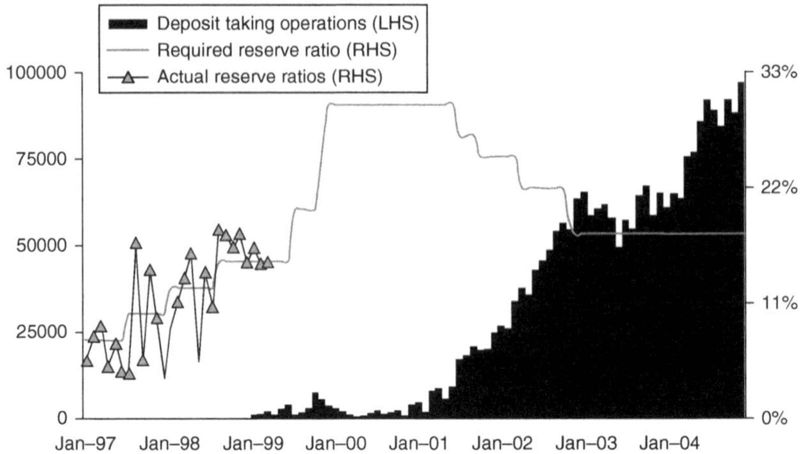

Figure 4.6 Deposit taking operations (outstanding daily average) and Required Reserves, Romania, 1997–2004

Source: Computed from the Statistical Section of the *National Bank of Romania Monthly Reports*.

(Gabor 2008). With access to international financial markets restored, deposit-taking operations became the main method for managing interbank liquidity.

Furthermore, during the 1997–1999, policy-makers were confronted with an apparently paradoxical situation: a structural excess of liquidity coexisted with highly volatile interbank interest rates. The one-week money-market rate fluctuated heavily throughout the period, a predictable outcome of the monetarist approaches where the central bank does not make it its policy objective to stabilize the inherently volatile interbank interest rate. It increased above 200 percent on three occasions, reaching highly positive real values. The NBR denied that the quantity-targeting strategy was ultimately the source of such substantial volatility on the interbank market, and instead advanced two explanations: excessive government expenditure and the speculative behaviour of the banking sector. Indeed, Antohi et al. (2003) described speculative attacks on the national currency as a method of putting pressure on the interest rates on central-bank and government securities, an argument Borc (2002) further linked to the structural changes on the treasury and interbank money markets.

Borc attributed the high interest rates throughout 1997–1999 to a combination of the following factors: the deployment of the exchange rate as nominal anchor, the historically high inflation after the fall of Communism and, third, the commercial banks' monopoly position in the interbank and Treasury markets. The first two arguments reflect the (rather Western-centric) claim that emerging countries' central banks are more likely to deviate from commitments to price stability and that investors require higher risk premiums to factor in deteriorating inflationary expectations (Mishkin 1999). These arguments fail to consider, however, that speculative activity responds to (expected) nominal returns rather than real returns on investments, as the short-term nature of speculation renders nominal values central to investment decisions (UNCTAD 2004).

Instead, starting with 1997, speculative activity would become a central element in the policy process. The central bank deplored the "speculative behaviour of some banks holding large amounts of foreign currency" (NBR 1998a). The commercial banks' behaviour in both the wholesale and Treasury markets increasingly reflected carry-trade activity. The implications for policy practice came into sharper focus during 1999.

4.4.1 The 1999 banking crisis

Concerned about capital outflows that would have threatened its inflation objective, the NBR took a net sale position on the currency market in the later part of 1998 and then the beginning of 1999, seeking to offset threats of a massive depreciation.

The NBR interpreted currency pressures as a signal of excess liquidity on the interbank market. On this market, banks were playing what Borc (2002) termed a bilateral bargaining game: on one side were banks with excess liquidity from the NBR's foreign-currency operations, and on the other were two state-owned banks (Bancorex and Banca Agricola), with severe liquidity problems. As the NBR downsized substantially its lender-of-last-resort function, complying with the IMF's demands, the sole source of liquidity remained the interbank market, where the asymmetric distribution of liquidity had produced a divide between banks with access to foreign capital and those (mainly state-owned banks) confined to local savers and international trade activity. With rising reserve requirements and a deteriorating loan portfolio (where the contractionary policies imposed during 1997 worsened balance-sheet positions plagued by problems of fraud and shoddy banking practices), the two state-owned banks were compelled to borrow at very high returns. Interbank lending became a very profitable activity for banks with excess liquidity. Once demand from these two banks was satisfied, excess-reserve banks turned to the currency market as the second source of speculative returns. The excess liquidity was used to fund currency positions, in a variation of the "sterilization game."

Under these circumstances, the central bank had several possible courses of action. It could allow the exchange rate to depreciate, with the attendant increase in inflation rates. A second option, using "moral suasion" to stabilize expectations, signalled a disposition to defend the currency that sought to discourage speculation without requiring actual interventions. Finally, the central bank could choose to intervene directly on the currency market, simultaneously absorbing money-market liquidity and bringing the market into the bank, as Bagehot would put it, by sterilizing at a high interest rate.

The first option reflected negatively on commitments to price stability, while the second could not withstand sustained speculative pressures. Consequently, to narrow the wild swings in exchange-rate movements throughout December 1998, and again in March–April 1999, the central bank resorted to both foreign currency sales and high interest-rate sterilizations. Indeed, increasing daily volatility in exchange rates since July 1998 went hand in hand with a trend increase in interbank short-term rates (see Figure 4.7). Once the critical moment of debt service was

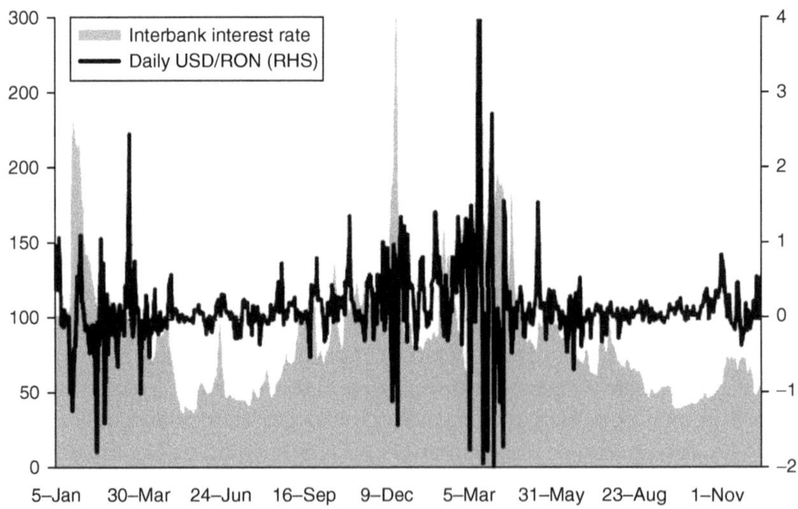

Figure 4.7 Daily currency and overnight rates dynamics, Romania, 1998–1999

Source: Computed from the National Bank of Romania statistics http://www.bnro.ro/StatisticsReportHTML.aspx?icid=801&table=642&column= for interbank data, and http://www.bnro.ro/StatisticsReportHTML.aspx?icid=801&table=702&column=, accessed December 20, 2008.

overcome, the NBR allowed the exchange rate to depreciate at a slow pace while simultaneously proceeding to rebuild its foreign-currency reserves. The additional liquidity injected through currency operations set the interbank rate on a decreasing trend.

Currency sales functioned as an antispeculative instrument but at the expense of overnight-rate spikes. The NBR would ask banks that were betting on a currency depreciation to buy a large volume of foreign currency at the quoted rate. Since regulations required banks to engage in transactions with the central bank at the quoted rate, the matching liquidity had to be raised on the interbank market, pushing overnight rates to record levels as, for instance, during March 1999 with second-round effects for banks with liquidity shortfalls. The central bank refused to smooth fluctuations not because of some monetarist impulse to allow markets to work but because the success of its antispeculation tactic depended on restricting banks' access to domestic liquidity for matching the foreign currency buying orders.

This "market mechanism" for discouraging speculation inflicted liquidity shortages and expensive refinancing on other banks in the system so that by the end of 1999 Romania avoided a default on its foreign-debt service at the expense of a banking crisis. The state budget absorbed the costs of restructuring two state-owned banks, while the NBR revoked the licence of several small private banks (NBR 1999a), successfully calming a series of incipient bank runs[75]. To tackle the vulnerability arising from the country's exposure to global financial volatility, the Romanian central bank accelerated the financialization of the banking sector. Its strategy of containing speculative pressures on the currency market sent a clear message: successful banking under neoliberalism required 'impatient' practices (market portfolios) rather than loans to production.

Romania contributed to an already substantial record of banking crisis in the region. Croatia had a crisis in 1996, recurring in 1998–1999; the Czech Republic between 1993 and 1997; Hungary and Poland during 1991–1995; Estonia between 1992 and 1995; Lithuania in 1996 and 1997, the Slovak Republic between 1996 and 2000; and Slovenia between 1992 and 1994 (Haas and van Lelyveld 2006). Government funding contributed to the restructuring and recapitalization of the affected banks, motivated by the view that balance sheets needed a "clean up" for privatization. Crises were framed, as in Romania, as a consequence of vested interests, asymmetric information, and the bad-debt problems associated with the widespread initial recessions (Caviglia et al. 2002; De Haas and van Lelyveld 2006). The liquidity policies of the central bank shaped by the excess demand narrative (privileged in the IMF's discourse in all its SBAs in the region) or the increasing exposure arising from capital-account liberalization (faster in other CEE countries than in Romania) received little attention, so that the only solution to banking crisis appeared to be a fast privatization of state-owned banks.

While the banking crisis also involved private institutions, governments committed the bulk of funds to the restructuring of state-owned banks. Implicit in the push for privatization was also the link that neoliberal discourses made between higher government spending and interbank interest rates, suggesting that crisis in the state-owned sector negatively affected private banks' ability to raise funds on the interbank market. Romania offered an interesting example of this argument.

The dynamics of interbank rates and a pattern of lending-rate movements that showed little sensitivity to short-term rate fluctuations (and thus to the NBR's liquidity policies) raised questions of what governed interest-rate movements. The NBR (1999a) pointed to the lack of confidence and uncertainty generated by conflicting policy objectives, a depoliticizing exercise that aimed to sideline the grip that speculative behaviour exercised on the money market. It also deployed that neoliberal argument par excellence, that irresponsible expenditure crowded out private investment[76]. Indeed, since the 1997 SBA, the government had been increasingly forced to finance its deficits on the domestic money markets, which, the NBR argued, kept interbank rates high. The cost of bank restructuring increased the burden on the expenditure side and opened up another source of speculative returns for the banking sector when the government's access to foreign borrowing all but disappeared toward the end of 1998. Since the NBR was legally forbidden to engage in purchases of government paper on the primary market, a Treasury desperate for liquidity was forced, on several occasions, to accept extremely high interest rates at very short maturities. For instance, throughout the first trimester of 1999, the government could only borrow at three months, above 120 percent yield (see Figure 4.8). Several high-volume auctions were not concluded as the Treasury deemed the commercial banks' offers unacceptable. Such a pattern of financing brought the 2000 public-debt service up to a staggering 14 percent of GDP.

Debt-related interest payments increased substantially, forcing the government to downsize social expenditure to achieve a significant primary surplus in both 1998 and 1999. Starting with April 1999, the Treasury decided to eliminate such costly intermediation, issuing

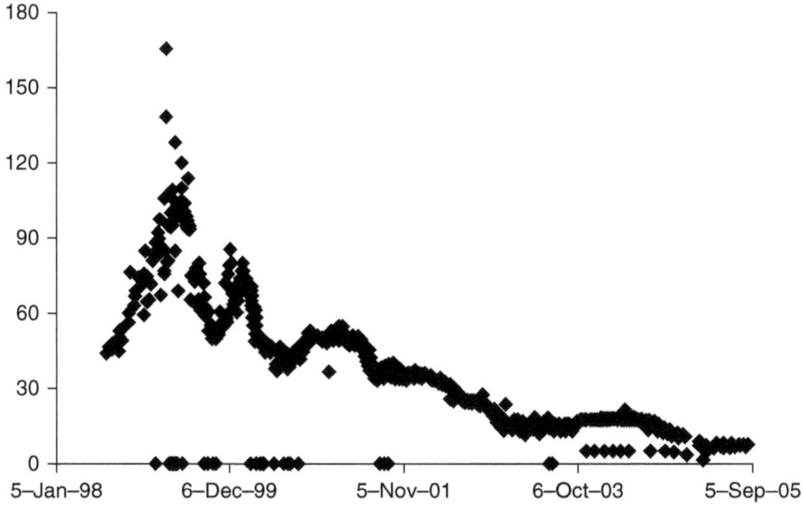

Figure 4.8 Yields on domestic debt, Romania, 1998–2005
Source: Computed form the Ministry of Finance data.

bonds directly to individual rather than institutional savers, so that the share of government paper held by banks fell from the near 100 percent throughout 1997 and 1998 to 63.1 percent at the end of 2000 and 18 percent at the end of 2005. This decision triggered a competition for savings that saw banks immediately responding with deposit-rate increases.

The relationship between commercial banks, the NBR, and the Treasury came to be described as a "guerrilla war" or "ambush" and the money market as the "cemetery of public money" (Capital 1999), as if the field of monetary management contained well-defined, antagonistic interests between different policy-actors. The central bank, in this representation, struggled to formulate policy in a captive position vis-à-vis the money market when throughout this period it engaged into a much more fluid, shifting set of alliances. To describe the relationship between the NBR and speculative finance, manifested primarily through the banking sector, as antagonistic downplays the fact that both participated in sterilization games, even if driven by different concerns. The strategy of targeting real exchange-rate appreciations drove the central bank to introduce sterilization operations that fostered speculative behaviour, including that of the state-owned banks which the IMF accused of sluggish adjustment to market behaviour!

Furthermore, the NBR's claims that fiscal domination hindered monetary-policy implementation must be assessed against its practices of sterilization. In a circle of mutual dependency, the high interest rates attending sterilized interventions increased the debt burden which would only be addressed by a procyclical pattern of primary surpluses accumulation during periods of economic recession. Debt management, on the other hand, was exposed to the procyclical nature of capital inflows (Kaminsky et al. 2004), which Togo (2007) further connected to the cyclical nature of the risk premium on public debt. The implication, Togo suggested, was that, under pro-cyclical risk premium and capital flows, the government ought to refrain from contracting short-term debt or minimize the concentration of maturing debt in one period. This technical expression of the policy trade-offs obscures the extent to which the priorities of the central bank shaped public debt dynamics. To argue that the government had not managed correctly either its debt or its fiscal stance sidelines the critical role in narrowing policy options played by both the IMF's push for money-market financing and the speculative behaviour of the banking sector. It also questions the extent to which policy coordination would have been possible, when the NBR's attempts to legitimize its policy stance generally involved a dichotomized representation that placed fiscal misbehaviour at the root of macroeconomic problems. The terms of agreement on a common goal, a process that indeed premises negotiation, have been constructed by neoliberal discourses to inevitably start from fiscal restraint.

Thus, the 1999 moment revealed how in fact policy success translated into a successful compliance with the rules of financialized globalization. It entailed a "purging" of the banking sector that further narrowed the potential (and policy instruments) for a different economic paradigm and legitimized a policy practice increasingly dependent upon speculative capital, where adjustment to the international rules of the game justified a deep recession and a further deterioration of the state's capacity for social provisioning.

4.4.2 The recovery years, 2000–2005

As explained earlier, the increasingly divided politics and the prolonged economic crisis resulted in a vacuum of credibility, particularly in what concerned politicians' ability to manage the economy. By the end of 1999, the Romanian President decided that the only way forward was to hand economic policy to technocrats. Mugur Isărescu's short premiership – he returned to the central bank a year later – marked a fundamental change in both his public image and that of the institution with which he was associated. The success in restoring stability and kick-starting the economy was attributed to Isărescu's ability to push the necessary economic reforms (EIU 2001).

Isărescu was trusted to speed up fiscal reforms and privatizations, particularly in the banking sector – a source of long-standing tensions with international organizations. However, in a moment of unusual candor, he later described the experience as prime minister as follows:

> I have to confess that I would have liked to go to the Parliament and declare: "In 2000, a decade after the December 1989 Revolution, the priorities of the government will include extensive investments in industry, agriculture and other economic sector, higher spending for health, schools, regional administration, army, substantial increases in income all in the context of a strong national currency." Unfortunately, I did not have that opportunity. It will certainly be for another prime minister, probably in 2009, two decades after the revolution. The train from Helsinki, which we have no right to miss, will take us there. (Isărescu 2006: 105[77])

The quote suggests first that the governor held a far less dogmatic position than it would appear from the usual public statements. It outlines a growth strategy closer to that of East Asian tigers but at the same time it invokes political priorities not to pursue it. The ultimate goal of responsible politics, it suggests, was EU membership (the train from Helsinki, where the start of accession negotiations was formally sanctioned) where that alternative growth path would be entirely possible. For membership to be secured, neoliberal policies had to be enacted: inflation remained the greatest enemy, not because of monetarist theorizing, but because the EU saw inflation control as a primary condition for declaring Romania a functioning market economy.

Ironically, during his time as prime minister, Isărescu made fiscal decisions for which he had criticized previous governments. The IMF suspended the SBA during his premiership (September 2000) because the government had broken the quantitative target on budget deficit and had also failed to meet the targets on bank privatization (EIU 2001). The Isărescu government had committed to higher than planned expenditures to finance an increase in pensions and public-sector wages.

The central bank's account of this period is more nuanced than the "Isărescu saved us" narrative. Without downplaying the role of domestic-policy decisions, it accepted that global liquidity conditions played a fundamental role in the return to stability. Indeed, the NBR (2003a) heralded 2000 as the year when it regained its dominion of the money markets and began recovering its credibility as inflation tempered gradually, aided by a favourable international environment that saw global finance increasing its appetite for emerging-markets investment. Foreign capital flows increased substantially, supporting the NBR's practice of gradual real appreciations. Accordingly, the magnitude of structural excess liquidity on the money market and the attending sterilization operations expanded considerably.

However, the central bank was not entirely able to eschew the ambiguity of its policy discourse. The monetarist foundations of its policy framework projected a clearly defined set of policy practices and outcomes. These involved monetary targets pursued through reserve control. However, by 2003, the NBR recognized, and the IMF (2004) concurred, that in fact monetary aggregates had little if any relevance for policy practices, while the exchange rate and, gradually, the policy rate, were better indicators of its policy stance[78]. And this is where the political character of the policy strategy reveals itself. Monetarism is predicated on the assumption that markets are the only viable mechanism for regulating activity, financial markets included. A rules-based policy removes discretion and allows markets to distribute resources efficiently. However, the increasing consolidation of the neoliberal rules of the game depended on a deeply discretionary policy practice that produced the necessary incentives for speculative capital.

The first challenge was to articulate a practice of tight monetary control, for how otherwise could the NBR explain the disinflation process? Maintaining a legitimizing representation required considerable work, for money-market dynamics rendered the impact of policy decisions on the intermediate target (broad money) unpredictable. To bring money-market dynamics in line with claims of tight liquidity control, the NBR altered its reserve requirements mechanism, reducing the maintenance period to 15 days in the first quarter of 1999. A daily floor and ceiling for reserves, practically amounting to a daily reserve requirement, was set simultaneously with the creation of an overnight interbank market (Gabor 2008).

The new accounting mechanism did not increase the effectiveness of the monetary targeting strategy. The introduction of the overnight interbank market expanded the commercial banks' avenues for a more efficient management of reserves and the attending volatility in overnight rates (see Figure 4.9). The high uncertainty triggered by the central bank's attempts to tighten liquidity during the first half of 1999 resulted in an increase of the spread between the bid (the rate at which

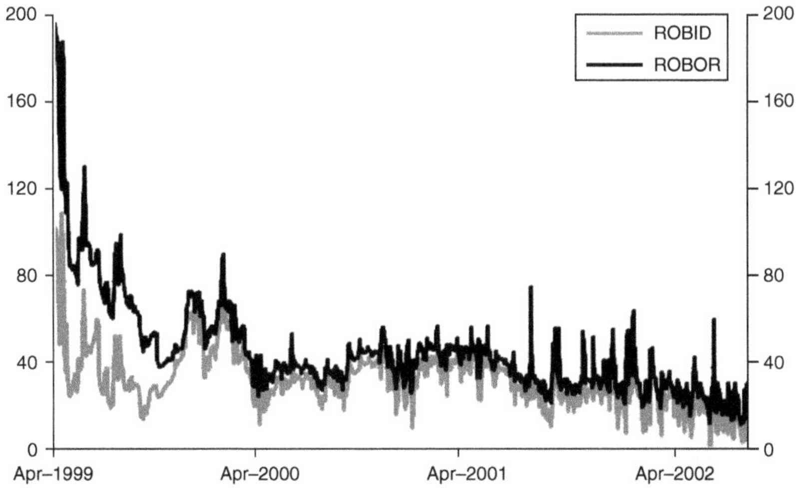

Figure 4.9 Overnight money market rates, Romania, April 1999–July 2002
Source: computed from the National Bank of Romania statistics http://www.bnro.ro/StatisticsReportHTML.aspx?icid=801&table=642&column= accessed December 20, 2008.

banks are willing to borrow) and the offered rate, to subsequently narrow once sterilization operations resumed.

In August 2002, the de-facto daily-reserves requirement was replaced with one month averaging, with the 23rd of the month as the cut-off date (Gabor 2008). The central bank sought to improve the effectiveness of its liquidity management, and, indeed, extending the accounting period reduced intra-period volatility (see Figure 4.10). Yet volatility persisted because of the lack of an explicit policy focus on stabilizing wholesale interest rates (Bagehot 1910). Towards the end of the maintenance period, excess reserves would push bid rates to the level of the standing deposit facility if reserves could not be placed on the interbank market or during (less frequent) liquidity shortages, (January and March 2003), both bid and offered rates would increase as banks turned to the interbank market to match reserve requirements.

Clearly, the monetarist assumptions underlying the policy strategy were invalidated by money-market dynamics, rendering not only the demand for money but also the money multiplier unstable. The liquidity effect of sterilization operations allowed commercial banks to make "asset decisions [...] largely independent of their reserve position" (Moore 1984: 106).

Should we take the failure of monetarism as self-evident? The question, again, is not whether monetarism worked or why the NBR did not

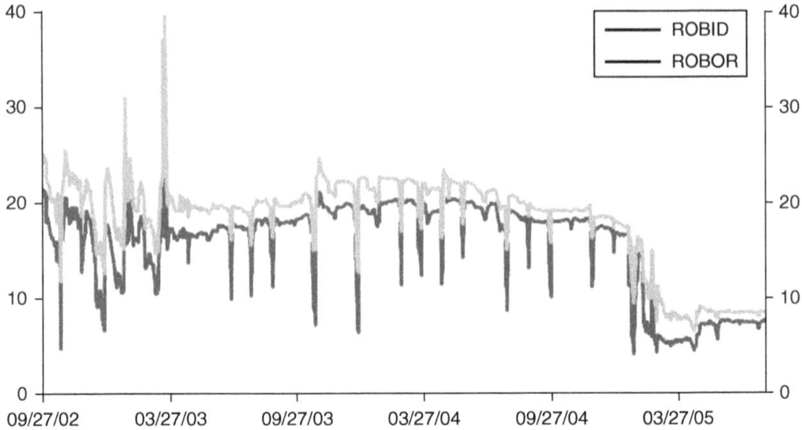

Figure 4.10 Overnight money market rates, Romania, August 2002–August 2005

Source: Computed from the National Bank of Romania statistics http://www.bnro.ro/StatisticsReportHTML.aspx?icid=801&table=642&column= accessed December 20, 2008.

accept an endogenous theory of money but how and why "success" was produced and sustained in the policy space. Here, David Mosse's (2005) research on development practices and policies is useful in exploring the NBR's policy. Mosse argues that the more interests are tied up within a particular interpretation, the more stable and dominant the policy model becomes. The need to sustain the relationship with the IMF, whose approval eased Romania's access to international finance, partly explains the endurance of monetary targeting against the NBR's open admission that the implementation of a pure monetary targeting regime was not within its reach. Even the IMF's country reports contain little, if any, reference to the monetary targeting strategy, while acknowledging that inflation control involved exchange-rate targeting. So what explains the resilience of this policy model, which the NBR's logic of practice routinely contradicted? Here, Mosse's warning against a linear conceptualization that represents practice as the result of the policy model is particularly relevant. Instead, he argues, policy models (and discourses) serve to mobilize and maintain political support, thus legitimizing rather than orientating practices (Mosse 2005: 14).

Indeed, the NBR was constrained to promote the view that its activities were the result of the implementation of official policy, when, in fact, practices of monetary management were increasingly subordinated to commercial banks' sterilization games. Remarkable in this period is the rapid expansion in the volume of liquidity sterilized through deposit-taking operations: from ROL300 million in 1999 to ROL10 billion by 2004 (see Figure 4.6). Increasingly large capital inflows arising from balance-of-payment surpluses (on account of privatization-driven foreign direct investments, foreign remittances, and foreign loans) produced exchange-rate appreciations. The central bank's attempts to contain appreciation led to a fast increase in money-market liquidity. Thus, a fundamental component of the monetary transmission mechanism, the money market, assumed to transmit the signals of the central bank through a competitive process, was in fact dependent upon the overwhelming participation of the central bank: the volume of liquidity deposited with the bank reached 90 percent of the overall interbank market by the end of 2002 (NBR 2002a). Commercial banks' liquidity positions no longer reflected traditional lending activities, as sterilization reoriented portfolio preferences toward short-term placements in central-bank instruments or the primary Treasury market.

Notwithstanding the policy discourse, sterilizations became a vehicle for attracting capital inflows, channelled through commercial banks' carry-trade activities. Thus, monetary targeting made coherent practices engendering an inherent contradiction: interventions to prevent excessive appreciations produced the policy "problem" (excess liquidity) and "the solution" (sterilization). Still, abandoning currency interventions and sterilization would have reduced arbitrage opportunities and narrowed the inflow of capital that produced the exchange-rate appreciations and disinflation. This inherent contradiction further questioned the narration of conflicting objectives: that policy practice produced confusing signals by gravitating from external stability concerns tailored to the exporter's interests to internal stability that would have justified less or no interventions to prevent currency appreciations. In fact, currency interventions, along with sterilizations, were a necessary practice for curtailing inflation, rather than a strategy of export promotion. The success of the central bank's neoliberal mission (the containment of inflationary pressures) crucially depended on the continuous engagement in "sterilization games," contributing to the financialization of both central-bank and commercial-bank activities.

By 2003, the NBR accepted that it was defending the indefensible (NBR 2003a). OMOs were difficult to rationalize through a monetarist discourse in the presence of a structural excess of liquidity. Seeking to adopt the conceptual apparatus of "modern banking" with its emphasis on signalling as a tool for stabilizing expectations, the NBR gradually switched policy argumentation to interest rates. Such a formulation overlooked the conditions under which the interest rate that determined the NBR's relationship with money markets could function as a signal to lending and spending decisions.

Indeed, interest-rate policy argumentation points to the power the central bank holds through its position of monopoly supplier of high-powered money. A day-to-day practice orientated at offsetting the volatility of autonomous liquidity factors allows it to maintain short-term rates within a corridor closely correlated to its policy rate (for instance the Bank of England maintains a fluctuation corridor for the overnight rate of 50 basis points). In this manner, the central bank controls the price of liquidity in the system. The short-term money-market rate functions as signal for the entire structure of the interest rates, aggregate demand and inflationary pressures. As longer term rates incorporate an additional expectations factor, an interest-rate policy strategy requires the central bank to influence expectations about future policy moves and thus to strengthen the link between short- and long-term interest rates.

Hence, the claim that the interest-rate policy functioned better as an indicator of the monetary policy stance has to be considered against the practice of sterilized interventions. Clearly, the only variable relevant for money-market dynamics was the rate at which the NBR mopped up money-market liquidity and not the reference rate in its statistical releases, which for most of the period remained consistently below the sterilization rate (see Figure 4.11).

However, the sterilization rate did not function as a policy rate in the traditional understanding (i.e. as the cost of liquidity in the system) but rather as an opportunity cost for banks constantly searching for the best arbitrage opportunities. One of the key figures of the central bank's monetary policy department, Dorina Antohi, admitted that the interbank market had "an insignificant role" in propagating monetary policy impulses (Antohi et al. 2003: 8). The neoliberal monetary management produced a paradoxical outcome: an interbank market largely dominated by the central bank but with little relevance in the monetary transmission mechanism. While the central bank influenced wholesale finance through its sterilization decisions, the "policy rate" was conditioned by currency and money-market dynamics. This appeared nowhere more clearly than in the evolution of the deposit-taking rate throughout this interval. After the extended volatility registered during 1997–1999, sterilization rates entered a rapidly descending trend. Nonetheless, these rate cuts were not autonomous policy decisions constructed through rigorous analysis of aggregate demand developments.

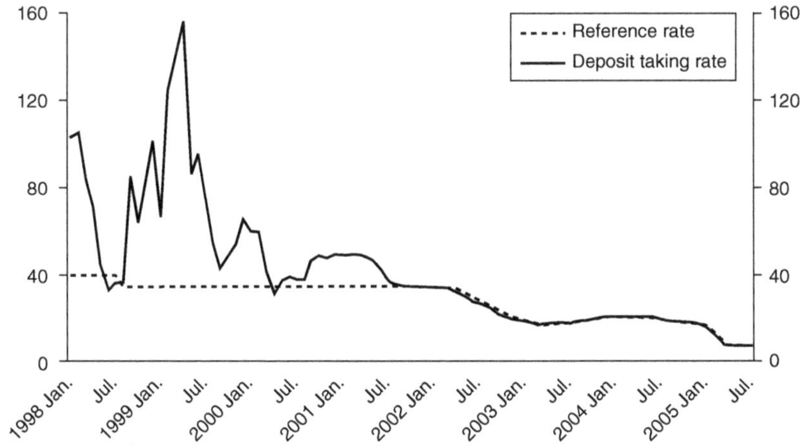

Figure 4.11 Official and sterilization interest rates, Romania, 1998–2005

Source: Computed from the National Bank of Romania statistics http://www.bnro.ro/Interest-Rates-on-Monetary-Policy-and-Standing-Facilities,-history-3337.aspx, accessed December 20, 2008 and the Statistical Section of the Annual Report, 2006.

In fact, the NBR (2002a) admitted that the quasi-permanent excess supply on the currency market and the Treasury's success in reducing the costs of financing on the primary Treasury-bill market were instrumental in its decisions to reduce sterilization rates[79].

The policy reversal during the second half of 2003 further confirmed this trend. After having reduced the policy rate by around 1,000 basis points since June 2002, the NBR decided to "tighten" monetary conditions by ending the easing cycle and increasing the sterilization rate in three steps, each of one percentage point. Two interrelated developments explained this move. First, the NBR (2003a) attributed its decision to balance-of-payments developments. It interpreted a reversal of capital inflows as evidence of an overshooting in its interest-rate cuts that depreciated the currency[80] and threatened disinflation

Second, it argued, the policies in place had unduly supported an expansion in demand, on the back of a fast increase in foreign-currency-denominated consumer credit. Indeed, between January 2000 and June 2003, domestic non-bank credit nearly tripled, albeit from a low base. In the first six months of 2003 alone it increased by 80 percent. The currency composition shifted toward foreign-currency credit: while, at the end of 1996, around 35 percent of the banking-sector assets were in foreign currency, by April 2003 this share had risen to 60 percent, reflecting expectations of a trend appreciation in the domestic currency and the interest-rate differential caused by high domestic interest rates. A post-Keynesian positioning would have described this process as the endogenization of the monetary transmission mechanism, where the productive sector's demand for credit and the banking sector's liquidity preference, based on the risk assessment of the creditworthiness of the borrowers and the level of perceived risk the banks are willing to assume, drive credit creation (Dow 2004). The central bank's control, in this scenario, narrows to influencing the cost of credit in the system (by setting the price of liquidity). Nevertheless, in the particular circumstances of a banking system awash with liquidity and a substantially euroized asset side, there was little scope for monetary control either on monetarist terms (reserves control) or post-Keynesian lines (interest-rate control).

Under these circumstances, the attempts to contract aggregate demand by raising sterilization rates would achieve the very opposite: shifting demand toward foreign-denominated credit. Clearly, explaining credit dynamics as the outcome of a monetary easing, as the central bank did during 2003, would have required a rather more substantial control of monetary conditions than the structural excess of liquidity allowed. Nevertheless, such a claim served a different discursive purpose: to articulate policy through interest rates and aggregate demand control. These discursive efforts reflected NBR's decision to shift its policy regime from (it claimed, an obsolete) monetary targeting toward inflation-targeting, whose adoption date was set for August 2005.

The regime shift has to be understood in the context of capital-account liberalization (see Appendix I). Because EU accession negotiations required Romania to allow non-residents access to local currency bank deposits by 2004, the central bank worried that this regulatory change would potentially increase exposure to speculative activity (Gabor 2008). A postponement to April 2005 was negotiated, a breathing space the NBR (2005a) demanded in order to adopt containing measures. On the one hand, it undertook a series of aggressive policy rate cuts to reduce the interest-rate differential: the sterilization rate decreased from 21.25 percent in January 2004 to 8 percent by August 2005. Viewed from a different angle, NBR's expectations of higher (speculative) capital inflows allowed it to substantially lower its sterilization rates, a move suggestive enough of the fundamental role that speculative capital played in structuring policy decisions. On the other hand, the NBR decided simultaneously to allow inflation-curbing nominal appreciations in the domestic currency by gradually withdrawing from the currency market, which it aimed to abandon by the fourth quarter of 2005. This stance, the NBR claimed, would offset the potential inflationary consequences of its monetary easing.

4.5 A second pause for reflection: The banking sector and foreign ownership

The OECD (2002: 43) described 1999 as the moment when financial-sector reform gained momentum in Romania. The restructuring process redefined the banking sector through the closure of one of the largest state-owned banks, privatizations, and several bank failures.

Restructuring, international institutions held, was highly overdue. Indeed, while the 1997 SBA committed the government to speed up the pace of bank privatization, by December 1998 state-owned banks still amounted to over 70 percent of banking activity. The politics of gradualism had maintained Romania on the dark side of the great divide, as a famous Berglof and Bolton (2001) article described an opening gulf between successful and laggard formerly planned economies. What opened the divide, they argued, was governments' failure (Romania unequivocally one of them) to break the cycle of unpaid enterprise debt, arrears, and pressures for monetization that worsened state banks' balance sheets. The large presence of the state in the banking sector continued to reproduce the Communist inheritance. The "gradualist" years' commitments to change the ownership structure and thus to stimulate market-driven processes of financial intermediation failed to materialize. This articulation of the banking-sector problem simultaneously identified the solution: privatization and private ownership as necessary conditions for crossing the divide – a premise underlying the constant pressures international organizations (the IMF, the World Bank) placed on accelerating banking privatization.

Neoliberal accounts of the changes in the banking system narrowed the explanations of the 1999 bank failures to serious governance problems and political pressure to extend credit to vested industrial interest, thus validating soft-budget constraints. Notwithstanding the many high-profile corruption cases which involved banks' top management, particularly in the state-owned sector[81], this narration of restructuring as a natural and necessary progress toward private ownership had two discursive effects It first sidelined over the NBR's practices during the years of normative neoliberalism. Its policies of maintaining historically high refinancing rates and restricted lending had a negative impact on the banking sector, particularly during 1999. Furthermore,

NBR's attempts to enforce neoliberal recipes for "restructuring" SOEs also contributed to the deterioration of state-owned banks' assets.

Second, it premises state-bank behaviour systematically tailored to the requirements of state-owned production, sidelining the increasing financialization of the relationship between finance and production. While indeed state-owned banks were repeatedly instructed to extend preferential credit, could this constitute conclusive evidence of their functioning (only) as a validation mechanism for soft-budget constraints? This representation cannot be reconciled with liquidity shortages and the three payment blockages described in the last chapter nor the industrial sector's repeatedly voiced concerns that state-owned banks were deliberately engineering operational blockages to "stimulate" demand for expensive credit.

The 1997–1999 crisis years provided a perfect opportunity for the further financialization of the banking sector. With the peak in debt service looming at the end of 1998, the IMF most helpfully advised Romanian authorities that a faster privatization of important state-owned assets could partially offset the foreign financing gap (Pop 2006). Pressed for foreign currency, the government initiated a fire sale of two large state-owned banks[82] (along with several other high-profile privatizations), further opening up the banking sector to international ownership. Simultaneously, the asymmetric distribution of liquidity on the interbank market, coupled with serious governance problems (EIU 1998) had immediate consequences for the liquidity and solvency of several state-owned and private banks. Thus, the two state-owned banks which had channelled preferential credit to the energy and agricultural sectors during 1995 and 1996 (Bancorex and Banca Agricola) found it increasingly difficult to finance a stream of nonperforming loans on the interbank market (amounting to 253 percent of the capital in the banking system in December 1998). Under the IMF and World Bank's specific requests, one state-owned bank was closed, and two other restructured for privatization[83].

Neoliberalism's impressive capacity to redefine itself is obvious here. Critical voices saw the 1997 Asian crisis and its spread elsewhere as a fundamental crisis in neoliberalism, when it quickly became clear that the dislocation was instead used as a platform for extending neoliberal logics (Peck and Tickell 2002). A similar outcome occurred in Romania: international volatility and pressures from multilateral lenders (IMF, the World Bank and the European Commission) opened up the banking sector in an unprecedented manner, marking a substantial reconfiguration of banking activity. By the end of 1999, the state banks had

Table 4.3 Banking sector structure, Romania, various years

	Number				Share in total credits		
	1990	1998	1999	2005	1998	1999	2005
State-Owned	5	7	4	2	75%	50%	6%
Domestic private capital	2	13	11	7	9.5%	6.1%	31%
Foreign private capital	0	16	19	30	15%	43.6%	62%
TOTAL	7	36	34	39	100	100	100

Source: Computed from National Bank of Romania Annual Reports 1992 (p. 37), 1999 (p. 45) and the Financial Stability *Report 2006* (p. 8).

lost 25 percent of market share, while foreign-owned banks extended their influence further at the expense of private banks with domestic capital (see Table 4.3), a tendency that would continue over the following years.

But this was not the only achievement: the government absorbed restructuring costs. The elimination of state-owned banks thus further increased the scope for speculative returns on the Treasury markets, functioning to increasingly structure banking behaviour through financialization. Indeed, during 1999 it became evident that the neoliberal policy-making punished credit activities and rewarded speculation. Banks obtained higher returns on money and currency markets than through long-term financing of productive activities – by 2005, the share of bank loans in corporate liabilities decreased to 10 percent (NBR, 2008b). What the NBR (2000a) called a paradoxical situation in fact reflected the shift towards market-based investment activity associated with the financialization of banking and supported through carry trade activities by favourable liquidity conditions in international financial markets.

That commercial banks' willingness to lend for productive activity diminished considerably throughout the period is an important explanatory factor for another 'challenge' of the transformation process: the culture of non-payment and arrears (IMF, 2004), affecting both the state-owned enterprises and private firms. Aside from political considerations (rent-seeking behaviour for instance), the IMF recognized that the systematic liquidity squeeze produced by a curtailing of directed credit contributed substantially to the consolidation of such behaviour. Nevertheless, the disappearance of directed credit cannot account for another interesting statistic the IMF (2004) report produced: enterprises financed around 8 percent of total requirements through bank credit, while arrears financing rose to 35 percent.

This tendency continued after 2000. The new practices of monetary management contributed to the financialization of banks. A strategy of targeting exchange rate appreciations combined with sterilization operations reconfigured the relationship between the money, currency and Treasury market, with the foreign-owned banks' speculative behaviour playing a central role on all three. While the NBR (2004a) acknowledged that the money market played an insignificant role in propagating monetary policy impulses to the productive sector, it refused to recognize that this was the consequence of its practices of liquidity management, increasingly subjugated to the requirements of transnational market actors.

Indeed, Western European banks increased their presence in the Romanian banking sector. Banca Agricola was sold to Reifeissen (Austria) in 2001. The privatization process of the largest Romanian bank, Banca Commerciala Romana (35% market share in total bank assets in 2003) is symptomatic of the intense international pressure to transfer state owned banks into private ownership. In 2003 the European Bank for Reconstruction and Development, the International Finance Corporation (the umbrella organization of the IMF and the World Bank) and the Romanian government signed a pre-privatization agreement that transferred 25% of the bank to the two international organisations for the sum of USD 222 million. In the previous year, BCR had total assets of €4.5 billion and had made a net profit of €99.5 million. The EBRD explained the process as follows:

> First, the project will enable the privatisation process of BCR to continue, which will be a major step towards achieving private sector ownership of the Romanian banking sector. The commitment of the Romanian State to continue the privatisation process for BCR should contribute to positive agreement with the International Monetary Fund (IMF) for the disbursement of the final tranche of the IMF standby agreement. In addition, the share purchase by the EBRD and IFC will have an important demonstration effect for the country, signalling confidence in the Romanian banking sector and in the overall investment environment. (http://www.ebrd.com/projects/psd/psd2003/29327.htm)

In other words, the Romanian government transferred a quarter of the shares in a profitable state-owned bank in exchange for a sum barely twice the profits made by the bank in the previous year. The EBRD reasoning built on a neoliberal appeal to the magic of private ownership. To remove any doubts about the validity of such reasoning (a difficult task since the bank had shown to be profitable in state ownership), the IMF conditioned the disbursement of the SBA tranche on the transaction. The privatization was completed in 2005, when the Austrian Erste Bank purchased the controlling shares for EUR 3.75 bn. The EBRD and the IFC together received EUR. 1.5 bn for their shares, about 800% return on their investment two years before. The Romanian Minister of Public Finance, Sebastian Vladescu, applauded the privatization:

> "You were asking at some point whether I would not like to make a phone call to a bank and impose a certain yield on Treasury bills. No, I would not like it. That is exactly why we sold BCR. It is wrong to have this option, because it opens up the possibility of abuse. One might say, I am very competent, I know exactly how much the bank should charge me and I am correct about it. Let us instead allow the markets to work, I am very happy that markets work. We have a functioning currency market. That the exchange rate is 4 (RON to the Euro), or 4.1 or 4.25 or 3.9, that is up to the market, not the Ministry of Finance. We have to adapt to the market. The interest rate (on government debt) is 4% or 8% because of market mechanisms. I would like it to be 1% or 0%" (Mediafax, 2010[84].)

The comparison of the two narratives of the BCR privatization contrasts the international discourse on bank privatization as necessary for the neoliberal economy with the Romanian government's open acknowledgement that state-owned banks had to be transferred into private hands to reduce the state's room for manoeuvre, particularly in what concerned the financing of the deficit. State ownership in the banking sector would allow the government to use banks as captive sources in order to support sovereign debt dynamics, which would obstruct market mechanisms in the determination of the appropriate yield and reduce private banks' scope for exploiting yield differentials. Had the Finance minister considered the structural characteristics of the Treasury market, dominated by several large banks in Romania (and elsewhere in Eastern Europe), he would have found the idea of yields established through competitive conditions much more difficult to defend. It also glossed over the well-documented tendency for speculation (particularly but not exclusively from non-resident investors) in domestic bond market that Grenville (2008) described for several East Asian countries with liberalized capital accounts, and domestic private banks' preference for short-term instruments. Indeed, Mihaljek (20000) observed a close correlation between private capital flows and debt markets in developing countries.

Furthermore, while the political economy of central banking might have been singularly colourful in Romania compared to its CEE neighbours, the outcomes for the financialization of the banking sector were not. Widely different approaches resulted in a remarkably similar financial architecture (Berglof and Bolton, 2001). After the collapse of socialist planning, international policy advice decried state-ownership in the banking sector as undermining efforts to restore allocative efficiency. It advocated foreign private ownership as key to increasing the availability of credit to private activities, improving competition and providing efficiency-improving technology.

The combination of banking crisis and the push for privatization produced a double movement, from state to private and from domestic to foreign ownership (Caviglia et al, 2001). It offered Western banks seeking to internationalize their activity a foothold in Eastern European markets. By 2007, the share of foreign ownership in CEE banking sectors was well above both Western Europe and other emerging markets levels (Aydin, 2008). A similar acquisition strategy saw Western banks (Austrian and German in Central Europe, from Nordic countries in the Baltic states) targeting large-state owned banks: by 2006, with the exception of Slovenia, foreign banks were controlling between three and five of the largest banks in every country across the region (see Table 4.4), increasing exposure to tension in the home-countries interbank markets.

Throughout Eastern Europe, banks were replacing long-term lending to businesses with short-term market activities such as government financing. For instance, by 2004, in the Czech Republic, one of the industrial leaders of emerging Europe, only 15% of bank credit was extended to the manufacturing sector, less than for households or government. Indeed, Berglof and Bolton's (2001) influential paper summed up well the increasing financialization of banking sectors in Eastern Europe. By the end of the 1990s, financial systems were dominated by commercial banks, increasingly foreign owned and lending primarily to government or for consumption. Enterprise financing came from retained earnings, while highly illiquid and volatile stock markets left foreign direct investment as the only external source for financing long-term capital investment. Similar to Romania, central banking

Table 4.4 Foreign banks participation in Central and Eastern Europe

Countries	Share of total assets		Ownership
	2001	2005	
Slovenia	15	22	Societe Generale (France), KBC (Belgium), Banca Intesa (Italy)
Latvia	45	58	DNB Norbank (Norway), SEB Bank (Sweden), Swedbank (Sweden),
Hungary	59	59	Erste Bank (Austria), Reiffeisen International (Austria), HVB (Germany), Banca Intesa (Italy), KBC (Belgium)
Romania	44	62	Erste Bank (Austria), Societe Generale (France), Reiffeisen International (Austria), AlphaBank (Greece), ING (Holland)
Poland	69	67	HVB (Germany), Comerzbank (Germany), Unicredit (Italy), ING (Holland)
Lithuania	76	84	Samplo (Finland), DNB Norbank (Norway), Swedbank (Sweden), SEB Bank (Sweden)
Czech Republic	77	93	Societe Generale (France), HVB (Germany), KBC (Belgium), Erste Bank (Austria)
Slovakia	92	99	Erste Bank (Austria), Reiffeisen International (Austria), HVB (Germany)
Estonia	98	99	Samplo (Finland), Swedbank (Sweden), SEB Bank (Sweden)

Source: Compiled from Aydin (2008) and Cavaglia et al. (2001).

approaches to liquidity management had produced a structural excess of liquidity on the wholesale money markets (Balogh, 2009).

4.6 Conclusion

This chapter mapped the further reconfiguration of the monetary policy space between 1997 and 2005, a period when the NBR formally adopted high-powered money targeting as its policy strategy. As Peck and Tickell (2002) so persuasively argued, the hegemony of neoliberal discourses cannot be reduced simply to an after-Keynesian, or in this case post-communist, outcome of spontaneously emerging market forces in the spaces opened up by the state's withdrawal. Instead, the process of neoliberalizing economic management saw a shift (or perhaps a cumulative change) from the 1990–1997 destructive emphasis that structured monetary policy as the primary instrument of neoliberal destruction, to a constructive phase where markets relevant to monetary management are shaped by pressures of financialization.

The usual account of the period attributes policy success to the increasingly technocratic mode of policy-making and congratulates the 1997 right-wing coalition's wisdom to withdraw (albeit hesitantly) from the process of policy implementation. Against the sustained efforts to clean up and systematize policy discourse, one of its defining, and I argued, necessary characteristics remained its ambiguity, whose source can be traced in the shift in policy rationalities operated by the 1997 SBA: sterilized currency interventions and a fiscal policy disciplined by the market. In the first instance, the redefinition of the relationship between policy discourse and practices is revealing. Thus the economics of stabilization predicated on the existence of excess liquidity translated into extended and highly detrimental liquidity shortages before 1997; afterwards a policy discourse that ascribed success in the disinflation process to a tight monetary control in fact saw policy practice and success dependant on a structural excess of liquidity on the money market.

The exchange rate constituted a second site of narrative ambiguity. The NBR claimed that its decisions were embedded in two conflicting objectives: export competitiveness, implicitly recognizing that export performance hinged on a competitive exchange rate as much as on productivity, and internal stability, sanctioning a pass-through from exchange rate to prices that it had refused to discuss, minimized or rejected altogether before 1997. This translated into a policy goal of sustainable real appreciations, which allowed the NBR to deny policy responsibility for a widening current account gap. Notwithstanding the NBR's claims, the intimate connection between the governance of the money markets and exchange rate movements point to a symbiotic rather than competing relationship, familiar to other countries dependent on capital inflows: sterilizations as a vehicle for commercial banks' carry trade activity.

The claims surrounding the interest rate policy constituted a third space of ambiguity. The massive sterilization volumes and the managed exchange rate contradicted the discursive anchoring of success in the monetary targeting strategy, so that by 2003 the NBR shifted its policy argumentation to interest rates. The successive cuts in sterilization rates, facilitated by the availability of foreign inflows, ushered in an argumentation linking interest rates to aggregate demand control. Nevertheless, the dominance of transactions with the central bank on the wholesale market and the little relevance of the sterilization rates for the cost of liquidity in the system simultaneously invalidated a monetary transmission mechanism rooted in the control of short-term interest rates. Once set in the context of the further liberalization of the capital account, this line of argumentation permitted the NBR to bring considerations of speculative inflows and financial stability into its interest rate decisions and begin the process of shifting to inflation targeting.

The ambiguity of the central bank's narrative is not surprising; it is in most cases a routine practice. Striking about this ambiguity was the governor's articulation of a growth model far closer to the 1990 Commission for Transition than to the neoliberal approaches. The governor also abandoned the neoliberal rhetoric of depoliticization, accepting that the policy priorities pursued were dictated by the requirements of the European Union membership rather than theoretical rigour. But pragmatism – which premised that such room for manoeuvre was only available *inside* the European Union – dictated that national autonomy alone would not be enough to tackle global pressures. Unfortunately, such a willingness to transcend the narrow confines of the neoliberal dichotomy state-market did not last for very long. On the contrary, Isarescu's effectiveness as a prime-minister reinforced the cult of the technocrat, giving weight to the central bank's long standing argument that its policies would have been successful had the government not interfered with implementation. It also reinforced the neoliberal idea that the central bank was the locus of economic competence and that irremediably incompetent politicians had to be constrained to make decisions consistent with the policy priorities established by the central bank.

But central banking throughout this period was not all about maintaining the appearance of control. The narrative of objective policy formulation glosses over the politics of monetary policy while simultaneously understating the global forces that shaped and defined domestic policy choices. Indeed, while the structural and institutional resistance to neoliberalism during the "gradualist years" produced localized outcomes (such as a uniquely intense relationship with the IMF), the post-1997 developments resist such narrow confinement. With the banking sector increasingly foreign owned and driven by carry trade concerns, practices of monetary management marked the following changes:

- The transformation of the relationship between wholesale banking and the central bank, as management of liquidity contributed to the increasing financialization of banks.

- A monetarist policy discourse engaged in feigning control, of legitimizing and normalizing practices tailored to attracting speculative capital, while simultaneously tying financial stability considerations into the choices of foreign-owned banks, further complicated, the next chapter will show, by the arrival of non-resident investors.

5
Inflation-targeting in the Run-up to the Crisis

The central bank explained that the policy shift had been driven by two factors (NBR 2005a). First, it recognized the ineffectiveness of setting monetarist-inspired monetary targets. Instead, it sought to join a growing consensus seeking to align the theoretical underpinnings of monetary policy strategies with developments in general equilibrium monetary theory. Second, it maintained that its practices of exchange-rate manipulation would no longer be sustainable under further capital account liberalization that allowed nonresidents to purchase Treasury bills and to hold bank deposits starting with April 2005 (Isărescu 2005). Tackling the increased vulnerability to speculative capital movements required interest-rate manipulation (NBR 2005c).

This chapter will map out the particular characteristics of the inflation-targeting regime in Romania, to then set the practices of central banking in the context of wider regional dynamics. It will explore both the ideological dimension of the policy framework – focusing on the construction on policy argumentation through the new conceptual domain offered by New Keynesian economics – and further ask how the new policy regime changed practices of liquidity management in response to the entry of nonresident investors on domestic markets. Furthermore, the period under analysis, August 2005 to December 2008, saw the unfolding of a fully blown global financial crisis that started as a meltdown in the US securitized markets in 2007. The chapter will ask to what extent inflation-targeting functioned to increase vulnerabilities to financial turmoil elsewhere, and whether the crisis as it unfolded by the end of 2008 changed the parameters that had previously circumscribed practices of monetary management.

5.1 Institutionalizing the new policy regime

The negotiations for EU accession carried two immediate consequences for macroeconomic policy: an accelerated pace of capital-account liberalization to allow the entry of nonresident investors combined with a narrowing of the scope for regulatory measures aimed at fostering financial stability (NBR 2005b). Furthermore, EU membership entailed an unconditional commitment to join the euro area upon fulfillment of the Maastricht criteria. New Member States were expected to define a time horizon for joining the European Exchange Rate Mechanism (ERMII) that specified a (15 percent) fluctuation band around a fixed parity.

For inflation-targeting New Member States (Romania, Hungary, Slovakia, Poland, and the Czech Republic), research on the optimal policy regime before the ERMII membership generally recommended flexible exchange rates. Orlowski (2005) suggested a stages approach, from a strict regime and floating exchange rates to a hybrid combination of well-specified inflation targets supported by exchange-rate targets. Diev and Kurtz (2006) identified a trade-off between either nominal interest/exchange-rates volatility under a free float or current-account disequilibrium under a fixed exchange rate. Given the emphasis on price stability in the Maastricht criteria, they recommended a flexible exchange-rate regime, a view to which the Romanian central bank subscribed.

At the time of adopting inflation-targeting, the NBR (2005c) argued that it had fulfilled the institutional criteria fundamental to a successful regime switch: it was both operationally and legally independent from any political pressures, fiscal dominance had disappeared as a threat to inflation, and, very importantly, its credibility had been reinforced through a continuous process of disinflation bringing inflation into single-digit territory.

The policy framework specified a consumer-price-index-based inflation target (7 percent for 2005 and 5 percent for 2006), set as a midpoint within a target band of +/{minus}1 percentage point and a forward-looking policy rule. This demanded that the policy instrument, the short-term interest rate, respond to forecast rather than current deviations from the target. Annual targets would be set for a longer time frame, in a joint announcement with the government, and a clear set of escape clauses was specified to detail the circumstances under which the NBR would not assume responsibility for missing the target. Furthermore, the NBR (2005e) explained that while it preferred market mechanisms in the currency market, it reserved the right to interfere occasionally when the exchange rate moved into undesirable territory.

This, to a certain extent, was consistent with inflation-targeting discourses, for intervention is (albeit reluctantly) sanctioned as a temporary practice if exchange-rate volatility threatens the inflation target, but interventions should not be a constant practice since they could distort expectations (Epstein and Yieldan 2006). Subsequently, the central bank's presence on currency markets became one of the most contested policy arenas.

The record of the inflation-targeting regime could be described as a mixed performance at best: only in one of the first four years did the NBR comply with its inflation target, an experience not uncommon to Eastern European inflation targeters (Daianu and Lungu 2007). Indeed, the 2005 level nearly missed the interval (8.6 percent annual increase compared to the 7.5 percent upper limit), while inflation in both 2007 and 2008 recorded levels substantially above the upper limit of the target interval (see Figure 5.1). The monthly developments show an accelerated disinflation during 2006 and until September 2007, after which consumer price inflation moved systematically above the targeted band. Policy responses saw an aggressive easing during 2005, a tightening cycle throughout 2006 to be followed by a cycle of fast easing that

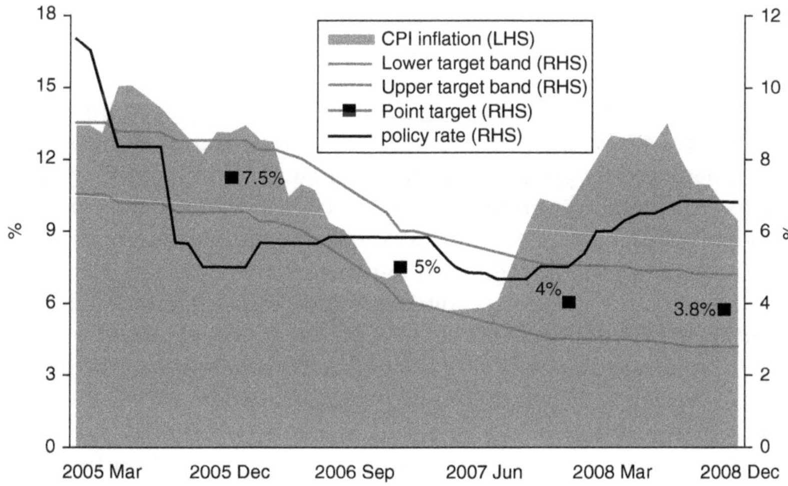

Figure 5.1 CPI inflation vs. Inflation target and the policy rate, Romania. 2005–2008

Source: Computed from National Bank of Romania data http://www.bnro.ro/StatisticsReportHTML.aspx?icid=801&table=665&column=3800,3801,3802, (accessed January 23rd 2009 and NBR, 2009a for the inflation data).

brought policy rates down by 150 basis points until September 2007. Subsequently, the NBR hiked its interest rate at every meeting until August 2008, bringing it to 10.25 percent, the highest level in the EU by the end of 2008.

The inflation reports constructed the policy stance around two driving factors: broad monetary conditions and liquidity management. A focus on broad monetary conditions, the NBR (2005f) claimed, would provide a broader mapping of aggregate demand pressures over the forecast horizon, by accounting for both policy rate decisions and exchange-rates influences. Second, the NBR (2006c) recognized that an adequate management of liquidity was required to improve the transmission mechanism from short- to long-term interest rates and to provide the appropriate signaling role for individual decisions.

The use of these two elements in policy argumentation brought together policy models and the central bank's strategies on money and currency markets.

5.1.1 Model(s) and policy rules

Inflation-targeting regimes are appealing for their promise of a scientific approach to policy formulation. While the process of modelling is essential for producing projections of future trends, the central bank's perceptions of model uncertainty might limit the extent to which these projections structure policy decisions, a point to which the analysis of the Romanian policy process turns.

While the narratives explaining policy reactions deployed inflation-targeting concepts, the NBR provided no explicit information on the models deployed for policy formulation, a first indication of the complications that model uncertainty raised for claims of transparent policy-making. Indeed, central-banking discourse (the European Central Bank [ECB], for example) distinguished between the limited knowledge of how the economy worked (Issing 2002) and fundamental (Knightian) uncertainty where the future could not be statistically derived from the past. In other words, policy could not always be anchored in the objectivity of models – in fact there was no "true" model of the economy. Central banks are generally reluctant to publicly formulate a policy rule, as was the central bank of Romania. The contradiction between the theoretical emphasis on transparent policy rules and model uncertainty was resolved by appealing to technocratic knowledge.

Indeed, whereas the IMF (2007a) produced the only fully specified New Keynesian model for Romania, various NBR presentations only offered a narrative explanation of the model specifications (NBR 2006c, 2006d).

The Monetary Policy Committee would prepare near and medium-term forecast and qualify model-based policy scenarios with "expert judgment." The near-term model forecasts two quarters inflation and GDP trajectories, which were further fed into a New Keynesian medium-term model.[85] Initially, the forecast horizon covered six quarters, modified in February 2006 to eight quarters to better reflect the lags in transmission. The short-term forecasting produced monthly projections for main components of the consumer price index[86]: food items, nonfood, and services, excluding those with administered prices. The near-term forecasting model reflected statistical relationships rather than standard New Keynesian economic theory, since it incorporated no forward-looking behaviour. Price dynamics were explained by exchange rates, net average wages, imported price inflation, and administered prices. Policy discourse acknowledged various sources of uncertainty arising from difficulties in forecasting the dynamics of exchange rates in the short term and unpredictable wage and administered prices policies. With these qualifications, projections were fed into the New Keynesian medium-term model.

The central bank further suggested that its interest-rate decisions responded to both deviations from targeted inflation and the output gap while simultaneously seeking to smooth interest-rate volatility (NBR 2006c). It considered the interest-rate channel to be relatively weak, reflecting sluggish reaction of lending and deposit rates to policy decisions. Whereas in policy terms an impaired transmission mechanism raises doubts about the decision to adopt inflation-targeting, in theoretical terms New Keynesian models pay little attention to the complexities arising from financial markets that depart from the neoliberal canon of efficiency. The transmission mechanism is modelled through a single interest rate (Gaspar and Kashyap 2006), a modelling approach questioned by central-bank practitioners because the direct impact of policy decisions operating through bank and market rates is as important as the discursive commitments that anchor expectations. In the context of the excess liquidity on the Romanian money market and the increasing shift away in banking activities toward short-term profit from market activity, the theoretical minimalism toward the banking sector becomes even more problematic. It also questions the typical position toward asset bubbles – Alan Greenspan's view that cleaning up after a burst bubble would be less market-disruptive than interest-rate decisions tailored to containing growing asset bubbles (Bernanke and Gertler 2001).

Exchange-rate concerns were absent from the policy rule, although the NBR (2006c) identified exchange-rate dynamics, along with the expectations, as the two critical channels in the monetary transmission mechanism. Instead, the exchange-rate discourse drew on the New Keynesian promise to open economies: a credible policy regime would stabilize prices and guarantee access to international finance necessary for exchange-rate stability. The Romanian developments in the run-up to the Lehman Brothers moment offer interesting insights into this proposition.

Policy narratives combined three main concepts underlying inflation-targeting discourses: expectations, the output gap and the broad monetary conditions.

Expectations

While the narration of policy models deployed by the Romanian central bank suggested that expectations were modelled as a combination of backward-looking and forward-looking expectations, policy decisions were articulated around the current policy rate. Policy discourse did not, at least publicly, assigned much relevance to the importance of publishing a forecast of the path of the instrument, a decision contested in the inflation-targeting literature (Svensson 2006). Indeed, inflation-targeting models assume that the ability of the central bank to influence expenditure critically depends on influencing expectations regarding the future path of the overnight instrument. In other words, current interest-rate decisions matter little for private-sector decisions, and only in as much as they influence expectations of the future path of the instrument rate. While the interest-rate assumptions are crucial to model projections[87], the NBR's policy argumentation involved what Svensson (2006) termed the paradox of forward-looking inflation-targeting regimes: most policy discussions focused on current instrument settings and levels, offering little guidance about the future interest-rate movements.

Furthermore, the relatively underdeveloped nature of bond markets and consequently the small range of maturities available limited the possibilities of capturing forward-looking expectations from the yield curve. Despite the discursive emphasis on expectations, incorporating these in modelling exercises proved complex. For instance, the IMF (2008) reported wide nominal deviations between expectations and actual values. For January 2008, consumer price inflation was expected to rise above 50 percent, ten times higher than the level registered. Nevertheless, the central bank refused to accept these patterns as either evidence of its failure to anchor expectations or as indication of the uselessness of the concept of expectations for the purposes of its inflation-targeting strategy. The governor instead deplored the lack of "economic culture and sufficient knowledge" (Isărescu 2008c) that prevented economic agents from acting like the rational agents of the New Keynesian models. Thus, forecasts of economic analysts gained prominence in policy discussions.

Indeed, the establishment and consolidation of a community that constructs and interprets the meaning of policy measures is essential for a policy discourse that assigns expectations and credibility an essential role. The relationship between the central bank and the interpretive community can be cast as a struggle over imposing a certain interpretation of policy measures given the various interests of policy actors. Thus, international institutions, particularly the IMF, engaged in policy argumentation through "objective" models. Commercial bank analysts articulated a different set of policy priorities, focused on liquidity management practices rather than models. The influence that these different interests played in the policy process, framed in inflation-targeting language as the importance of anchoring market expectations, produced a complex interaction mechanism to which I will return later.

The output gap

Policy narratives stressed the crucial role of the output gap. The deployment of output gaps to substantiate policy decisions required efforts to narrow the argumentative field and command credibility, to reframe policy to conceal signs of ambiguity or inconsistency regarding either empirical estimations, questions of spare capacity or policy responses to projections.

Indeed, the central bank recognized on repeated occasions that the methodology for computing the potential output suffered from shortcomings arising from the short time period and the massive structural changes since 1990. Uncertainties would particularly affect recent period estimations, as GDP data were usually subjected to substantial revisions[88]. The reliability, or indeed significance, of output gap data could be further questioned by the volatility of agricultural output, where production patterns, broadly involving small-scale or subsistence techniques, implied a high vulnerability to weather conditions. IMF (2007a) chose to exclude agricultural fluctuations from output gap estimations.

Furthermore, the NBR's argumentation of the output gap displayed inconsistencies with New Keynesian assumptions. For instance, it linked the investment component of aggregate demand to potential output dynamics (NBR 2008d), when the underlying theory assumes that aggregate demand does not shift potential output (Fontana and Palacio Vera 2004). Furthermore, estimating natural levels from historical data assumed businesses operating at full capacity, when even IMF statistics suggest that capacity utilization gradually increased from 72 percent in 2003 to 80 percent in 2007 (IMF 2008). The existence of spare capacity in the manufacturing sector was not surprising given the higher levels of capital formation driven by foreign direct investment in the run-up to and aftermath of EU membership.

Notwithstanding these complications, the central bank held that expert judgment and comparison with IMF's assessments would complement econometric techniques, so that output gap forecasts could provide a useful guide to policy formulation. The NBR (2008c) research thus sanctioned a 6 percent level for the potential output growth between 2006 to 2008 (Galatescu et al. 2008).

The central bank's estimations raised an empirical puzzle: on several occasions, its projections suggested that substantial excess demand coexisted with a fast disinflation process, as, for instance, between the end of 2006 to mid-2007 (see Figures 5.2 to 5.7). Indeed, the graphical representations of the output gap produced by the central bank contradicted somewhat the focus on perennial demand–pull inflationary pressures. For instance, the February and November projections for each year were strikingly similar, describing a positive output gap during the current period and the following few quarters, followed by a negative

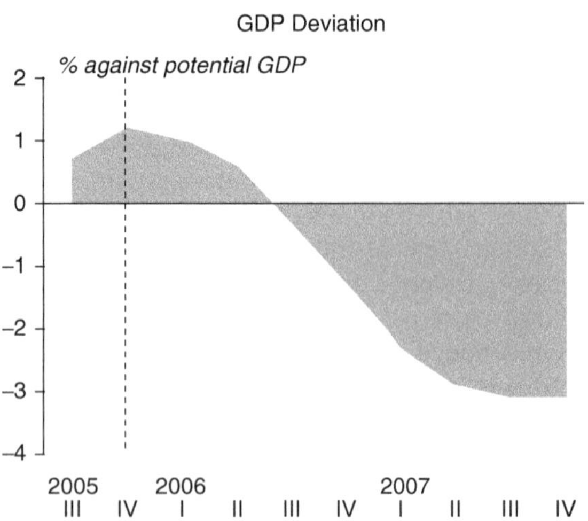

Figure 5.2 Output gap. NBR Inflation Report Feb 2006

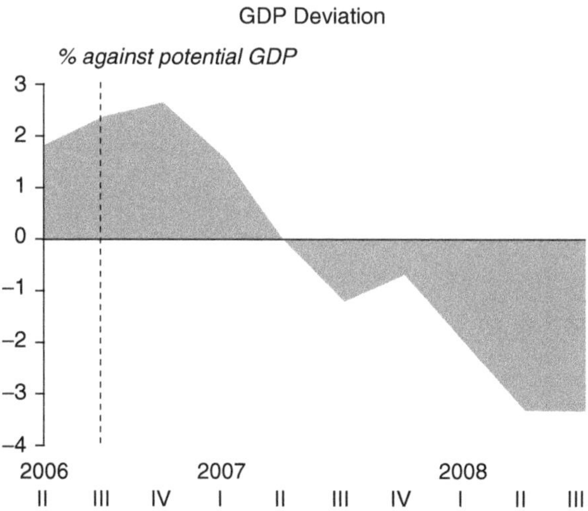

Figure 5.3 Output gap. NBR Inflation Report Nov 2006

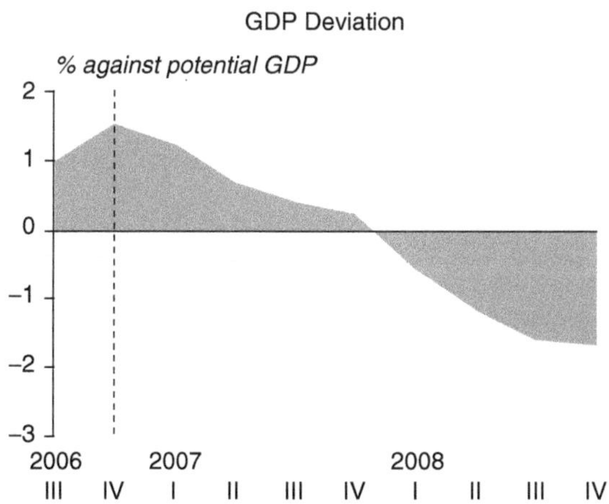

Figure 5.4 Output gap. NBR Inflation Report Feb 2007

output gap toward the end of the forecasting horizon. Of course, projections should not be expected to depict future outcomes perfectly, as unpredictable "shocks" imply a significant likelihood that forecasts would be incorrect. Nevertheless, for policy to be consistent with the underlying model, instruments should be adjusted to the projections constructed given all information available.

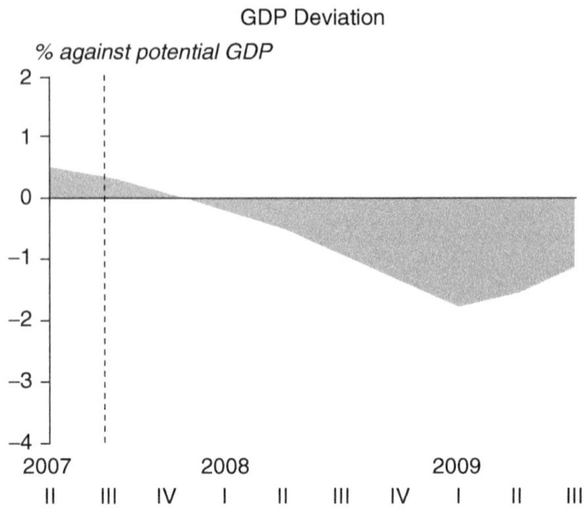

Figure 5.5 Output gap. NBR Inflation Report Nov 2007

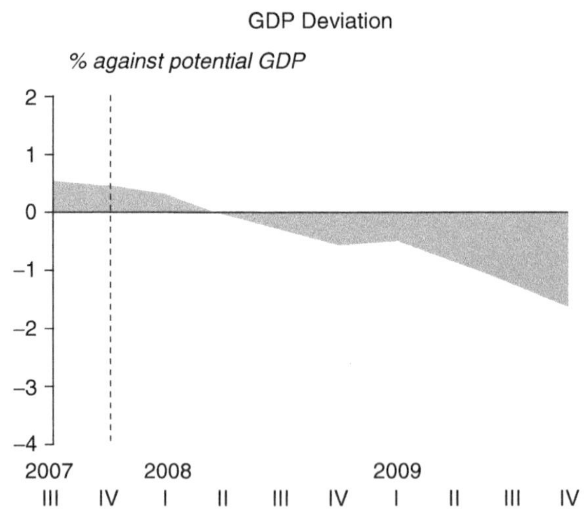

Figure 5.6 Output gap. NBR Inflation Report Feb 2008

Thus, if policy takes into account the lags in the transmission mechanism, as implied by forward-looking strategies, then policy responses would have consistently required monetary easing or at least no change in the policy stance in the case of a very low stabilization "bias" (the

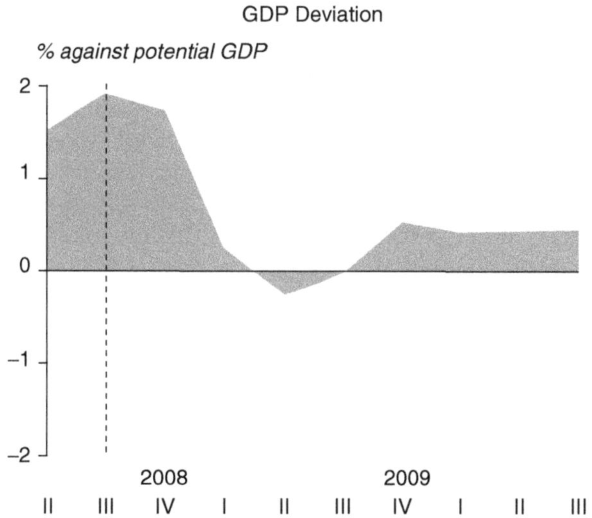

Figure 5.7 Output gap. NBR Inflation Report Nov 2008

Source: The *National Bank of Romania Inflation Report*, February 2006 (p. 46), November 2006 (p. 13), February 2007 (p. 45), November 2007 (p. 46), February 2008 (p. 45), November 2008 (p. 44).

central bank's concern with output volatility). This was not the case in February 2006, when a tightening cycle started against a projection of a large negative output gap toward the end of the forecasting horizon, unlike February 2007, the start of an easing cycle against a similar outlook for the output gap.

To reconcile these conflicting accounts, policy argumentation sought to redefine the representation of policy stances. This would no longer reflect interest-rate movements (particularly given the impaired transmission mechanism) but had to be judged against developments in broad monetary conditions. In this representation, excessive aggregate demand is consistent with a fall in price inflation if the real exchange rate appreciates, tightening monetary conditions. For instance, the August 2005 inflation report explained that the substantial interest-rate cut operated since the beginning of the year (of 800 basis points) should not be constructed as expansionary policy because of the substantial real currency appreciation[89].

The central bank interpreted the systematic appreciations of the real exchange rates (consumer price index deflated) between 2005 and 2007 as exercising a contractionary effect on excess demand (NBR 2006, 2007), and vice versa, starting with 2008. It premised a causality from real exchange-rate dynamics to aggregate demand that denied the opposite effect was equally possible. For instance, with confident expectations, an appreciation of the exchange rate could positively affect domestic demand by stimulating foreign currency loans (as indeed happened throughout this period). This possibility would suggest some caution in deploying the monetary conditions index as a reliable indicator of policy stances and, indeed, of producing forecasts of future output gaps. However, rather than economic rigor, this line of argumentation had two strategic functions:

1. It suggested that policy formulation accounted for exchange-rate dynamics mainly through the aggregate demand, rather than the cost-push channel.
2. It worked to legitimize policy decisions, particularly at the beginning of an easing cycle.

While policy narratives accepted that the exchange rate could be a significant source of cost-push pressures, inflationary concerns were articulated around income policies, a tendency shared by the IMF policy argumentation. The privileging of wage dynamics in explaining inflationary dynamics was endorsed by empirical claims that wage policy in the public sector appears to have influenced wage settlement in the private sector (NBR 2007a, 2007c; IMF 2007b), so that, by 2007, both the IMF and the NBR were claiming that wage increases in the public sector were behind inflationary dynamics and threatened the target.

While for most of the inflation-targeting period productivity gains outpaced industry wage growth (NBR 2008d), the labour-market tightening following large-scale labour emigration (after EU membership) saw industry wages tracking public-sector increases. Whereas fast wage increases could indeed translate into a wage-price spiral, the central bank's forecasting models were ill equipped to account for such dynamics. Indeed, the near-term model specified net average wage dynamics as a measure of aggregate demand pressures, with no wage-productivity differential incorporated to account for cost-push pressures. The medium-term structural model, on the other hand, had yet to take into account labour market dynamics by the middle of 2008[90]. As with the monetarist framing of the early transition years, policy narrative again privileged wage dynamics as the key source of inflationary pressures in order to marginalize considerations of other cost-push pressures affecting price dynamics.

Second, the central bank tended to connect interest-rate decisions with current or near-term projections rather than projections over the forecast horizon, an approach common to most inflation targeters (Goodhart 2005). For instance, the August 2007 inflation report explained the decisions to cut the policy rate by 150 percentage points during the first two quarters as an outcome of improving short-term projections for inflation (to the end of 2007). Such an approach was partially conditioned by analysts' narratives, which tend to explain changes in the policy instrument or construct expectations of near-term instrument path in connection with past price developments or near-term projections[91]. Against such a framing, policy decisions are contestable, and might appear inconsistent, when the change in the policy instrument contradicts the inflation-targeting normativity: for instance, analysts questioned the decision to substantially reduce policy rates at the beginning of 2005 while inflation was accelerating (Ziarul Financiar 2005).

It would appear that policy models derive legitimacy from success in enrolling certain interests, of the interpretive community in this instance. The central bank's decisions were somewhat constrained by the meaning attached to policy decisions by market players. However, there are tensions in this process, for policy decisions are interpreted differently by different policy actors. A good example was the summer of 2007, when a resurgence in inflationary pressures pitted the IMF's model against the NBR's and financial analysts' interpretation, revealing how the politics of modelling inflation played out in policy argumentation involving actors with (relatively) similar estimative capacity.

The IMF's inflation-targeting model for Romania was published in the June 2007 country report (IMF 2007a). The coefficients of the model, arrived at through what is claimed to be a sophisticated calibration process, were similar to those in the standard model developed for Canada (Berg et al. 2006), suggesting that universalism remains the modus operandi in the IMF's policy advice. Overlooking the complexities of model uncertainty, the report outlined two possible policy scenarios:

1. In the baseline scenario, the NBR maintained rates at current levels and the government its fiscal deficit at 2.8 percent of GDP. The additional excess demand would drive output above its potential and inflation above its target, requiring substantial interest-rate increases in the following year, 2008.
2. In the adjusted scenario, the NBR would take firm action by raising interest rates by 50 percentage points, while the government reduced

current spending to contain the deficit 1 percent of GDP and kept wage demands under control. This would contract the excess demand.

In other words, the central bank's decisions to postpone an immediate tightening would only magnifying disequilibria and require more contractionary future policy responses.

The IMF (2007a) linked public wage policies to its forecasts of excess aggregate demand, although data showed that the execution of the budget was substantially lower than projected up to that point. Fund policy analysis failed to consider how to tailor policy responses to different types of shock and recommended, in usual fashion, fiscal tightening and interest-rate increases. Despite the earlier recognition of the significant exchange-rate pass-through, the IMF paid little importance to a series of cost-push pressures: a bad agricultural season, rising international commodity prices, and massive labour emigration attending EU membership (January 2007) tightening the labour market and creating wage pressures. Furthermore, the global liquidity pressures triggered by the US subprime market crisis and investor concerns about the sustainability of the two-digit Romanian current-account deficit saw higher exchange-rate volatility (Gabor 2010).

The central bank's policy response appeared to have factored in a broader range of inflationary pressures than the IMF's emphasis on excess aggregate demand. It thus resisted calls for interest-rate increases until November 2007, when it became clear that the target would be missed (again suggesting that policy responded to current or very near forecasts). Similarly, several analysts acknowledged that the assessment of the type of shock, and its projected impact on the target at the end of the targeting horizon, would warrant different policy responses (Ziarul Financiar 2007a).

In sum, policy argumentation struggled to impose some coherence onto a policy regime with several problematic domains. Furthermore, the central bank's practices attempted to reconcile the narrative of close liquidity control underlying inflation-targeting discourses with the pressures arising from both the financialization of the wholesale money markets described in the previous chapter and the arrival of nonresident investors on the domestic policy scene.

5.2 Practices of monetary management

The new policy framework premised the use of a short-term interest rate (NBR 2005e), usually the overnight interbank rate, as the operational target of the new policy rule. Against this requirement, the 2005 policy shift was accompanied by sustained attempts to consolidate the overnight rate as an operational target and inscribe policy practice within the logic of inflation-targeting: the control over short-term market rates, through OMOs, as the avenue for influencing long-term interest rates relevant for spending and saving decisions.

Policy practice during the monetarist period sought to induce exchange-rate appreciations. With structural current-account deficits, the central bank developed a series of practices for achieving capital-account surpluses. While foreign direct investment played an increasingly important role in supporting exchange-rate appreciations, central-bank interventions on the money markets provided a second channel for attracting foreign capital. As the last chapter argued, the bulk of NBR money-market operations were focused on the speculative segment, inducing real appreciation through sterilization operations and an attractive interest-rate differential. It created an excess of liquidity on the interbank market, limiting the relevance that the policy instrument could have as a cost of liquidity, and hence for aggregate demand control.

This placed the central bank in a rather uncomfortable relationship with the foreign-owned commercial banking sector, the main players on the currency market and the source of speculative capital. It produced a vicious circle where banks reaped profits not only from expectations of exchange-rate appreciations but essentially from the risk-free high returns NBR offered on its sterilization operations (Gabor 2008), a recipe for the financialization of banking activity. The reduced control over the money markets raised doubts about the scope for influencing long-term interest rates.

Despite rhetorical commitments, liquidity management practices under the new policy regime failed to forge a closer relationship between the policy rate (on sterilizations) and short-term money-market rates. While overnight-rate volatility remained a systematic feature of the period, the patterns of volatility shifted, mirroring changes in money-market liquidity (see Figure 5.8). The adoption of the new policy strategy saw wholesale rates falling to the level of the deposit facility for most of 2005, a sign of excess liquidity that further characterised market dynamics in 2006, when overnight rates would fall to, or even below, the deposit facility rate toward the end of the maintenance period (the 24th of the month).

Indeed, the first inflation report, in August 2005, outlined the necessity of devising appropriate tools to cope with capital account

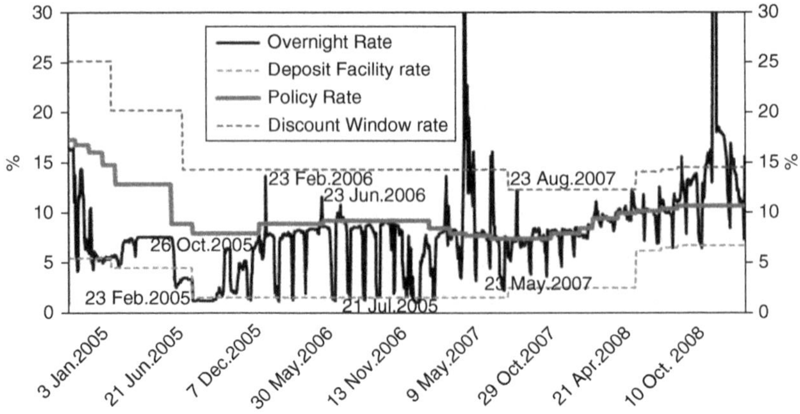

Figure 5.8 Policy and money market rates, Romania, 2005–2008

Source: Computed from http://www.bnro.ro/Interest-Rates-on-Monetary-Policy-and-Standing-Facilities,-history-3337.aspx, for NBR interest rate data and http://www.bnro.ro/StatisticsReportHTML.aspx?icid=801&table=642&column= for money market data, accessed December 22, 2008.

liberalization (NBR, 2005e). Without questioning, or differentiating, the impact of various types of capital inflow, the NBR discourse referred to a "sustainable" rate of capital inflows and acknowledged a trade-off, to which it referred as the Tosovski dilemma: the policy instrument, a signal for inflationary expectations, also functioned to attract investors in search of yield differentials.

5.2.1 A timid attempt to decouple from financialization

Consequently, the NBR attempted to decouple policy practice from speculative inflows and to bring it in line with inflation-targeting specifications. A better control of money-market liquidity required that the central bank redefine the relationship between speculative capital inflows, excessive liquidity, and sterilizations (Gabor 2008). To do so, immediately after the August 2005 regime switch, the central bank proceeded to reduce the rate at which it compensated banks for depositing liquidity overnight at the standing facility (Figure 5.8) and the sterilization volumes (Figure 5.9).

The central bank's refusal to continue offering vehicles for speculative returns saw overnight interest rates plunging to the level of the standing-deposit facility, where banks were forced to deposit the excess liquidity at a dismal 1 percent return. This signalled the substantial presence

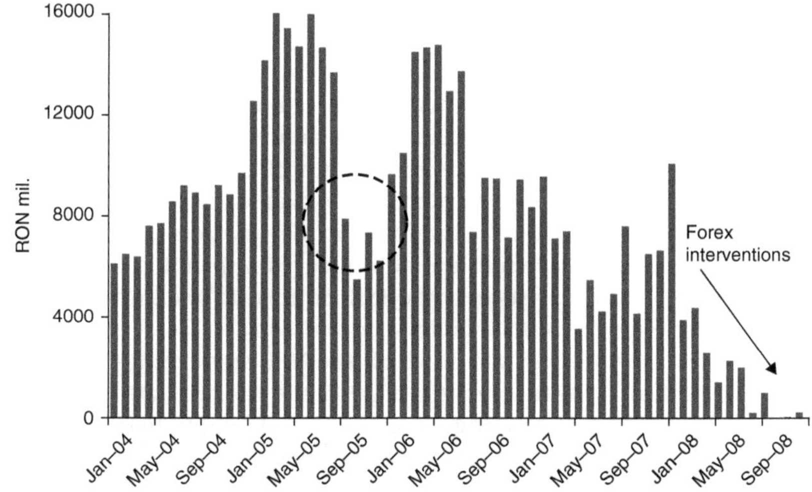

Figure 5.9 Sterilization operations, RON bn, Romanian, 2004–2008
Source: Computed from the statistics section of *the National Bank of Romania Monthly Report, 2004–2008.*

of speculative capital on Romanian money markets: in September and October 2005 commercial banks took around €60 billion to the NBR's deposit facility, forty times the amount registered in August 2005 and 200 times higher than in July 2005.

Policy rhetoric toughened considerably as the governor explicitly linked the shift in money-market interventions to speculative flows and announced that sterilizations would be resumed when excess liquidity originated from normal banking activity (i.e. deposit-taking) rather than participation on currency markets. A cursory look at the banks' balance sheets, he maintained, sufficed to identify speculators. The central bank would refuse to validate speculative activity from banks with a low deposit base (Chiru 2005). He put it as follows[92]:

> We will resume sterilizations when placements will reflect deposit-taking activity rather than currency trading. When I sterilize, I check three elements of the balance sheet: liabilities, assets, and volumes bid for sterilization – and I cannot accept sterilizations bids from banks with a very low deposit base. (Isărescu in *Ziarul Financiar*, October 6, 2005)

The change of attitude triggered policy contestations, framed by both commercial banks and the IMF through the inflation-targeting discourse. The collapse in short-term interest rates, they argued, was both stimulating excess aggregate demand and feeding inflationary expectations (IMF 2006; Adevarul 2005). This argument, in typical New Keynesian fashion, failed to take into account that the policy rate was not the marginal cost of liquidity for the banking sector given the structural excess of liquidity on the interbank money markets (Antohi et al. 2003) and could not have substantial influence on spending decisions. Furthermore, both analysts and the IMF pointed to the growing differential between the official policy rate and what the NBR called the effective rate: the average rate at which the NBR sterilizes liquidity in the system. During the first months of 2005, the effective rate fell faster than the official rate, reflecting an approach to liquidity management constrained by currency developments on the one hand, and the normativity of the inflation-targeting regime on the other. This solution was interpreted as subverting the signalling role of the policy instrument, the IMF (2007a) urging a reunification of the two rates.

Nevertheless, the efforts to institutionalize some degree of policy autonomy were short-lived. Money market rates collapsed under the level of the deposit facility (see Figure 5.8), while the outflow of speculative capital quickly translated into currency depreciations that threatened the inflation target. Concerned about the credibility of its newly adopted policy regime, the central bank resumed its liquidity management practices: by November 2005 the central bank had returned to the interbank market with increasingly large sterilizations. Speculative flows returned, and, by the end of the year, the interbank money market was functioning exactly as it did under the old policy regime: stable throughout the maintenance period and hovering around the deposit facility level at the end except in a few cases of unexpected changes in autonomous liquidity factors. The attempt to reverse the financialization of the money markets by decoupling central-bank practices from volatile capital inflows failed, partly due to a discourse structuring policy action through its emphasis on expectations.

Up to the 2008 crisis, policy practice confronted the same predicament: interest-rate decisions tied into exchange rates and speculative flows. After the 2005 episode, the NBR was reluctant to adopt measures that would alter the structural characteristics of the money market. However, the crisis quickly engulfing the world economy from 2007 onwards marked another substantive change in money-market liquidity, redefining the monetary policy space and NBR's practices. The global

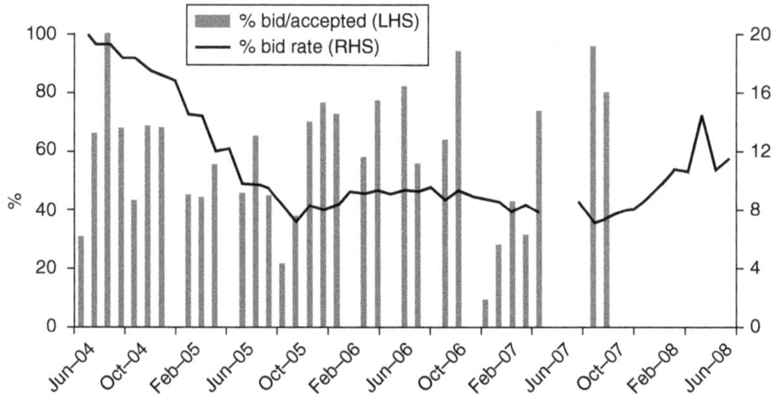

Figure 5.10 Certificates of deposit, volume and yield, Romania, 2004–2008

Source: Computed from the National Bank of Romania data (http://www.bnro.ro/StatisticsReportHTML.aspx?icid=800&table=805&column=, accessed March 26, 2009).

deleveraging and diminishing risk appetite saw excess liquidity disappearing from the Romanian money market. Indeed, sterilization volumes decreased systematically to virtually disappear in September 2008 (see Figure 5.9).

The interest rates demanded on reverse repo operations, an additional sterilization method through three-month instruments, further suggested that banks were increasingly reluctant to deposit liquidity with the NBR, demanding returns between 300 and 500 basis points higher than the policy rate. At the last auction for which data are available, in June 2008, there were only two banks bidding for the NBR's offered volume, a number substantially lower than the twelve banks that participated in the January bid (see Figure 5.10). The new dynamics on the interbank money market reflected increased liquidity preference in the banking sector against a very uncertain economic outlook and the central bank's operations on the currency market.

5.3 The financialization of currency markets and vulnerability: A Eastern European story

The common theoretical proposition underlying inflation-targeting regimes requires central banks to abandon the exchange rate as a policy objective in order to preserve the credibility of a single objective: price stability (Taylor 2000). Such a policy stance is, however, complicated in circumstances where the exchange-rate exercises a systematic influence on costs and prices and the extent to which policy-rate decisions can be freed from exchange-rate considerations, as premised by inflation-targeting discourses, is not entirely straightforward (Miguel and Savastano 2001). As Epstein and Yeldan (2006) pointed out, there is a very clear distinction to be made between what warrants an intervention and what does not. The "strict" interpretation of inflation-targeting, as put forward by Bernanke et al. (1999) or Fischer (2001), restricts interventions to cases where volatility affects the ability to forecast and target price inflation. Any concerns about levels or, in other words, any central-bank preferences about the path of the exchange rate, implies multiple policy objectives and undermines efforts to stabilize expectations. An inflation-targeting central bank ought to leave competitiveness to the market, a discourse to which the NBR subscribed.

Once inflation-targeting was adopted, policy discourse rejected responsibility for external competitiveness. Exchange-rate movements were framed in terms of national productivity (i.e. export performance), sidelining the impact of speculative inflows on short-term exchange-rate dynamics. Nevertheless, the exchange rate still entered policy rate decisions, which both the NBR and the IMF constructed as a trade-off between internal (fuelling aggregate demand) and external (moderating real appreciations) considerations. Indeed, the IMF accused the central bank on several occasions of allowing exchange-rate concerns to interfere with its inflation-targeting objective and endangering inflationary expectations (IMF 2007b). This is precisely where the ideological function of the inflation-targeting model lies: it suggests that exchange-rate considerations, and speculative activity, are best addressed through market mechanisms.

The central bank's attitude toward exchange-rate movements changed with the site of policy contestation. During periods of sustained exchange-rate appreciations (such as 2006), increasingly vocal policy contestation pointed to NBR's obsession with inflation at the expense of the productive sector, as suggested by expanding current-account deficits. The central bank had repeatedly sacrificed competitiveness to accelerate the pace of disinflation (Serbanescu 2006). The NBR maintained that export performance was driven by productivity and that a worsening of the current-account performance reflected the exporting sectors' failure at technological upgrading. Nevertheless, policy argumentation turned to financial stability concerns, and credit markets dynamics, to counteract the IMF's charges that its policy decisions reflected exchange-rate concerns.

Indeed, in policy practice, the NBR's attitude was far more nuanced than the inflation-targeting discourse would have suggested. The shift to inflation-targeting was accompanied by a public commitment to withdraw from the currency market as required by the inflation-targeting framework, a qualified withdrawal conditional on the NBR's perceptions of "unsustainable trends." Even where such circumstances arose, policymakers were required to decide what type of interventions to undertake. The literature on emerging-market inflation targeters acknowledges that it is possible, and at times unavoidable, for inflation-targeting to coexist with exchange-rate management (Benes et al. 2008). Such a choice can be played out in two institutionally different ways. The central bank can first choose to affect the exchange rate by incorporating it in the policy rule. It would target a certain level through interest-rate manipulation, rationalizing exchange-rate dynamics through the uncovered interest-rate parity condition, a fundamental assumption underlying open economy general-equilibrium models. Alternatively, it could opt to conduct interventions independently of interest-rate management, a choice generally rejected by theoretical conceptualizations because it violates the uncovered interest-rate parity condition and the forecasting properties of the model. The first choice is by definition of a more systematic nature, for it explicitly recognizes certain preferences for exchange-rate levels. Direct interventions are less preferable as these could exacerbate short-term volatility, if market players can anticipate interventions and take speculative positions. Thus, infrequent, unannounced interventions are generally intended as a signal rather than market-making.

Analysts suggested that the central banks had been deploying both (Ziarul Financiar 2007). Indeed, after the October 2005 failed attempts at regaining control over money markets (at least) twice throughout the period analysts speculated that the NBR had interfered directly in the market, during July 2007 and then in October 2008. Except for two short depreciation episodes (one in late 2005, produced by the NBR's attempts to deflect speculative inflows, and the other in May/June 2006, when foreign investors sold short all Eastern European currencies), the exchange rate had experienced a sustained nominal appreciation (see Figure 5.11). By the middle of 2007 it had gained 25 percent in nominal terms, despite the repeated cuts in the interest rate that analysts contextualized with the sustained trend appreciation. Whether driven by an expanding trade deficit or concerns of excessive credit growth, analysts suggested that the NBR was interfering indirectly through the trading desk of a major domestic bank. The central bank governor later confirmed the allegations (Isărescu 2009).

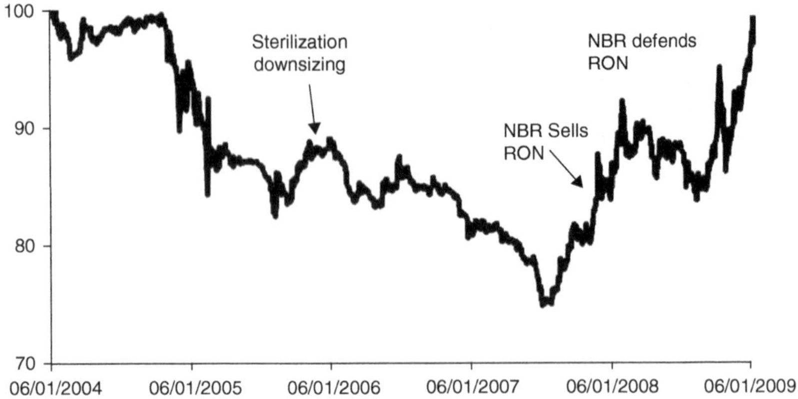

Figure 5.11 Foreign exchange dynamics, Romania, June 2004=100

Source: Computed from European Central Bank data (http://sdw.ecb.europa.eu/browse.do?node=2018794, accessed February 12 2009).

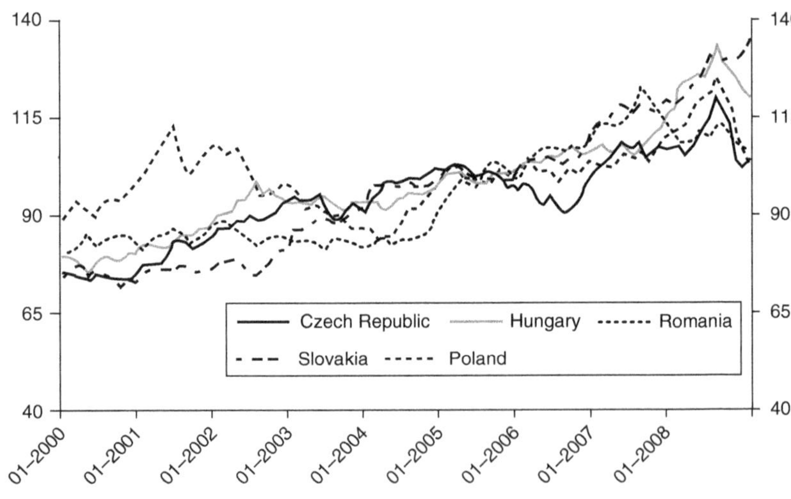

Figure 5.12 Real exchange rates, CEE countries, 2005=100

Source: BIS (2009) statistics.

The Romanian central bank was not alone in its concerns with developments on currency markets. The inflation-targeting countries (Romania, Poland, Czech Republic, and Slovakia) experienced real exchange-rate appreciations similar to those operating fixed exchange-rate regimes[93] (Figure 5.12). Hungary presented a special case: from 2001 to 2007 its inflation-targeting regime coexisted with a managed float (similar to the fluctuation band required by eurozone entry), which it abandoned in February 2008. As in Romania, sterilizations accompanied the trend appreciations. The Bank of Hungary (2007) further reported that central banks across CEE were struggling with structural excesses of liquidity on domestic money markets, despite substantial sterilizations[94]. Indeed, central banks across the region intervened in currency markets to stem fast appreciations arising from large capital inflows and EU structural funds.

The region-wide trend appreciation was narrated as a natural outcome of the catching-up process, a correction in relative prices through increasing marketization and productivity gains, described as the Balassa–Samuelson effect[95] (IMF 2006). The Balassa–Samuelson effect explained cumulative appreciation as an equilibrium process, not through exchange-rate movements per se but rather through price movements that change real levels, including exchange rates. While empirical research produced mixed evidence of its magnitude (see Egert et al. 2002 for a survey), the Balassa–Samuelson effect was widely used in policy discussions. For instance, the IMF's inflation-targeting models for formerly planned economies specified a long-run real exchange-rate equilibrium that allowed for an appreciation trend (IMF 2007a).

The insistence on equilibrium processes and the framing of exchange-rate movements through productivity growth endorsed the emphasis on flexibility and set aside concerns that overvaluations hampered growth (Gala 2008). Invoking Balassa–Samuelson, the usual causality was reversed: productivity gains drove exchange-rate appreciation, an argument strengthened by record growth in the region (Rahman 2008).

However, the narrative of productivity-driven adjustments to equilibrium could not account for the puzzle of systematic surpluses in the balance of payments registered across the region despite large current-account deficits. Romania, Bulgaria, and Latvia, for instance, ran current-account deficits above 10 percent of GDP (Figure 5.13) yet their reserves increased by an average 5 percent of GDP between 2004 and 2007. In other words, flows on the capital account were the source of exchange-rate appreciations.

In neoliberal discourses, the balance of payment dynamics revealed an important benefit of fast international financial integration. The region's success in harnessing globalized market forces allowed it unprecedented access to foreign capital to finance improvements in standard of living (Fabrizio et al. 2009). Of course, increasing reliance

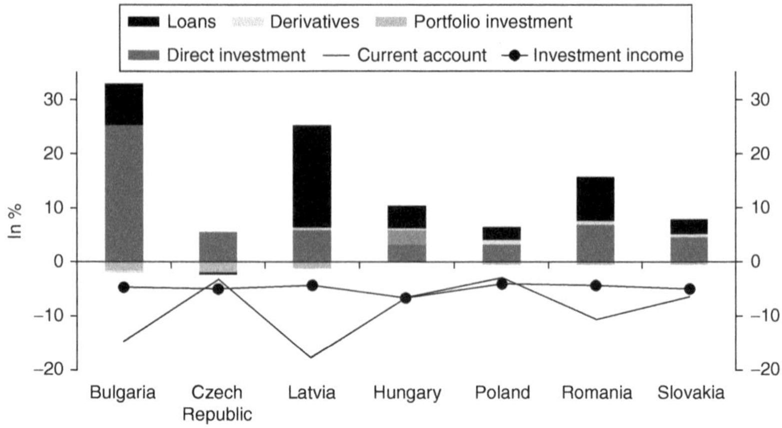

Figure 5.13 Balance of payments (percent of GDP), average 2004–2007
Source: Eurostat data.

on international financial markets had its challenges, yet in the neoliberal narrative market credibility was sufficient to put concerns to rest. Growing imbalances, a trade-off characteristic to fast convergence, would be mitigated through an adequate mix of fiscal discipline and monetary tightening (Rahman 2008).

The income component of the current account offered a first indication of what it meant to depend on foreign capital: large capital inflows increased both external debt service and profit remittances[96]. In the most extreme case, Hungary, the trade surplus was outpaced by the income account deficit (above 6 percent of GDP on average over 2004–2007). Furthermore, higher deficits on the income account reflected the increasingly large role played by debt-generating capital inflows. Except for a few countries (Bulgaria, the Czech Republic, or Slovakia), loans became the largest form of channelling foreign capital to CEE: during the three years previous to the crisis, the Baltic countries were borrowing from abroad at around 10 percent of GDP on average, closely followed by Romania and Bulgaria (Figure 5.13).

The structural changes in CEE banking sectors were partly responsible for this pattern of indebtedness. The foreign-owned banking sectors identified a window of opportunity in the region. As detailed for the Romanian case, while sterilization operations offered a risk-free source of returns for commercial banks, volumes and returns depended on the central banks' individual approach. Instead, the process of convergence opened up new profit opportunities: optimistic consumers, keen to revenge years of credit rationing and austerity. The shift away from lending to production continued, as banks turned to higher risk and higher return segments, with the attending bubbles in consumer and housing credit. Financialization produced and was in turn accelerated by fast growth.

In the early stage, foreign-owned banks operated under the same constraints as domestic banks (Aydin 2008). But with capital account liberalization, the ability to attract domestic deposits lost importance. In pursuit of market shares in host countries, foreign-owned banks turned to parent banks or, building on the credibility of parent banks, to foreign interbank markets. The short-term nature of such sources of financing shifted the maturity structure of external debts toward shorter maturities. Thus, by the end of 2008, Baltic banking sectors raised more than half of the funds through foreign loans, followed by Romania, Hungary, and Bulgaria (Figure 5.14). Latvia's experience was different because of the lower share of foreign ownership (60 percent compared to 97 percent in Lithuania and 85 percent in Estonia). Yet, domestically owned banks responded to competitive pressures by increasing reliance on short-term forms of finance, mainly nonresident deposits (IMF 2009b). Thus, 60 percent of Latvian banks' short-term debt was to nonresident investors.

An important point to note is that banks preferred to use this foreign borrowing to extend credit in foreign, rather than host-country

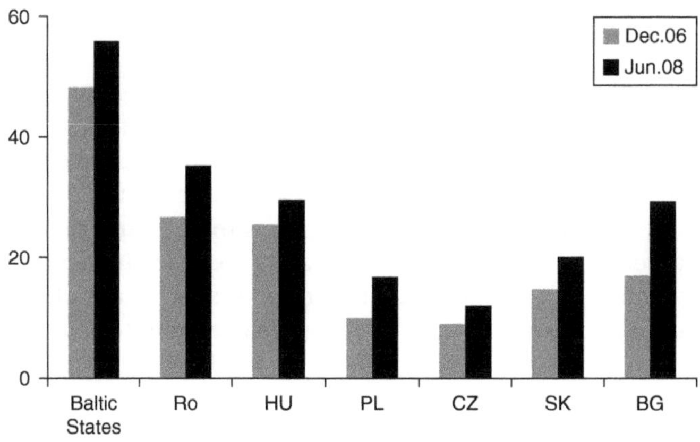

Figure 5.14 Foreign loans to the banking sectors of selected CEE countries (percent of total funds)

Source: Data from the National Bank of Hungary Financial Stability Report 2009.

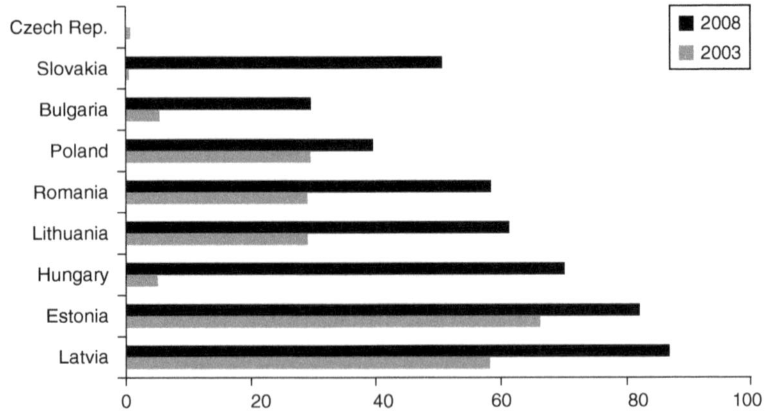

Figure 5.15 Share of foreign currency loans in total credit to households
Source: Data from National Bank of Hungary.

currency. By the end of 2008, 70 percent of Hungarian household credit was denominated in foreign currencies, mostly in Swiss francs – a low-yielding currency. Comparable levels were registered in the other two New Member States under an IMF agreement: 90 percent of Latvian banks' outstanding loans were in foreign currency, and around 60 percent for Romania (Figure 5.15). In Romania, the share of exotic-currency credits (predominantly denominated in Swiss francs) in total foreign-currency credits expanded from 8 percent in 2006 to 23 percent in 2008. The Czech Republic and Slovakia registered almost negligible shares.

I will call this strategy for exploiting yield advantages a single-currency carry trade. Because exchange-rate volatility can quickly erase profits, carry-trade investors want to be able to liquidate positions quickly. To put it differently, investors seek to match maturities on both legs of investment. Because housing or consumer loans are less liquid (in the absence of securitization), if banks were to finance domestic currency credit by borrowing abroad on the short term, they would face a maturity mismatch that increased exchange-rate risk exposure. A solution was found: foreign-currency lending, which effectively transferred the exchange-rate risk to domestic borrowers. For borrowers, the attractiveness of foreign-currency credit rested on the combination of low interest rates compared to lending rates in domestic currency (which explains the small exposure in the Czech Republic, where interest rates were at comparable levels to those in Western countries) and the expectation that exchange rates would continue to appreciate. Central banks could have prohibited this form of lending – the Romanian central bank, for instance, flirted and eventually abandoned the idea, unsuccessfully attempting to moderate the pace of household foreign currency borrowing through tighter prudential regulations. Yet, for most countries, regulatory measures were constrained by the reluctance to probe the European Commission's emphasis on market processes. Only two countries tightened reserve requirements on foreign currency liabilities (Romania and Latvia) but with limited success in containing growth.

The single-currency form of carry trade reflected expectations similar to those underlying the unprecedented growth in subprime mortgages in the USA. Securitization practices were treated as a one-way bet because the investors expected house prices to continue rising. Similarly, European banks poured money into emerging European markets because the perception of borrower risk was moderated by expectations that (a) asset prices would continue to rise given the process of convergence and (b) even if exchange-rate risk was transferred to borrowers, the expected trend appreciations would reduce the debt burden for households with revenues in domestic currencies. Single-currency trades weaved policy-makers further into global dynamics because they reinforced policy dependency on exchange-rate appreciations and interest-rate decisions in funding currency countries. Sharp reversals in exchange-rate trends threatened borrowers' ability to repay their loans and the bursting of asset bubbles.

Structural changes in currency markets induced by the presence of nonresident investors further complicated the challenges of managing currency markets. For Romania, this tendency first manifested during 2006, when nonresident currency transactions grew four times year on year, driven by substantial carry-trade returns. As Figure 5.16 suggests, leveraged cross-country positions that speculate on interest-rate differentials provided a profitable source of carry-trade returns, starting at 5 percent for most of the period.

The Romanian dynamics were symptomatic of regional currency markets. By 2007, a substantial share of currency transactions originated from carry-trade activity. Non-resident trading in derivatives drove currency movements, accounting for around or more than two-thirds of all transactions. Whereas the data per se are not "proof" that nonresident activity was driven by carry-trade motivations, the short-term maturity of the instruments (except in the Czech Republic) does not suggest that derivatives served as hedging instruments for exporters (Table 5.1).

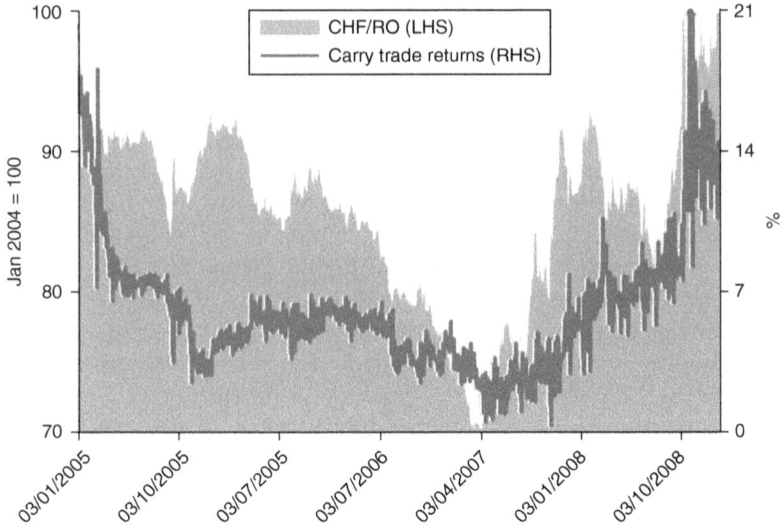

Figure 5.16 Carry trade returns vs. RON/Swiss francs exchange rate, Romania, Jan 2004=100

Source: Computed from Swiss Central Bank statistics for CHF exchange rate and 3 month Libor data (http://www.snb.ch/en/iabout/stat/statpub/zidea/id/current_interest_exchange_rates, accessed May 26, 2008 and April 12, 2009) and National Bank of Romania statistics for 3 month ROBOR and exchange rate statistics (http://www.bnro.ro/Raport-statistic-606.aspx, accessed January 23, 2009).

Table 5.1 Foreign exchange market structural characteristics, selected CEE countries. April 2007

	Volume (daily avg.)	Derivatives		of which non-residents		Instruments with maturity <7 days	
	US$ mil	US$ mil	percent	US$ mil	percent	US$ mil	percent
Romania	2510	1508	60	1351	90	1224	81
Poland	8813	6820	77	5404	79	5274	77
Hungary	6715	4658	69	3945	85	3632	78
Czech Republic	4947	3631	73	2995	82	2110	58

Source: Adapted from the National Bank of Romania *Financial Stability Report*, 2007.

Carry-trade activity further altered patterns of vulnerability. Indeed, unlike household carry trades, financial institutions' foreign-currency exposure is more likely to unwind quickly against market turbulence, particularly where nonresidents occupy such an important position.

The policy challenges came to the fore in October 2008, when regional currency markets suffered a coordinated depreciation in the aftermath of Lehman Brothers. The Romanian response (yet again) surpassed its neighbouring countries in drama, as the governor appeared in public to declare the successful defeat of a speculative attack.

5.4 The October 2008 speculative attack in Romania

Just before the Lehman debacle in September 2008, the Romanian governor criticized analysis that bundled Romania with the Baltic countries as the likely victims of a hard lending in Eastern Europe (Isărescu 2008a). Despite similar characteristics, such as booming construction and housing sectors, a credit-driven consumption boom, and large current-account deficits, Isărescu maintained that there was one essentially different macroeconomic feature that would prevent Romania from repeating the Baltic story: the monetary policy regime, relatively autonomous compared to the currency board of the Baltic countries that had transformed their central banks into statistics institutes. Monetary policy, he implied, would be instrumental in sheltering Romania from global volatility, particularly since the Romanian banking sector had not indulged in profit-making along the "originate and distribute" paradigm. In fact, the banking sector was adequately capitalized, with insignificant exposure to "toxic assets" as it held the assets it originated on its balance sheets. Developed financial markets might have been experiencing a "Minsky moment," but not Romania.

The first signs of the wishful thinking behind the Governor's arguments emerged in October, only one month later, when volatility in the money and currency markets rose substantially in the aftermath of the Lehman Brother's bankruptcy in the USA. In the preceding four months, large short positions had set the domestic currency again on a depreciating trend, a tendency the NBR sanctioned as a market mechanism for a soft landing and increased export competitiveness when demand in export markets, predominantly in Western Europe, was tightening. This benign attitude toward exchange-rate dynamics changed radically in the third week of October 2008. In no uncertain terms, the Governor claimed victory over offshore investors' speculative attack on the domestic currency (Ziarul Financiar 2008).

The attack had begun on October 15, when a series of hedge funds and foreign banks sought to speculate on an expected depreciation of the domestic currency, expectations partly arising from Standard & Poor's downgrade to sub-investment grade status (BB+), the only EU member with such a low profile. Around €2 billion RON short positions were opened, to be settled two days later (ING 2008). While the success of such operations depends on realized expectations of depreciation, offshore investors required access to domestic liquidity in order to close positions. These could be obtained either from wholesale markets or through currency swaps. And this is where the central bank intervened, in a move reminiscent of its 1999 antispeculative tactics: between October 15 and 17 the NBR drained liquidity from money markets by selling euros so that on the October 17 no domestic liquidity was to be had. Interest rates on the overnight market climbed to above 50 percent, while swap rates went as high as 500 percent (ING 2008), as speculators attempted (and some failed) to close positions. Ironically, the RON strengthened as offshore players resorted to foreign-currency sales to obtain domestic liquidity. Short-term interbank rates remained high for the rest of the month, as the central bank would only provide liquidity through the discount window, where access was restricted by collateral requirements.

The significance of the episode was twofold. First, it brought into the public domain the question of adequate practices of liquidity management during times of crisis beyond the bland commitments to "adequate management of liquidity" repeated in the central bank's inflation reports. And here two conflicting interpretations emerged, pitting the central bank against most players in the money markets. Indeed, sustained criticisms of the NBR's approach consolidated around the claim that its refusal to stabilize interbank rates by providing the necessary liquidity was symptomatic of its heavy-handed approach, particularly ill judged when central banks around the world were engaging in aggressive liquidization of wholesale and securitized markets as a first necessary response to a fast-spreading crisis (Catu 2008, Paun 2008). High interbank rates would have a damaging effect on economic activities as these increases would be transmitted to loan rates. By refusing to address interbank liquidity shortages, the central was effectively engineering a recession. Such a suggestion the NBR rejected in no uncertain terms. Liquidity injections were not necessary simply because there was no shortage of liquidity in the market but a hoarding of liquidity driven by the same speculative intensions behind the October attack. True to its position, the NBR publicly identified three big commercial banks where liquidity positions did not justify the high quotes on the interbank market and hikes in loan rates and threatened administrative sanctions (Ziarul Financiar 2008).

Second, such an unexpected shift in the previously cozy relationship between market players and the central bank revealed the pressures financialization places on monetary policy. The investigation of post-1997 practices suggested that these were increasingly subjugated to the concerns of financial actors, with short-lived attempts at decoupling policy decisions from speculative capital dynamics on the currency and money markets. Nevertheless, during 2008 it became increasingly apparent that such a representation does little justice to the complex dynamics produced by neoliberal articulations of the relationship between various transnational actors and central banks. Practices changed in response to a multiplicity of interests, and when confronted with the possibility of a massive depreciation, the NBR hesitated little to reverse its strategy toward speculative capital and exchange-rate dynamics. The unfolding crisis changed practices of monetary management toward a more autonomous approach.

5.5 Conclusion

This chapter aimed to interrogate critically the institutionalization of inflation-targeting as the new monetary policy regime in August 2005. It opened up questions of power and politics in inflation-targeting discourses, asking how this regime shift has changed practices from the days of monetary targeting. It appeared that, while models cannot easily be turned into practice, they function according to a political logic to mobilize support and enlist different interests – particularly from policy actors in the banking sector. Policy documents, analysts from commercial banks, and the IMF acknowledged, in various forms, that the theoretical centrality accorded to interest rates in influencing domestic demand was nowhere matched by a transmission mechanism that functioned as described by inflation-targeting models. Despite a few short-lived attempts, the NBR did not take control of money markets consistent with the premises of the model.

Nevertheless, interest-rate decisions were systematically, though not solely, interpreted through an aggregate-demand frame. Interpretive communities in monetary policy spaces functioned, as Sayer (1994; in Li 1999: 298–299) observed them in development policies, to enroll supporting actors with reasons "to participate in the established order as if representations were reality." Still, interpretations were not entirely fixed, as the interests they were tied up with had at times been antagonistic to the policy measures announced by the central bank. Hence, instrument decisions were also linked to foreign-exchange dynamics, interpreted to signal the central bank's (excessive) concern for competitiveness.

The policy model(s) were not the most contested policy space, despite numerous inconsistencies:

1. the incoherencies in responses to output gap estimations;
2. the expected impact of broad monetary conditions;
3. the responses to current rather than future variables;
4. the unresolved question of how expectations are formed and to what extent they influenced price dynamics.

Instead, policy contestations were strongest where practices of liquidity management deviated from commitments to financialization. While, for most of the period, sterilization operations confirmed to this role, during September/October 2005 and then in October 2008 the central bank attempted to decouple from global liquidity pressures. Indeed, the central bank's interventions on money and currency markets, that signalled its refusal to validate speculative returns, triggered intense contestations. In turn, very few voices asked whether a structural excess of liquidity was consistent with aggregate demand control.

The full liberalization of the capital account and the switch to inflation-targeting saw the consolidation of a financialized monetary regime similar to other inflation targeters in the region, with the following features:

- A strategy of real exchange-rate appreciations, through direct currency interventions and/or substantial yield advantages. The central bank's practices of liquidity management, rationalized in policy discourse through monetarist concerns toward the structural excess of liquidity on money markets, functioned to attract speculative capital inflow. Excess liquidity further enabled banks to act as counterparty to nonresident activity on currency markets with limited scope for central bank control.
- The further financialization of the banking sector, engaged into a multiplicity of carry-trade activities. Driven by processes of internationalization and privatization, commercial banks increasingly replaced long-term traditional lending with market-based investment activities. In emerging Europe, the financialization of banks involved in trading in central-bank sterilization operations, government securities, and the foreign-currency financing of asset bubbles in consumer credit and housing through cross-border loans from parent banks and foreign interbank markets. The inflation-targeting regime contributed to vulnerability by maintaining high interest-rate

differentials (except for the Czech Republic) that saw demand for loans switching to lower yielding foreign currencies. In developing countries, inflation-targeting regimes thus operate according to the traditional political economy understanding that links high yields to rentier interests.

- The increasing financialization of currency markets, where trading is no longer driven by traditional commercial activity but instead reflects carry-trade activities of nonresident investors and foreign-owned commercial banks.

Such practices of central banking increase vulnerability to external volatility and complicate liquidity management during crisis because commercial banks become counterparty to nonresident activity. Bagehot's (1876) famous advice that the first response to a financial panic should be to stabilize interbank markets by satisfying banks' demand for liquidity becomes problematic if it funds speculative currency positions. The central banks grappled with Bagehot's advice throughout 2009, the year when CEE (briefly) became subprime.

6
Coping in the Subprime Region

Up to February 2009, the global deleveraging pressures appeared to have affected European banks only relative to the degree of the exposure of their investment banking arms to the convulsions of Anglo-Saxon financial markets. But during February 2009 the threats of a homegrown crisis were increasingly visible, at its roots the European commercial banks' strategies of internationalization in CEE. Western European banks had entered banking systems in the region through privatization processes, keen to exploit markets with confident consumers, pent-up demand, and booming activity. As parent banks channelled foreign-currency loans through their subsidiaries, cross-border exposures increased to around €600 billion (*The Economist* 2009). Concerns revolved around the maturity mismatches between short-term borrowing in international money markets and long-term lending in Eastern European consumer and housing markets. From growth tigers, the region suddenly became subprime.

As Western banks' potential losses from investment banking surprised even the pessimists, it appeared plausible that parent banks might not be willing to roll over credit lines to their CEE subsidiaries. Historical experience did not provide an encouraging answer. While foreign ownership had positive effects for host economies during benign periods, problems at the parent bank reduced subsidiaries' willingness to lend (Martinez-Peria et al. 2002), and problems in the host economy usually induced foreign banks to reduce exposure, further compounding the capital flight (Caballero 2002). The 2008 crisis combined these two scenarios in the CEE region: Western European parent banks deeply affected by financial turmoil and host economies suffering from falling export demand.

The ensuing developments offer a fertile ground for exploring what happens to the central-bank practices underlying financialization when its inbuilt instabilities produce a crisis. In CEE, the global crisis of financialized capitalism threatened the seemingly harmonious relationship between central banks and financial markets, breaking down the traditional methods for negotiating policy processes, now replaced by panicked flights to safety or speculative bets in currency markets. From partners willing to support the process of convergence, foreign-owned banks embodied the threats that financial integration posed for emerging markets.

The chapter sets regional dynamics within the broader shifts in global liquidity conditions. It identifies three different stages in the global financial crisis, marked by the Lehman Brothers bankruptcy in September 2008 and then the shift to quantitative easing in March 2009. These shifts, it argues, had important consequences for the region both through the dominant presence of European banks and the changing risk perceptions of nonresident investors, especially given similar vulnerabilities to financialized, roll-out neoliberalism.

Romania offers an interesting opening point for understanding regional dynamics. The terms of its agreement with the IMF renewed policy commitments to private finance, both through direct macroeconomic commitments to austerity and through new institutional setups such as the European Bank Coordination Initiative (EBCI). Yet a comparative analysis of the practices adopted by the central banks of Romania and Hungary points to an emerging and somewhat contradictory politics of resistance to financialization.

6.1 Policy responses to crisis and global liquidity conditions: The return of the carry trades

The New Keynesian paradigm dominating macroeconomic policy formulation before the crisis defined "normal" policy as a combination of inflation-targeting, limited fiscal activism and a laissez-faire approach to financial stability informed by the efficient market hypothesis. The crisis brought a new macroeconomics of stabilization that combined unconventional monetary policy measures with fiscal activism and increased policy attention to financial fragility. Where policy autonomy allowed it, crisis package was applied in some form of the above, reflecting distinct periods in the macroeconomic of crisis.

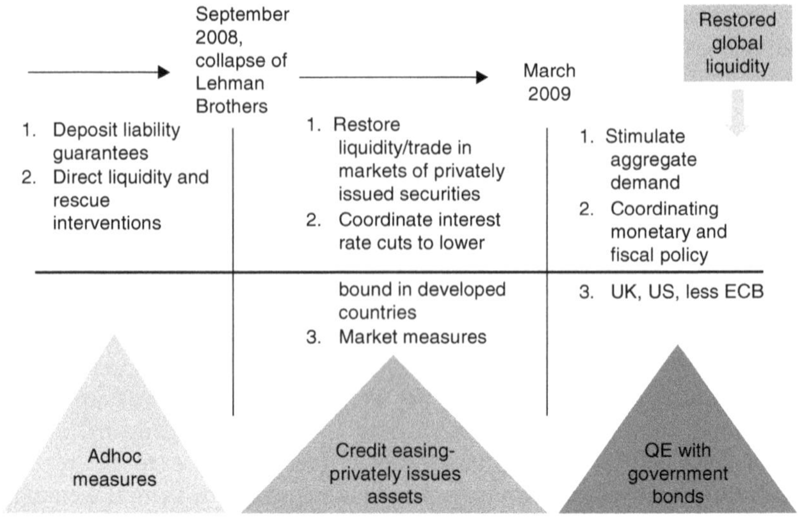

Figure 6.1 Timeline of crisis responses in developed countries

A timeline of the crisis responses in developed countries identifies three qualitatively distinct periods since 2007 (see Figure 6.1). Up to the Lehman Brothers bankruptcy in September 2008, ad-hoc measures were deployed to counteract the threats to the usual functioning of financial markets. Bank-liability guarantees sought to restore public trust in banks and to prevent the embarrassing repetition of the Northern Rock bank run in the UK. Direct liquidity and rescue interventions (ranging from outright nationalization to stabilization and recapitalization funds) aimed at containing the systemic threats associated with the unprecedented liquidity problems across a broad spectrum of financial institutions. However, the collapse of Lehman Brothers shattered any illusions that the financial turmoil could be contained from transforming into a fully blown economic crisis that would transcend the boundaries of developed countries. A startling period for financial markets began, marked by unprecedented volatility which Marvin and Taylor (2009) explained as a consequence of the dramatic worsening in perceptions of counterparty risk. In fact, the post-Keynesian differentiation of risk and uncertainty aptly applied to the situation. The Lehman bankruptcy produced a situation of fundamental uncertainty that prompted investors to unwind leveraged positions (with the first round effects transmitted to emerging countries through reversals of carry trades in currency markets) and to seek refuge in safe havens (gold, the US dollar or the Swiss franc).[97] Policy-makers appeared at a loss, unsurely navigating in uncharted waters, temporarily unable to produce the systematic and coordinated actions that would have restored confidence. Central bankers lamented the "casino" turn in capitalism, which rendered securitization from an eminently beneficial financial innovation to address risk into speculative practice that amplified volatility (Trichet 2009). The disorder lasted until March 2009 when increasingly coordinated and highly unconventional policy responses restored global liquidity. It became apparent that the financial crisis produced, to follow Jessop's (2009) distinction, a crisis *in*, rather than *of*, neoliberalism. Central banks played a key role in avoiding the collapse.

Day-to-day "conventional" techniques of liquidity management involve OMOs to maintain the short-term interbank market rate close to the policy rate – the cornerstone of the New Keynesian transmission mechanism. Once interest rates hit the zero lower bound (or are kept unchanged at a certain level), central banks have three mechanisms for easing financing conditions (Bernanke and Reinhardt 2004). The first acts on a purely discursive level to influence market expectations of future inflation rates, linking policy commitment to a reduction in real interest rates. Alternatively, the central bank could act directly on its balance sheet, to either change its composition (narrowly defined as credit easing) and/or to expand its size (quantitative easing). There is a qualitative difference between the two strategies: while both are paid for with high-powered money, only quantitative easing reflects an explicit intention to increase liquidity in the system.

During the first stage of the crisis, policy efforts directed at stabilizing interbank markets were informed by New Keynesian concerns with the transmission mechanism. It was no coincidence that the tensions in the US subprime market first manifested in interbank markets. These constituted the first instance locus of confidence losses because leveraged investments crucially depended on the possibility to mobilize liquidity quickly (and cheaply). Although emergency interventions to stabilize interbank markets increased in both size and frequency throughout 2008, central banks refused to treat these as symptoms of systematic failure. The clearest signal of such a reading was sent by the Federal Reserve's decision to sterilize the effects of its emergency liquidity provisioning (direct liquidity support, swaps, and loans to other central banks). Between December 2007 and September 2008, it sold Treasury bills of around US$250 billion, guided by New Keynesian concerns that excess liquidity injections might unduly relax credit conditions and feed inflationary pressures à la Friedman. The Federal Reserve appeared to be dealing with two different sets of financial markets. The first, of a New Keynesian imagination, transmitted monetary-policy decisions to the economy and required sterilizations. The other, severely strained, required repeated liquidity injections to address a "temporary" instability that could be amplified by "rational" investors' flight to safety.

The narrative of exceptionality changed in the second stage of the crisis. Central banks inaugurated a series of credit-easing measures that sought to avoid the near disaster of the post-Lehman moment when interbank markets dried up, setting in motion a large-scale deleveraging process that threatened to bring international financial markets to a standstill. Coordinated cuts brought interest rates in most developed countries close to zero, while central banks recognized that financial markets needed protection from themselves: regulatory measures temporarily prohibited short-selling activities, of a highly speculative nature, across most jurisdictions. In November 2008, the USA announced that it would directly purchase asset-backed securities, followed by Japan (commercial paper) in December and the UK (£50 billion worth of high-quality private-sector assets) in January.[98] The purchase of privately issued financial instruments was intended to change risk spreads across different assets rather than as an explicit stimulus to aggregate demand à la Keynes. A temporary public intrusion would thus correct failures and restore normal functioning to various segments whose functioning was impaired by the growing uncertainties of counterparty risk and deleveraging.

By February 2009, policy-makers felt increasingly uneasy about the effectiveness of such measures. Instead of the desired "return to normal," emerging anxieties focused on CEE and the possibility that European banks might pull out. Regardless of whether this functioned as a trigger or just an added concern, in March 2009 central banks in UK and US adopted the Japanese approach to restoring confidence: quantitative easing, or liquidity injections through the purchase of government bonds. This strategy of injecting liquidity, it was explained, had two added benefits compared to credit-easing (Smaghi 2009). It offered a faster, more effective method of bringing down yields in markets with privately issued securities because sovereign debt acted as benchmark for higher-risk instruments. As returns on holding government debt reduced, portfolio preferences would shift to riskier assets, lowering the cost of funding for private (especially productive) sectors, and would stimulate long-term productive investment and aggregate demand. Even where uncertainty led investors to shun riskier assets, the increased liquidity would be deposited with commercial banks and increase the deposit base from which to issue loans. This channel, the Bank of England (2009) warned, effectively depended on the banks' willingness to lend. If deleveraging pressures or banks' liquidity preference remained high, excess reserves created through quantitative easing would be parked with the central bank, lessening the desired impact on aggregate demand.

As central banks expressed concerns about impaired transmission mechanisms, governments in the "developed" world abandoned any neoliberal pretence of fiscal discipline. Keynes, the master, was back: Western governments would spend their way out of the recession. Ironically, the global liquidity surge after March 2009 essentially depended on (however reluctant) abandoning the cherished neoliberal insistence on central-bank independence and recognizing the post-Keynesian position that the central bank, and not markets, was ultimately responsible for public debt dynamics (Arestis and Sawyer 2004). Policies of quantitative easing not only boosted global liquidity but also acted on market expectations of interest-rate movements. If the Japanese experience between 2001 and 2006 was anything to go by, quantitative easing added to the central bank's reluctance to increase policy rates from the zero lower bound (Sheng and Pomerleano 2009). "Mrs. Watanabe," the famous household figure behind the Japanese carry trades, was going global.

With expectations that interest rates would remain at the lower bound for a considerable period of time, low yielding currencies (the US dollar in particular) became funding currency for "the mother of all carry trades" (Roubini 2009). Since March 2009, Roubini calculated, a weak US dollar combined with quantitative easing drove a large and synchronized rally across risky assets that produced returns at around 50–70 percent to November 2009. Carry trades retuned to emerging markets with high yield differentials on such a scale that Brazil chose to impose capital controls in October 2009.

The ECB constitutes an interesting exception to the developed countries' approach, with important implications for the New Member States. The peculiar institutional make-up of the eurozone combined the remarkable absence of a supranational fiscal authority with a conservative commitment to keep the Euro "stabil wie die Mark." One expression of this commitment was written in the Maastricht Treaty as an explicit prohibition of central-bank monetization of public debt. Consequently, the ECB named the unconventional measures adopted after September 2008 "enhanced credit support." Instead of purchasing privately issued securities as elsewhere in developed financial markets, the ECB chose to inject liquidity through the banking sector. Different measures, it argued, were warranted by different institutional features (Smaghi 2009). Banks dominated the European financial system, in opposition to the market-led system of Anglo-Saxon countries.

Immediately after Lehman, the ECB relaxed collateral and liquidity constraints on its operations with eurozone credit institutions. It instituted unlimited liquidity provisioning at maturities of up to six months ("fixed-rate full allotment") and expanded the range of acceptable collateral on its liquidity provisioning to banks. The insistence on the banking sector solved another dilemma: aside from the potential allocative distortions which the ECB decried, the purchase of either private or public securities had a key political economy dimension: preferential treatment of a member state's industry or government debt. Even when the ECB finally set to directly purchase private assets in May 2009, it chose debt securities (covered bonds) issued by banks (Trichet 2009). Bank-focused measures were less susceptible of discriminatory treatment because banks, driven by processes of internationalization, had a strong European dimension to their operation.[99]

For Eastern Europe, the ECB's strategy of providing banks with ample access to liquidity was less beneficial than it expected. In a highly unusual episode, on February 23, 2009, the *Financial Times* reported a joint statement by Poland, the Czech Republic, Slovakia, Romania, and Bulgaria that expressed concerns about speculation diverted from fundamentals in their currency markets (Kaminska 2009).[100] Indeed, regional currency markets had seen substantial pressures since the summer of 2008, which in the light of the central banks' statement could no longer be read as a straightforward consequence of global deleveraging. Hungary, at the time viewed as the basket case of emerging Europe, made several unsuccessful diplomatic attempts to secure the assistance of the EU during February 2009. It first proposed a regional rescue package under the coordination of the EBRD. But the EU and several New Member States refused. Then Hungary suggested that the ECB accept non-euro assets (Hungarian bonds) as collateral for loans. The ECB declined. CEE, the developing region most thoroughly engaged with international financial integration, was threatening to collapse under its contradictions with little assistance from the EU (an experience sadly repeated later in Greece).

The contradictions of a financialized model of banking came to fore in the aftermath of Lehman. As the joint statement of several CEE central banks suggested, commercial banks' activity in currency markets, both through direct trading and as counterparty to nonresident activity, threatened sharp devaluations. Yet devaluations increased domestic borrower risks and exposed bank balance sheets to the vulnerability inbuilt by single-currency carry trades. The countries with the highest exposure set to convince parent banks to roll over credit to subsidiaries, in the context of the Vienna Initiative (in its official formulation the EBCI) intermediated by the IMF during its negotiations with Romania throughout March 2009.

6.2 The IMF program in Romania

After the October 2008 speculative attack, the Romanian central bank's relationship with the money markets was driven by concerns that a substantial easing of liquidity conditions would have immediately aggravated an already strained currency market. The central bank worried that commercial banks' role as counterparty to nonresident activity might see liquidity injections funding speculative activity. Russia and Ukraine offered instructive examples: throughout 2008, commercial banks used liquidity obtained from the central banks to finance short-selling of the domestic currencies (Bloomberg 2008b).

As international financial markets were struggling through the post-Lehman gloom, CEE currency markets came under pressure from diminishing risk appetite and unwinding carry trades. For instance, the NBR reported that throughout November 2008, trading in the Romanian currency market declined by a staggering 60 percent as nonresident operators withdrew. In Hungary, nonresident investors reduced holdings of government securities by US$3.5 billion between October 2008 and February 2009, almost a fifth of the country's foreign reserve assets (IMF 2009b). Similarly, nonresident call deposits with Latvian banks fell by almost 15 percent between September and December 2008.

The Romanian central bank temporarily suspended its public commitments to flexibility to defend the currency. However, the €2.1 billion of central-bank reserves failed to arrest the depreciation, and by February 2009 the Romanian leu lost 20 percent of its nominal value, losses of similar magnitude to other New Member States with flexible exchange-rate regimes. It seemed the worst was yet to come, as global concerns about the European banks' position in CEE markets identified the region as the next hot spot of the crisis. Romania appeared particularly vulnerable, given the trend deterioration of the maturity structure in its external debt: in February 2009, gross international reserves only covered 75 percent of the short-term debt (from more than 170 percent in 2003). While foreign public debt halved to 7.5 percent of GDP, private foreign debt nearly doubled to 46 percent of GDP between 2005 and 2008.

A domestic-policy consensus called for IMF assistance, to avert a currency crisis given the uncertainties that commercial banks were willing to roll over short-term debt (NBR 2009a); or, according to the government, to avert a social crisis, as its reduced access to international financial markets effectively implied that it might not be able to raise sufficient liquidity to cover the public wage bill. Ironically, Romania turned to the international lender of last resort as the financial crisis was entering its third stage and quantitative easing restored appetite for risk and emerging markets.

The agreement, approved in April 2009, narrated the crisis as follows: an economy overheating through capital inflows and procyclical fiscal policies became vulnerable to global deleveraging and exchange-rate volatility (IMF 2009a). The IMF applauded the NBR for its attempts to contain foreign-currency credit growth after 2004, undermined by loose fiscal/income policies and capital inflows, and glossed over the extent to which the NBR's strategy of real appreciations and sterilizations had contributed to financial fragility. The €19.9 billion financing package (to which the IMF contributed €12.95 billion, the European Commission €5 billion and the World Bank and EBRD the rest) was conditional on a two-pillar approach:

1. **A strong policy program** that defined fiscal contractions as key to restoring confidence, along with an improvement in bank supervision and recapitalization, and continued exchange-rate flexibility.
2. **Large external financing assistance** to be directly desimbursed into NBR's foreign reserves, acting as an external financial buffer. In other words, the central bank, and not the government, would receive the IMF funds. Simultaneously, the IMF and national authorities obtained commitment from the Western parent banks to roll over short-term debt.

The emphasis on fiscal contractions reframed the crisis: while policy-makers initially explained the request for emergency multilateral assistance through the vulnerability to short-term foreign debt, the program identified government spending as the primary tool for adjustment. In fact, the IMF Board only accepted to consider the SBA terms once expenditure cuts amounting to 1.1 percent of GDP were implemented. Furthermore, the IMF program sought to renew policy commitments to private finance. Policy advice reflected concerns to protect the banking sector's profits, switching the burden of adjustment to the public sector. The concerns for bank profits could be traced in two policy fields: the exchange-rate advice and the mechanism for desimbursment.

First, despite rhetorical commitments to flexibility, the IMF argued that policy options were severely limited by the need to prevent currency depreciations in order to protect banks' balance sheets. Monetary policy responses were thus tied into exchange-rate stability: since monetary policy easing would precipitate capital outflows, the central bank was encouraged to maintain a high interest-rate differential, on a par only with Hungary in the EU. The IMF policy advice recommended more of the same: exchange-rate dynamics driven by speculative activity, without considering the extent to which such a strategy had contributed to making Romania, and Eastern Europe, "subprime."

The refusal to consider the destabilizing role of financialized practices also reflected in the design of the IMF loan disbursement. Although the insistence on fiscal adjustment recognized the government's financing difficulties, the IMF did not consider it imperative that its funds would provide direct budget support (for which the European Commission had committed €5 billion) nor did it draw attention to the importance of macroeconomic policy coordination. Instead, the program was designed to channel the IMF funds to the central bank, in exchange for which the institution reduced reserve requirements on banks' long-term foreign currency liabilities. The measure, the NBR hoped, would restart foreign currency lending and contribute to restoring the long-term health of the banking sector (NBR 2009c).[101] Yet this account was puzzling: before the crisis the central bank had repeatedly expressed concerns that foreign-currency lending fuelled consumption and housing booms. Part of the answer is to be found in the negotiations between the central bank, the government, and parent banks concluded in the Vienna meeting on March 26.

6.2.1 The European Bank Coordination Initiative

The Vienna Initiative, the IMF explained (Andersen 2009), reflected the global lender's search for potential methods of engaging the private sector in bailout operations. The intention was not new: after the charges of moral hazard directed at its interventions during the East Asian crisis, the IMF had introduced the concept of "burden sharing" as a prerequisite for its lending. The strategy failed, the IMF later acknowledged, because it premised vulnerable countries could finance from private sources at reasonable returns. Instead, the global economy needed a lender of last resort because uncertainty about a country's prospects translated into high risk premiums and unserviceable debt. This painful lesson nearly brought Romania to a default in 1999, when the IMF refused to lend before private financing had been secured. Ironically, 10 years later the IMF announced that its Romania program constituted a breakthrough in its new approach to coordinated policy responses, the EBCI, subsequently used in Bosnia, Hungary, Latvia, Serbia, and Ukraine.

That the IMF initiated and then oversaw the proceedings reflected the complex political economy of the EU. First, aside from ECB's emphasis on restoring banking-sector liquidity, the EU lacked an institutional framework for coordinating policy responses. The crisis in its old member states had triggered ad-hoc coordination, applauded by Quaglia (2009) as Europeanization in action. However, in the New Member States, the European Commission relied on the IMF to ensure that the EU's emergency assistance (smaller in volume) would trigger the "appropriate" policy adjustments.

In Vienna, the IMF brought together what it identified as key stakeholders: parent banks, home country authorities (the central bank and the government), and several European (the European Commission, the ECB) and international institutions (the EBRD, the World Bank). Remarkably absent from the list were civil-society groups or trade unions, although foreign banks' decisions were crucial to the well-being of borrowing households. The participants' list instead lends strength to Sassen's theorizing about global governance that no longer opposes globalization to the nation-state but where certain components of the nation-state (the central bank an interesting example) are denationalized, weaved into complex networks of global governance alongside other supranational institutions and private commercial banks. The Vienna Initiative can thus be read as an attempt to restore the (fragile) institutional arrangements for economic control, increasingly destabilized by the crisis.

The EBCI documents expose a notable contrast between the emphasis on restoring the private sector's confidence and the silence on what it would take to do so, as if the IMF's endorsement of policy reforms offered sufficient guarantee for parent banks to meet their commitments on debt rollover.[102] If parent banks only needed the IMF's assurance, then the EBCI would have little *raison d'être* because countries had already entered agreements with the IMF. Yet past experience showed banks failed to comply with commitments to rollovers during similar IMF initiatives in East Asia, Turkey in 2001 or Brazil in 2002 (Andersen 2009). That banks had explicit demands in return for commitments appeared from the laconic reference to "the availability of appropriate investment instruments" alongside adequate lending opportunities, a reference repeatedly reaffirmed in subsequent EBCI meetings for every country under an IMF program.

This reference, I will argue, offers a more complex reading of the central banks' role in the Eastern European crisis, and the contradictions embedded in its institutional orientation toward global agendas and systems. To expose these contradictions, the following sections will develop a comparative analysis of Hungary and Romania, both New Member States operating with an inflation-targeting regime and under an IMF program.[103]

6.3 Nine months after: A comparative analysis of Romania and Hungary

Nine months after the "subprime" moment, a puzzling situation was emerging in the currency markets of New Member States with flexible exchange-rate regimes. Currency dynamics broadly traced the three identified periods of qualitatively different global liquidity conditions. Up to the collapse of Lehman Brothers, regional currency markets suggested that investors' portfolio choices were informed by the decoupling thesis, with strong tendencies toward appreciation reflecting expectations that the region would weather the crisis better than its neighbouring developed markets. Romania temporarily bucked the trend, partly because the central bank was quietly intervening to stem what it perceived as excessive appreciations (Isărescu 2009). Between Lehman and March 2009, global deleveraging and currency speculations pushed currencies sharply lower, with Romanian leu the worst affected followed by the Polish zloty and Hungarian forint. The Czech koruna's pace of depreciation has to be considered in the light of its role as a low-yield, funding currency for carry-trade activity for several years

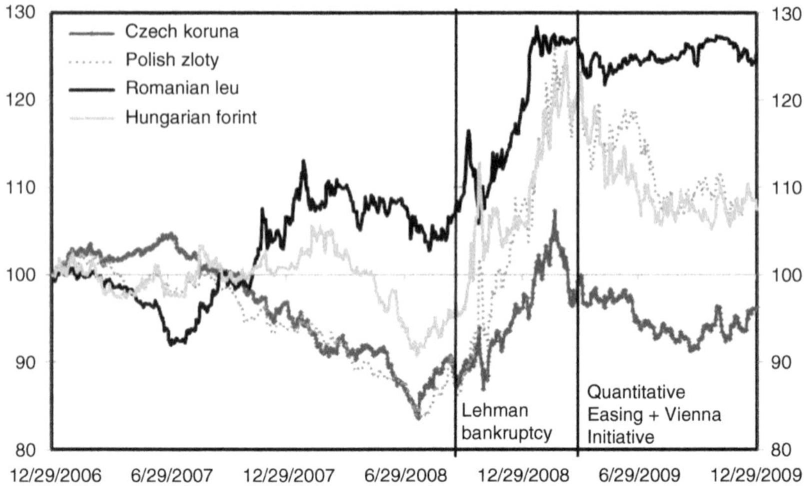

Figure 6.2 Nominal exchange rates, Dec. 2006=100
Source: Eurostat data.

before the crisis. As with the Japanese yen, the unwinding driven by deleveraging increased demand for koruna and moderated the overall pressures toward depreciation. Once global liquidity and carry trades were restored, regional dynamics changed again. Whereas Poland, Hungary, and the Czech Republic experienced a coordinated appreciation, Romania's currency remained broadly around its March 2009 level (see Figure 6.2).

The divergent performances of Hungary and Romania deserve a closer investigation; after all, during the first months of 2009 the global deleveraging appeared to have condemned both countries to similar fates. Shunned by nonresident investors and international rating agencies, with interest rates at the highest levels in the EU, both were forced to appeal to the IMF's assistance (Hungary in November 2008, Romania in March 2009) to avoid a currency crisis and had to subsequently commit to substantial fiscal contractions.

By the end of 2009, Hungary appeared to have recovered more quickly. A rally in Hungarian bonds prompted the government to announce it would forgo external assistance. In turn, the Romanian government was struggling to finance its expenditure through domestic commercial banks, paying interest rates nearly twice as high. The divergent performance, it was commonly argued, reflected the Hungarian commitment

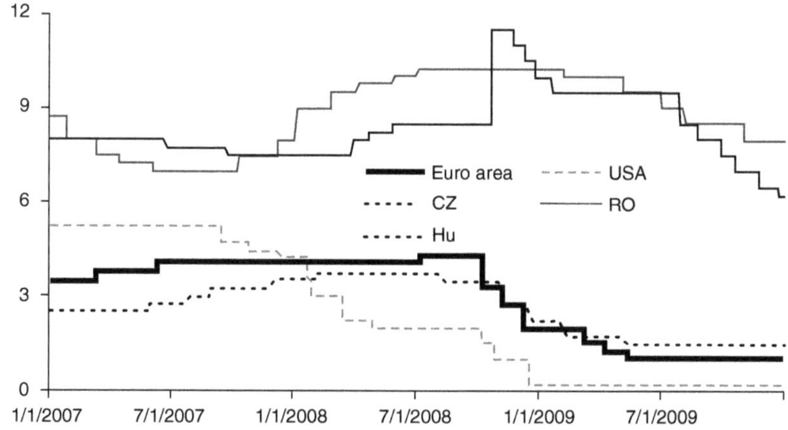

Figure 6.3 Central bank interest rates, 2007–2009
Source: Central bank websites.

to fiscal retrenchment. Despite a far higher than expected economic contraction, it maintained its initial 2009 targeted budget deficit (3.8 percent of GDP). The Romanian government instead chose to adjust its deficit target in line with the output fall (doubling the 2009 target to around 8 percent of GDP) amid increased political tensions since September 2009. Fiscal rectitude allowed the Hungarian central bank, Magyar Nemzeti Bank (MNB), to accelerate monetary easing in the second half of 2009, bringing the policy rate 200 basis points below that of Romania (Figure 6.3).

Could politics explain the Romanian currency puzzle? The answer is to be found in the central banks' liquidity management strategies in two interrelated domains: unpredictable liquidity operations, driven by concerns of speculative pressures in currency markets, combined with the neglect toward public debt sustainability. Politics notwithstanding, such different trajectories were the consequence of central-bank policies. MNB institutionalized a transparent and predictable response to the crisis on the money markets, blending concerns of public debt sustainability with sustained efforts to restore the attractiveness of Hungarian markets to international investors.

To start with, central banks faced similar challenges during October 2008. While the Romanian central bank inflicted liquidity shortages to deter further currency speculations, MNB responded to similar pressures on its currency markets by raising its policy interest rate by 300 basis points. Afterwards, crisis policies became increasingly different.

6.3.1 Monetary management in Romania before the IMF negotiations (March 2009)

In the aftermath of the October 2008 speculative attack, the central bank changed its liquidity policies. It abandoned the traditional instrument of monetary policy, sterilizations through deposit-taking operations. Higher liquidity preference in the banking sector and the asymmetric distribution of liquidity implied that the plentiful days of the structural excess of liquidity were over. Tensions in the interbank market intensified, as the central bank limited liquidity provision to its discount window (along with swap operations[104]). Nevertheless, the width of the corridor around the policy rate, of ±4 percentage points (compared to the usual ±0.5 percentage points in other countries) and the very short term of these liquidity operations (usually overnight) turned discount window access into an expensive method for covering liquidity needs.

For instance, during December and January 2009, banks paid 14 percent for overnight loans from the central bank. Furthermore, the banking system faced pervasive collateral constraints as EU membership allowed the government to finance its expenditure gap from structural funds (alongside privatization revenues) since 2007. With less need to finance the deficit on the domestic money market, limited securities issuance resulted in illiquid bond markets. Against such structural conditions, commercial banks charged, the NBR was deliberately amplifying volatility by refusing to ease liquidity tensions. The dynamics of the standing facilities appeared to support this claim (see Figure 6.4). During the first nine months of 2008, standing facilities were used asymmetrically to park excess liquidity. The interbank tensions triggered by the central bank's reaction to nonresident activity during October 2008 drove commercial banks to borrow heavily from the discount window. In fact, throughout the second period of the global crisis, the lender-of-last-resort facility remained the key source of liquidity for the money markets – overriding concerns of counterparty risk rendered banks with excess liquidity reluctant to lend to other banks, preferring instead the central bank's overnight deposit facility (remunerated at 400 basis points below the policy rate). After March 2009, the central bank switched to net liquidity absorptions through standing

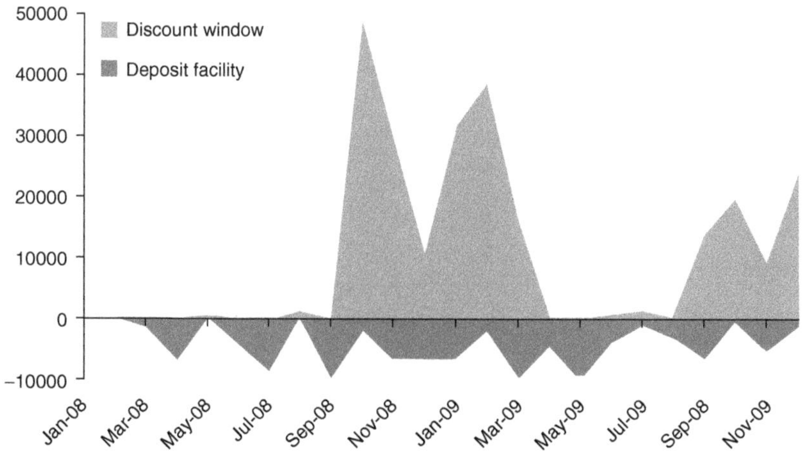

Figure 6.4 Access to standing facilities, Romania, 2008–2009

Source: Data from the National Bank of Romania, Monthly Report, December 2008 and 2009.

facilities, a pattern to be reversed again starting with September 2009 (in the context of the political crisis).

Indeed, commercial banks' use of the central bank's standing facilities suggests that liquidity was asymmetrically distributed. While banks simultaneously faced with liquidity and collateral constraints drove overnight rates on the money market at or above the Lombard rate on several occasions (as during February 2009), by the end of the maintenance period the interest rates regularly fell to the level of the deposit facility (see Figure 6.5). The high liquidity preference reflected both concerns of counterparty risk and the uncertainties engendered by the NBR's highly discretionary approach to liquidity management. Banks maintained "safety cushions" to safeguard against unpredictable liquidity policies.

However, such an approach to monetary management failed to arrest the RON depreciation despite the central bank's supportive interventions because it altered the traditional channels for commercial bank profits. The tight lid on liquidity limited profit opportunities from either the central bank's liquidity-mopping operations or from counterparty operations in carry trades (even with restored nonresident interest). Liquidity tightening affected another source of profits for commercial banks: the government's increasingly large financing needs.

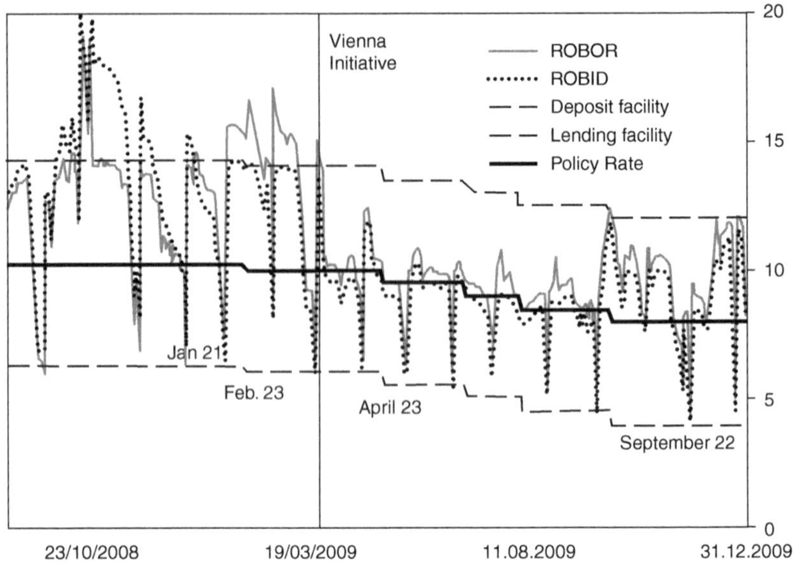

Figure 6.5 Policy and money market interest rates, Romania, 2008–2009
Source: National Bank of Romania.

The method of financing budget deficits impacts on banking-sector liquidity. If the Treasury chooses to raise funds in domestic currency, no extra reserves are created. The temporary fall in banking liquidity from the purchase of new issues is eventually offset because government spending returns into bank deposits. If the Treasury chooses to borrow in foreign currency (either domestically or through international loans), the impact on the banking-sector liquidity depends on the central bank. Where the central bank acts as the government's foreign-exchange agent, the government's foreign-exchange revenue will expand the central bank's balance sheet, a form of quantitative easing. The increase in net foreign asset will simultaneously reflect in an increase of the Treasury's deposit account with the central bank. Government spending eventually increases banking-sector liquidity. If the central bank refuses to take an active part, then the Treasury will exchange its foreign currency on the interbank currency market. The increased demand appreciates the domestic currency without changing the overall liquidity in the banking sector (Balogh 2009).

The Romanian Treasury financed its deficit exclusively through RON issues on domestic money markets up to July 2009 (around RON

50 billion, four times higher than in 2008). Because the May 2009 IMF tranche went directly to the central bank, it had no impact on banking sector liquidity. The central bank refused to support public-debt dynamics, even though the government finances had become severely strained over the last quarter of 2008 due to a combination of reduced access to foreign borrowing, worsening revenue collection, and higher expenditures attending parliamentary elections. The Treasury was forced to turn to domestic sources, as it did during the 1999 crisis. While that episode had demonstrated that non-banking institutions were a more cost-effective form of financing because banks had exploited the Treasury's captive position, a high liquidity preference arising from increased uncertainty left the banking sector as the main source of liquidity. Between November 2008 and March 2009, banks' claims on the government doubled to 8 percent of total claims.

In a disheartening repetition of the 1999 episode, the Treasury succumbed to the ping-pong between the central bank and the commercial banks. Before the IMF agreement, around 65 percent of new debt was contracted at three months maturity or less and yields at around 12 percent (Figure 6.6). The government found it nearly impossible to borrow the long term. The Prime Minister declared that in the absence of IMF support, the government might find it impossible to sustain public-sector wage payments (Wall Street 2009).

Yet the high yields on short-term treasury operations attracted considerable demand from banks with excess liquidity: all short-term auctions

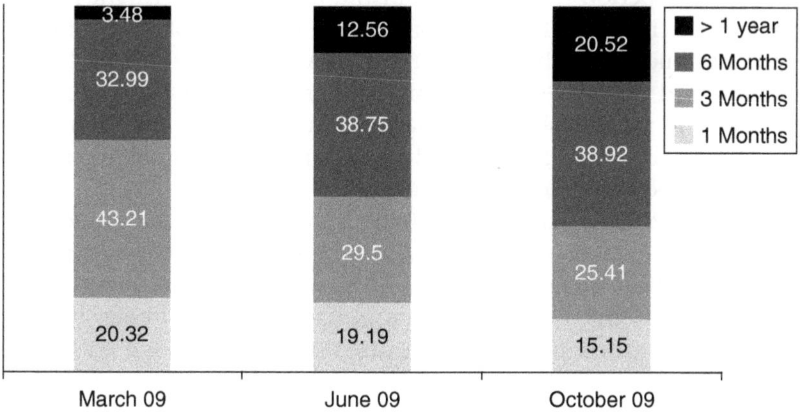

Figure 6.6 Composition of newly issued government debt, Romania. 2009
Source: Romanian Ministry of Finance.

throughout the first quarter of 2009 were oversubscribed. While the NBR's statistics make it difficult to assess the net liquidity position in the banking sector, it appears that the severity of the crisis combined with the unpredictability embedded in the central bank's discretionary tactics curtailed commercial banks' willingness to commit their own resources in the long term. The central bank's decision to limit liquidity injections to discount-window operations or to swaps (at high interest rates and short maturities) narrowed commercial banks' profit opportunities.

As the Vienna discussions unfolded, commercial banks sought to exploit the increased leverage in policy negotiations. The oblique reference to "appropriate investment opportunities" expressed the wish for a change in the approach to liquidity management. The substantial yields on Romanian assets could not be exploited without the central bank's cooperation.

6.3.2 Liquidity policies after the IMF agreement: Banking on the Romanian state

The IMF agreement secured this cooperation, bringing the central bank back into the money markets. It marked a change in the strategies of liquidity management, rendering the central bank more responsive to demands of the banking sector. During March, the central bank offered several liquidity-mopping operations through reverse repos or deposit-taking operations. The absorption, at the policy rate, of around RON 2 billion at one week maturity just before the end of the reserve requirement period (Figure 6.7), and the fall of the overnight rate to the level of the deposit facility confirm the existence of excess liquidity, if asymmetrically distributed. Then, in April 2009, the central bank reintroduced auction repo operations with one month maturity and full allotment to provide short-term liquidity at the policy rate. Improved liquidity conditions also impacted on debt management, allowing the Treasury to borrow at longer tenures.

The NBR (2009b) narrated the changes in its operational framework as part of a broader strategy to strengthen the monetary transmission mechanism in line with New Keynesian theoretical premises. It explained that the international crisis had increased money-market volatility and disrupted its normal functioning, and along with that the transmission mechanism from the policy rate to short-term market rates and then to the range of assets relevant for aggregate demand control. In its new quality as creditor to the banking system, the central bank regained control over the previously impaired transmission

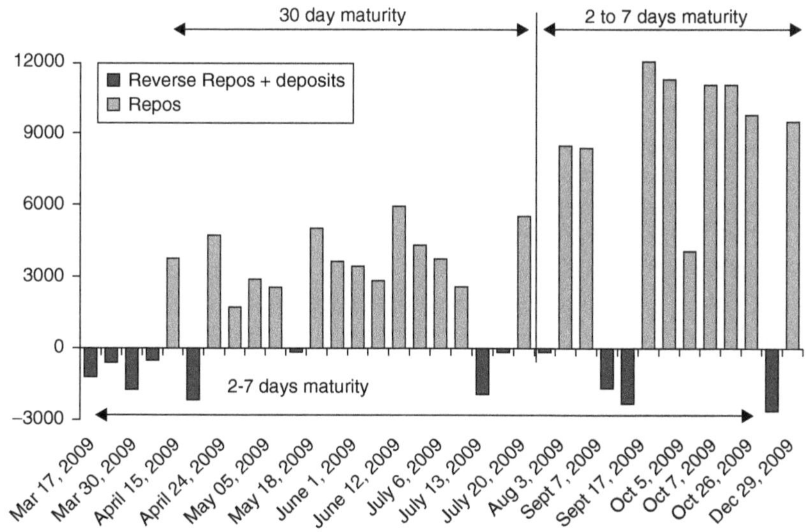

Figure 6.7 Open Market Operations, 2009. Mil. RON
Source: Author's computation, NBR data.

mechanism. However, rather than improved control, for five months (until September 2009) after the Vienna agreement, the pre-crisis normality was reinstated. Interbank money markets suggested improved liquidity conditions: neither bid nor offer rates approached the upper limit of the fluctuation interval (the marginal lending rate) but fell to the floor (the deposit rate) at the end of every maintenance period as banks tried to dispose of excess liquidity (see Figure 6.5).

How then to reconcile the pattern of overnight rates (implying excess liquidity) with the central bank's new declared position of net creditor to banks? For years, it had pointed to its net debtor position to explain its difficulties in bringing market rates in line with its policy rate. What was the obstacle now? The key, I suggest, is to be found in the relationship with the Treasury's debt management strategy. As lingering monetarist sensitivities prevented direct monetization, with the IMF's blessing the NBR inaugurated a neoliberal approach to quantitative easing. The repo operations introduced during April combined the Federal Reserve's approach to quantitative easing with the ECB's insistence on the banking channel in order to expand the funding available for commercial banks' operations on the Treasury market.

Traditionally, quantitative easing has been regarded as a crisis option: once policy interest rates are very low, the central bank purchases government or commercial paper, a policy solution proposed by Keynes to reduce the cost of borrowing and to induce increased business investment. After April 2009, the NBR chose an indirect route: through repo operations at the policy rate, it allowed commercial banks to access liquidity to finance primary Treasury bills issues. For instance, on April 15, commercial banks borrowed RON 3.7 billion from the NBR at 10 percent return and one month maturity, of which they used, on the same day, RON 2.76 to purchase a new issue of Treasury bills at three-month maturity and 11.5 percent return. Throughout April 2009 only, commercial banks lent RON 6 billion to the government, financed through RON 10 billion repo operations (Figure 6.7), a strategy with potentially increasing returns as the NBR would reduce its policy rates. This pattern of liquidity injections continued until September 2009, when a political crisis again changed the central bank's strategy.

Liquidity management remained dominated by exchange-rate concerns. While the increased global liquidity saw the return of carry trades on regional currency markets, the Romanian leu remained around its March 2009 level even though it offered the highest yield advantage in the EU. Despite the concession it made banks for public-debt financing, the NBR remained reluctant to validate speculative activity on currency markets. To counteract the pressures of financialization in currency markets, the central bank offered commercial banks a trade-off: "appropriate investment opportunity" in primary Treasury issues.

That the central bank prioritized exchange-rate dynamics over the sustainability of public debt was also revealed in its reluctance to act as the government's foreign-exchange agent. The first foreign-exchange revenues for the government came in July 2009 when the European Commission disbursed the first €1.5 billion of its €5 billion commitments, further supplemented in August with €1.65 billion foreign-currency loans from domestic banks (a syndicated loan plus euro-denominated bonds). Nevertheless, the government perceived these as insufficient to offset financing pressures and negotiated a change in the IMF's mechanism of disbursement. Finally, on September 22, the IMF accepted to divert half of the second tranche (US$1.36 billion) from the central bank to the government. Yet such substantial foreign-exchange revenues marked no substantial change in domestic liquidity conditions.

The pressures on the public debt combined with the highly contractionary macroeconomic stance agreed with the IMF contributed to a political crisis. In September 2009, the government was dissolved, and Romania held presidential elections in November 2009 without a prime minister endorsed by both president and parliament. While it is tempting to link the social and political tensions to a singularly divisive political system, Cordero (2009) found the same patterns in three other countries under an IMF agreement at the time (Hungary, Latvia, and Ukraine). He attributed the unrest to the strong economic contractions imposed by the IMF programs in the three countries. Thus the political crisis can be read as a *consequence* of contractionary economic policies. As the country prepared for presidential elections in November 2009, the economic crisis became a hot potato, as no party wished to assume responsibility for unemployment and the cuts in public-sector wages. With the political crisis, the Romanian press and public opinion again called for the appointment of the central-bank governor (reappointed in September 2009 for another five-year term) as prime minister. Isărescu refused, according to his adviser Adrian Vasilescu, for personal, political, and economic reasons. The experience of the 1999–2000 mandate showed that a strong prime minister required the backing of a strong political party, and, most importantly, the economic battle facing Romania in 2010 was primarily fought on the central-bank front. The Governor was needed to guide the central bank in the battle (Simionescu 2009).

Indeed, the central bank's response to the political crisis demonstrated how fresh the October 2008 speculative attack remained in institutional memory. Concerned that the political crisis would ignite speculative behaviour, the NBR tightened liquidity even further. To increase banks' dependency on its liquidity operations (and to contain their activity as counterparty to nonresident interest), it reduced the maturity of its liquidity injections to two days (see Figure 6.7). Consequently, despite growing international risk appetite and substantial yield advantage, exchange-rate pressures and financing conditions worsened. Reuters (2009a) reported that the government rejected a series of oversubscribed bids at several RON denominated tenders during September and October, considering the yields demanded too high. Additionally, commercial banks voiced increasing complaints that, despite a series of policy-rate cuts, the central bank was tightening money-market liquidity to limit currency trades. Indeed, by September, Romania was again experiencing liquidity shortages, driving banks to borrow record high volumes from the NBR's expensive discount window (see Figure 6.4). Confronted with such uncertainties, commercial banks would only lend to government at rates above the policy rate (around 10 percent, 2 percent above the policy rate). In contrast, the Hungarian government's short-term financing rate (around 6.4 percent) was below the central bank's policy rate (7 percent) during the same period.

Thus, the central bank's approach to quantitative easing turned Keynes's advice on its head: its approach to liquidity management constructed public debt financing as an important source of returns for private financial capital. Still, the relationship between the central bank and commercial banks remained frayed by concerns of potential pressures on currency markets. Such an outcome can be interpreted in two different ways. If the fear of nonresident speculation was the driving force, then the central bank's approach to liquidity management during 2009 could only be described as self-defeating strategy. To exploit investors' risk appetite, liquidity policies have to be supportive. A second possibility would be that behind the unpredictable changes in liquidity management hid a new attitude toward exchange-rate dynamics. As appreciations were no longer viewed as a benign phenomenon, the central bank chose to resist the carry-trade activity driving regional peers post-March 2009.

The second explanation would constitute a commendable attempt at tackling the pre-crisis patterns of vulnerability if it did not inflict such damage on the public-sector expenditure. But could the central bank be held accountable for public-debt dynamics (where it is not formally required to do so)? The mainstream reading, well exposed by the IMF, casts questions of public-debt dynamics in terms of market preferences and rational behaviour. An expanding fiscal burden leads market players, particularly in less developed financial systems, to demand higher returns on government bonds to compensate for risks to debt sustainability, further crowding out private investment (Spilimbergo et al. 2008). Through this framing, the high returns paid by the Romanian treasury arose from its failure to adjust expenditure to prevailing economic conditions in the short run and insufficient progress on the financial liberalization front in structural terms. Hence, it was questionable that Romania chose to nearly double its targeted deficit when its economy contracted by 8 percent throughout 2009. A more energetic fiscal adjustment would have improved public debt sustainability, to be complemented by structural policies to address the institutional drawbacks affecting an optimal functioning of financial markets.

On the contrary, Post-Keynesians have long argued against the framing of public-debt issues through all powerful markets. As Keynes had successfully argued, coordinating monetary and fiscal policies is crucial. Crowding out then arises from the deliberate policy choices of the central bank (Arestis and Sawyer 2004). In other words, it is in the central bank's reach, although not in its mandate, to shape questions of debt sustainability. In the last instance, the strategies of monetary management, rather than the fiscal activism per se, are responsible for the crowding out.

Would a different approach be possible? MNB's monetary management provides a good example.

6.3.3 Central banking during Hungary's 2009 crisis

Hungary was the first EU country to receive IMF assistance in November 2008. The emergency bailout reflected increasing concerns with the level of public debt and commercial banks' foreign-exchange lending. At the time, Hungary's public debt amounted to 80 percent of GDP (reflecting previous years of large budget deficits), compared with Romania's 20 percent of GDP. Similarly, over 70 percent of household debt was denominated in foreign currency, mostly in Swiss francs. The structural characteristics of its currency markets amplified vulnerability to global liquidity pressures: nonresident activity in portfolio investments amounted to 38 percent of GDP, twice higher than any other CEE country (IMF 2009b). The dangers of this exposure materialized throughout the post-Lehman stage so that during March 2009, a difficult month for Eastern Europe, Hungary appeared singularly ill equipped to weather the crisis. Standard & Poor's downgraded its debt outlook, signalling its concerns at the pace of the reforms agreed with the IMF in November 2008. Bond yields rose to a record high. Nevertheless, three months later, the country successfully launched a €1 billion bond on international money markets, and six months later it was enjoying a bond rally that cut yields on government debt by half (Reuters 2009b).

Hungary succeeded better than Romania in defeating pessimistic expectations (even if the social adjustments and output contractions were similar) because of the radically different set of policies adopted by the central bank: quantitative easing combined with a highly predictable strategy of liquidity management that sought to restore nonresident interest and to enable nonresident transactions in Hungarian assets.

The MNB adopted inflation-targeting in 2001. As early preparation for the Eurozone entry, it chose to peg the forint to the euro in a fluctuation band similar to the ERMII mechanism. Yet in early 2007 the central bank voiced concerns that the exchange-rate mechanism was conflicting with its inflation-targeting regime. Although cast in terms of credibility and instrument independence, the central bank implicitly acknowledged that the trading band did not allow the currency to appreciate at a speed that would support the inflation target. A second twist came from the considerable fiscal tightening pursued after 2006, when the budget deficit rocketed to 9.2 percent of GDP, the highest in the EU. The argument that an exchange-rate appreciation would limit the need for matching interest rate hikes eventually won, and Hungary moved to a flexible exchange-rate regime in February 2008. The desired appreciation followed swiftly.

Before the crisis, MNB's day-to-day practices of monetary management broadly replicated the Romanian approach. Since 1995, its exchange-rate strategy produced a structural excess of liquidity on the money market. The main policy instrument, two-week MNB bills, was used to mop up money-market liquidity. The overnight money-market rate, as in the Romanian case, moved at times outside the standing facilities corridor, reflecting unpredictable autonomous liquidity factors (see Figure 6.8). Unlike Romania, the MNB imposed a much tighter standing-facilities corridor: excess reserves parked overnight in the deposit facility were rewarded with 50 basis points less under the

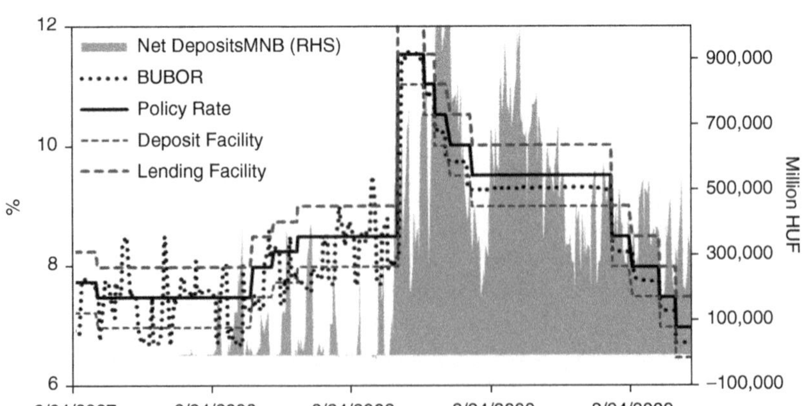

Figure 6.8 Policy, money market interest rates and net overnight deposits with the central bank, Hungary, 2007–2009

Source: Compiled with data from the National Bank of Hungary.

policy rate, while discount window lending was charged at 50 basis points above the policy rate.

In the tense aftermath of the Lehman collapse, the MNB radically changed its approach to liquidity management. Similarly high liquidity preference immediately after October 2008 saw banks substituting interbank market transactions with the MNB overnight deposit facility (see Figure 6.8). The MNB's immediate policy priority was to restore interbank liquidity. It proceeded to inject forint liquidity and simultaneously instituted a series of temporary measures to ease credit conditions[105] (IMF 2009b). Essential to this newfound activism was the relationship with public debt management. Against the NBR's explicit refusal, the MNB set to monetize public debt, either through direct purchases of government paper from primary dealers or indirectly by exchanging the governments' foreign borrowing for forint liquidity. Put differently, since October 2008 the MNB engaged into quantitative easing. By June 2009, its balance sheet had doubled year on year, with the increase on the asset side driven by external assets, and by two-week MNB bills on the liabilities side (Balogh 2009). During the same period, the Romanian central bank's balance sheet contracted.

A far more harmonious relationship between the central bank and fiscal authorities also reflected in the negotiations with the IMF. Whereas the Romanian central bank insisted that IMF money be disbursed into its reserves, Hungary successfully convinced the IMF to lend directly to the Treasury (the first two tranches). Since the central bank acted as the government's foreign-exchange agent, all foreign-currency loans were exchanged for forint liquidity. The asset-side expansion thus occurred because the central bank monetized external public debt. When improved sentiment allowed the government to return on international money markets, any accompanying issue of foreign currency bonds would further increase forint liquidity in the system (Balogh 2009).

According to Balogh (2009), the government's financing decisions, monetized by the central bank, determined banking-sector liquidity (government forint spending increased banks' reserve accounts with the central bank). In contrast to its Romanian peer, the MNB offered a predictable vehicle for the banks' excess liquidity: it accepted all bids of banks wishing to deposit liquidity at weekly auctions with a two-week instrument priced at the policy rate. Sterilization volumes tripled throughout 2009 (see Figure 6.9). As the MNB's net position vis-à-vis the money markets reflected increasingly large forint

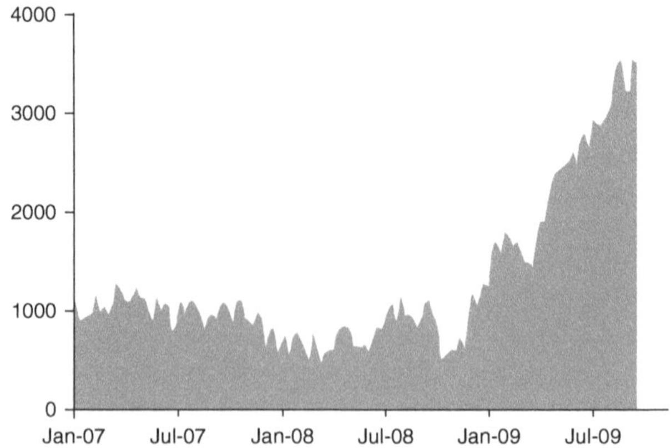

Figure 6.9 Sterilization operations, 2weeks MNB bills (HUF bn)
Source: Compiled with data from the National Bank of Hungary.

absorptions, overnight market rates stabilized close to the policy rate (see Figure 6.8).

It is important to emphasize that the Hungarian strategy proved successful in restoring carry-trade activity only when global liquidity conditions improved after March 2009. The MNB's willingness to offer "appropriate investment opportunities" allowed it to engage in an aggressive interest-rate-easing cycle below pre-crisis levels without reducing foreign interest. In fact, the IMF reported increases in nonresident demand for HUF-denominated assets (IMF 2009c). The improved outlook, combined with expectations of continued monetary easing further translated into better financing conditions for the government, driving yields across the maturity spectrum below the policy rate (Reuters 2009b).

The MNB tailored its strategy to restoring the attractiveness of its domestic markets. As with its developed (neoliberal) counterparts, coordination with the government's debt-management strategies proved crucial. Unexpectedly, the IMF did not raise any real opposition to the blatant contradiction of monetarist ideas embodied by quantitative easing. This allowed the central bank to harness higher public financing requirements to restore banking-sector liquidity and to provide vehicles for exploiting yield advantages once the global tensions passed their peak. This could be interpreted as a tacit endorsement of measures to restore processes of financialization. On the contrary, the Romanian policy responses have been defined by the central bank's attempts to reconfigure its relationship with financialized money and currency markets. While it did eventually set to ease liquidity pressures, the compromise has been uneasy, perhaps a proof of the difficulties involved in retaking control of domestic money markets. The NBR maintained a highly discretionary approach to monetary management, varying the maturity of its liquidity injections in line with its perceptions of potential downward pressures on the domestic currency. The public sector fell victim to the central bank's attempts to redefine its relationship with wholesale banking. Debt management, inadequate by omission or commission, has offset increasing debt-servicing costs with cuts in public-sector spending and unemployment.

6.4 Conclusion

The analytical focus on the central bank's practices enriches both theoretical and political economy discussions of crisis. Interest-rate decisions or political risk alone are not enough to interpret exchange-rate movements, either along or against the uncovered interest-rate parity. Strategies of liquidity management are equally important.

Thus, the third year of crisis in international financial market proved the worse for CEE. The regional vulnerability to crisis arose from the normalization of financialized regimes of monetary management with very few exceptions (the Czech Republic a notable one). This combined the pursuit of exchange-rate appreciations with an increasing financialization of banking sectors and currency markets. To protect banks' balance sheets, the IMF programs in the region sanctioned interest-rate decisions geared to exchange-rate stability. The advice proved successful after March 2009, once quantitative easing undertaken by central banks in developed countries restored risk appetite and carry trades in the region. The only new member state (of the EU) that bucked the coordinated strengthening across the region was Romania.

Several conclusions can be drawn from a comparative assessment of Romania and Hungary. The first refers to the political economy of the IMF's SBAs. As the previous chapters explored in detail, the IMF's leverage in policy negotiations depends on the configurations of power on the domestic policy scene. The above comparison suggests that countries have more room for manoeuvre than commonly acknowledged – perhaps only for policy measures aimed to re-establish financialization such as the quantitative easing strategy that Hungary developed. Indeed, in other policy fields, the IMF retained its dogmatic concern with fiscal contractions and public wage bills, seeking to prevent a turn to full-blown Keynesian fiscal activism. It also insisted on tailoring interest-rate decisions to exchange-rate stability, contradicting its earlier insistence (documented in the previous chapters) that exchange-rate concerns had no place in an inflation-targeting regime.

Indeed, both countries had to commit to aggressive demand contractions, even more pronounced in the case of Hungary (who maintained the highly contractionary 2009 budget-deficit target even when data confirmed output contraction was far worse than estimated). From a global standpoint, the IMF's approach (contraction in effective demand through overvalued exchange rates, fiscal tightening, and wage cuts) forces borrowing rather than lending countries to adjust (see Cordero 2009 for a critical account of the IMF programs in Hungary, Latvia, and Ukraine).

Another important question to be asked is whether the above analysis suggests a return to pre-crisis rules constitutes a better policy choice than seeking to redefine the old rules of engagement. The Hungarian strategy was to offer short-term investment opportunities in the sovereign debt market and the sterilization operations of the central bank. Resuscitating financialization required government institutions to participate in the political (re)construction of markets and financial relations. Such trust in the ability of finance-led growth regimes to avoid future volatilities is puzzling. If anything, the CEE's subprime moment confirms the vulnerability of growth models grounded in consumption and credit booms, especially if inflation-targeting regimes tying interest-rate decisions into speculative activity in currency markets lead to real exchange-rate appreciations. A more nuanced position toward exchange-rate dynamics is important not only for competitiveness considerations but also to reduce the incentives for single-currency carry trades and foreign-currency borrowing.

The Romanian central bank's strategy throughout 2009 was not equally consistent. First, the central bank recognized that the financialization of currency markets posed threats to exchange-rate stability. Policy speeches became a platform for warning "the banks in London" (i.e. nonresident investors) that the central bank would not be fooled again (Vasilescu 2010). The Romanian approach to liquidity management can hardly be construed as a systematic attempt to de-financialize. The central bank rehashed its 1999 crisis strategy: tighten money market liquidity to contain currency speculations, so that again money markets became "the cemetery " of public debt management – just as it did in 1999. Without central bank support, volatility in global liquidity can result in sovereign debt crisis. If the central bank continues to commit the same errors it made after 1999, then it is most likely that Romania will have to go back to the IMF (or some lender of last resort) yet again unless it adopts the Euro. The difficulties that Greece was experiencing at the time of writing (May 2010) might lessen enthusiasm for surrendering policy autonomy to the ECB.

7
Conclusion and Implications

Monetary policy choices are inevitably political under any economic or political paradigm and policy regime. Central banks cannot vanish from "technocratic" policy processes, as either automatic adjustment narratives or the rhetoric of free markets triumphantly suggest. Instead, the central bank functions within, and works to reproduce, ideologically informed strategies of economic management.

Critical to substantiating this claim, it was shown, was to integrate conventional economic analysis with a discursive approach that treats policies as contested and contingent, linking struggles over the construction of the "crisis" and its "solutions" to configurations of power and interest groups in policy spaces. Karl Niebyl had already pointed in that direction with his methodological proposition (1946) for studying central banking as a three-dimensional process: theorizing, policy, and the reality of institutions of finance and production. Niebyl's framework was combined with a politics of meaning to develop a nexus of theory, policy narratives, and practices of central banking. Such a redefinition allows conceptual precision by acknowledging that policy and "reality" are mutually constitutive, while retaining Niebyl's fundamental insight that policy does not arise from rational choices between various scenarios. As a methodological tool to this epistemological position, a narrative approach allows mapping the discursive frames involved in the production of a crisis. Narratives have homogenizing effects, imposing a certain order of interpretation over a collection of events. Its ideological function, then, resides not in what it includes but in what it leaves out of the story, a point well illustrated by the consolidation of fundamental paradigms of monetary policy through Keynes and Friedman's policy advocacy.

With neoliberalism and financialization as standpoints, Romania provided a fertile case for a critical scrutiny of the role played by its central bank in the reconstitution of the post-socialist economies as neoliberal economies from 1990 to 2008 – starting from the premise that even though domestic politics mediates the translation of neoliberal ideas into policy measures so that each country has its own trajectory, neoliberal paradigms of economic management will produce a core of macroeconomic characteristics common across the region. This analytical angle allowed to position CEE within the crisis in financialized globalization.

7.1 On Romania, models and practices

An emphasis on power and discursive struggles in the policy space prompted a different set of reflections on the process of institutionalizing a central bank after the fall of the Romanian communist regime. Standard monetary-policy analysis, described as an instrumentalist approach in policy studies, would have produced an account of the successes or failures of the three policy strategies deployed in Romania and subsequently assessed the validity of the underlying theoretical conceptualizations. It would have attempted to elucidate whether the shifts in policy regimes – from broad money targeting (1990–1997) to high-powered money targeting (1997–2005) to inflation-targeting (2005–2008) could be constructed as attempts to improve policy. To formalize economic dynamics in formerly planned economies would have raised considerable but not insurmountable methodological challenges. However, a different (epistemological) route was proposed.

The historical changes in the dominant narratives of monetary processes, underlying changes in economic paradigms along Kuhnian lines, saw the Romanian transformation beginning at a time when monetarism dominated international policy discourse. Its equilibrium discourses and advocacy of rules-bound monetary policy dovetailed well with and legitimized neoliberalism, a discourse committed to market mechanisms, deregulated economies, and private finance.

Critical conceptualizations distinguish between various phases in neoliberalism: an initial normative (Hay 2004) or roll-back stage (Peck and Tickell 2002) focused on dismantling the foundations of the Keynesian state and economic paradigm, to a roll-out stage that normalizes neoliberal practices of economic (and social) management which further reflect in institutional reconfigurations. The degree of success in permeating developing countries depended on the dynamics of interaction with international development interventions of the Washington Consensus type. In CEE, Smith (2002) argued, international policy advice has been instrumental in scripting post-socialist transformations as naturalized processes of neoliberal marketization, in a first instance through the IMF's strategic positioning in crisis management. Indeed, IMF's monetarist policy advice constructed the central bank as a point of entry for neoliberal agendas of economic management, according to the principle that "rational" policies will prevail if formulated without the intervention of politics (Woods 2006). Central-bank independence has served this depoliticizing operation well, substantiating claims of depoliticized central-bank expertise against the politics of government expenditure and taxation.

Yet a neoliberal economy does not simply arise from spontaneously emerging market forces or neoliberal institutions, as critical studies of neoliberalism as rule of governance sometimes imply (Hart, 2006). The messy process of implementation as Mosse (2005) put it, suggests a complex relationship between policy practices and policy intention that recasts the policy narratives of the period as follows.

(1) The 1990–1997 period could be broadly read as the era of normative, roll-back neoliberalism. Monetary policy measures engendered concerted efforts to discredit the idea that any form of planned economic activity, as embodied in the SOEs, could function under market principles. Indeed, in policy discourse, SOEs emerged as a powerful political force that resisted restructuring and ascribed a quasifiscal objective to exchange-rate and monetary-policy choices.

A first step in this direction was to redefine the "transition macroeconomic problem" through an excess aggregate demand narrative. This constituted a generic, centrally planned economy through two theoretical concepts: the monetary overhang that premised an excess of liquidity arising from pent-up demand in consumer markets, and the soft-budget constraint, which would have reproduced such excess liquidity even after price liberalizations unless the appropriate contractionary monetary policy was firmly in place. These legitimized the austerity discourse underlying the IMF's policy advice and translated into tight monetary targets specified as quantitative performance criteria in the four IMF SBAs.

Throughout the period, the NBR engaged in a continuous struggle to defend its monetarist interpretation of macroeconomic dynamics. This was a complex task, for notwithstanding discursive commitments, monetarism was translated to policy practice in different degrees.

Indeed, while monetarist-informed measures created liquidity shortages where policy discourse saw excess liquidity, produced repeated payment blockages instead of liberating a "repressed" financial system, contracted industrial production instead of producing growth, and fed exchange-rate devaluations into inflationary pressures, the repeated failure to conclude IMF agreements was interpreted as evidence of insufficient commitment to monetarist principles.

However, governments throughout this period showed a remarkable initial willingness to comply with IMF conditionality. That such commitments vanished has to be understood against the IMF's well-documented tendency for overly contractionary targets so that program completion is the exception rather than the rule in IMF programs. Indeed, there comes a point, as the Romanian experience has shown, where no rhetoric of discipline or the desirability of markets can rationalize, or indeed legitimize, the profound economic (social and political) dislocations produced by austerity policies. At that point, measuring policy performance in terms of compliance with IMF conditionality becomes necessary for the construction of the "good" policies/"bad" politics dichotomy. It is not only a necessary argumentative technique against policy contestations but also essential for rearticulating the necessity of neoliberal reform. Dislocations are thus attributed to micro "distortions" and domestic politics rather than the economics of the policy advice (Bofinger et al. 1997).

The central bank's reactions to repeated SBA failures were twofold. Policy learning and institutional reflexivity expanded the policy repertoire in order to continuously (re)produce and legitimize the monetarist narratives. On the one hand, its policy argumentation focused on interpreting the past measures as accommodative and formulating the future policy stances as necessarily tightening. The dynamics of high-powered money, for instance, brought into question such an articulation, for they suggest accommodative liquidity practices and tight-money discourses, and vice versa. On the other hand, every SBA expanded policy repertoires, not always in accordance with monetarist logics and sometimes rather against them, a sign that not the monetarist model per se but the overall push for neoliberalization was structuring policy action. Nevertheless, these extensions outside the monetarist discourses opened policy to contestation. For instance, when the interest rates on central-bank loans were raised to levels unusual even for very high-inflation environments, it prompted strong criticism from the government, the productive sector, and policy analysts.

The ambiguity characterizing the relationship between policy discourse and practices was even more evident in exchange-rate decisions. Policy texts went to great lengths to dismiss, deny, or marginalize the extent and speed to which exchange-rate devaluations were transmitted to prices, without questioning whether the search for price stability was consistent with a market-determined exchange-rate or devaluation decisions structured through equilibrium discourses. However, the NBR repeatedly intervened to prevent a fast depreciation of the exchange rate, its practices constrained by conflicting demands: the control of inflation, which required exchange-rate stabilization against a structural trade deficit, and the IMF pressures for complying with commitments to flexibility.

Industrial interests were important, and at times powerful, policy actors. Yet a coherent industrial strategy that recognized the crucial role of the exchange rate and of a financial system orientated toward recapitalizing the productive system, as the early Commission for Transition proposed, was not pursued consistently. Instead, monetarist discourses and practices sought to subject large-scale state-owned industries to the disciplining hand of the market. A policy package systematically targeting every avenue for protecting profits not only contributed to the decapitalization of large state production but transformed liquidity problems into solvency problems. The emergence of impatient finance in the state-owned sector, underpinned by the central bank's practices of liquidity tightening, played an important role in the deindustrialization of the Romanian economy.

(2) The 1997–2005 period the 1997 SBA was instrumental in producing the shift to neoliberalism's constructive phase. Redefined policy narratives sanctioned a managed exchange-rate policy, albeit one confined to the requirements of high-powered money targeting, and a fiscal policy disciplined by the market. Whereas the economics of stabilization predicated on the existence of excess liquidity before 1997 instead resulted in liquidity shortages, afterwards claims of tight monetary control to explain policy successes contrasted the structural excess of liquidity on wholesale money markets which the new practices of sterilized currency interventions produced.

Essentially, starting with 1997, the banking sector's carry-trade activity would become central to monetary-policy processes. Underlying this was a reconstitution of the relationship between money, currency, and the treasury markets, shaped by the NBR's practices of monetary management and the increasing role played by global finance present in this stage through foreign-owned banks. Sterilizations consolidated as the primary vehicle for speculative returns, locking currency and money-market interventions into engineering exchange-rate appreciations.

Indeed, this period saw the normalization of a neoliberal mode of economic governance. The exchange-rate strategy aimed at ensuring real appreciations set in motion the financialization of the currency market: capital flows would become the primary driver of exchange-rate movements, a trend reflected in the growing importance (and volume traded) of the interbank foreign currency market. Practices of sterilized interventions combined with currency appreciations and expanding current-account deficits increased vulnerability to international sentiment. Further, banking rationality shifted toward financialized accumulation. During the years of normative neoliberalism, the activity of the state-owned banking sector was constrained on the one hand by the NBR's attempts to tighten liquidity and by the government's attempts to revive the agricultural and productive sector through directed credit on the other hand. Coupled with a low confidence in the domestic currency and, consequently, a low monetization of the economy, banks were dependent on central bank refinancing and the bank's willingness to assume the lender-of-last-resort function. After 1997, the discourses and practices that rewarded speculation and punished credit for productive purposes produced an asymmetric distribution of liquidity on the wholesale money market that would further consolidate the financialization of banks. Access to foreign capital became fundamental to profit-making and even survival, as the 1998–1999 episode suggested. The narration of 1998–1999 as a moment of crisis not only hinted to the vulnerability associated with the increased exposure to global finance but revealed how practices of monetary management addressing speculative pressures contributed to further subjugating the management of liquidity to the exigencies of transnational financial actors. The NBR's "market-driven" solution for discouraging speculation inflicted liquidity shortages and expensive refinancing on money markets, producing a banking crisis, and the associated privatizations, that further opened up the banking sector to transnational actors. The high-yield differential combined with expectations of continuous exchange-rate appreciation further contributed to the changing configuration of credit and debt, with an increased euroization of the assets side of the banking sector that belied claims of tight monetary control and bubbles in consumer credit and housing markets. Competitive pressures saw banks innovating single-currency trades – borrowing abroad from parent banks/interbank markets and lending in host countries in the same currencies. Currency risks were thus transferred to optimistic consumers, simultaneously producing new challenges for central banks – any competitiveness enhancing effects of devaluations would be offset by the destabilizing impact on domestic borrowers.

In sum, this period saw monetarist narratives legitimizing practices tailored to attracting speculative capital and thus tied financial stability considerations into the choices of transnational market actors. Normalized neoliberalism consolidated its institutional effects, producing institutional configurations where central-bank practices respond to the exigencies of financialized accumulation and its ideological effects: economic management depicted as a "technical set of devices" (Hay 2004) for managing an open economy. The public trust in the Romanian central-bank governor – the apolitical technocrat – testifies to the appeal of technocratic explanations of policy-making. The shift to inflation-targeting, in Romania and elsewhere, marked a further move in this direction. The global success of rollout neoliberalism was simultaneously changing discursive regimes in international financial markets. Inflation-targeting, the monetary policy regime that explicitly incorporates interest-rate management as a technique for managing aggregate demand, promised scientific methods for building international consensus on optimal policies and safe integration into global financial markets. The NBR switched to inflation-targeting in August 2005.

Exploring the shifts in policy discourses and practices produced by the new policy regime suggested that, as in the period of high-powered money targeting, policy models function at best to legitimize rather than provide a consistent guide to policy actions. As elsewhere, the NBR couched policy rhetoric through inflation-targeting discourse. Yet efforts to bring institutional "reality" in line with theoretical conceptualizations had a limited success before the global crisis of financialized accumulation. Prior to 2008, the central bank failed in its few attempts to reconstitute liquidity management according to inflation-targeting requirements. However, despite the contradictions inherent in the rhetorical deployment of inflation-targeting models, these functioned to enlist interpretations and to stabilize the discursive system. Inflation-targeting rhetoric substantiated contestations where practices of liquidity management deviated from commitments to financialization, as, for instance, in September 2005 and, more pronounced, in October 2008.

Everything changed in 2008. Global financial dynamics showed the inherent contradictions and vulnerabilities engendered by neoliberal accumulation strategies, but manifested differently on the Romanian policy scene.

The last stages of capital-account liberalization that allowed nonresident activity marked a new stage in the financialization of currency and money markets. The banking sector lost its primacy in channelling speculative activities on money and currency markets, as an increasingly heterogeneous trader community produced different patterns of investment behaviour. By 2007, carry-trade activity dominated currency trading, increasing the likelihood of unwinding in periods of market turbulence. Simultaneously, demand for liquidity on the interbank money market also reflected commercial banks' activities as counterparty to nonresident investments. Such changes, it turned out in October 2008, produced new challenges for the central bank.

On the back of substantial carry-trade returns, the domestic currency appreciated systematically until the summer of 2008. However, increasing speculative pressures against the domestic currency produced patterns of volatility unseen since the 1999 episode. Short-selling evolved into a fully-blown speculative attack in October 2008, and the central bank's response echoed its 1998–1999 tactics. It took buying positions on the currency market and simultaneously drained liquidity from wholesale markets, with the attendant substantial increases in overnight and swap rates. The contradictions embedded in neoliberal rationalities of financialized accumulation became apparent during this episode: while neoliberal structuring of liquidity-management practices contributed substantially to increased financial instability in times of steady speculative inflows, in October 2008 the NBR refused to validate speculative returns precisely because these would have endangered financial stability. Thus, while central banks in developed financial systems were engaging in aggressive liquidity injections in wholesale and securitized markets, the Romanian central bank presented liquidity tightening and the attending hikes in the cost of liquidity as the only solution to tackle speculative attacks.

7.2 On Central and Eastern Europe: Same old game?

The timeline of crisis responses in developed countries suggest that all the compromises, inconsistencies, and contradictions have yet to produce a crisis *of* neoliberalism. As the 1990s Anglo-American recession or the Asian crisis transformed, rather than subverted, neoliberal paradigms of macroeconomic governance (Peck and Tickell 2002), the 2007–2009 crisis has again transformed rather than destroyed neoliberalism.

The IMF's chief economist summarized the lessons of the crisis: a return to the New Keynesian consensus with a more explicit focus on regulation once unconventional policy measures have produced the desired outcome (Blanchard et al. 2010). The crisis in financialized globalization is increasingly explained as a failure of regulation, rather than policies or accumulation regimes while central banks have stepped in (through quantitative/credit easing) to regenerate finance-led growth regimes. The reports that CEE was the most attractive region for the large carry trades underpinning the March 2009 change in global liquidity conditions further confirms that the region chose not to decouple from its embracement of international financial integration – with the possible exception of Romania.

The Romanian experience, particularly when considered in contrast to neighbouring Hungary, revealed that central banks can refuse to play the role of vehicles for neoliberal intentions and financialized practices. Even where neoliberalism successfully permeated policy spaces (and it has done so in Eastern Europe more than anywhere else), resistance to its pressures is possible. Yet the Romanian central bank's flirting with resistance unfortunately resumed to currency markets.

In contrast to Hungary's highly transparent and predictable approach to liquidity management combined with quantitative easing, the Romanian central bank (a) limited the government's access to IMF loans and (b) let the government take its foreign-exchange revenues (eventually obtained from the IMF, European Commission and private sources) on the interbank currency market to avoid the expansion in its balance sheet because (c) it took a highly discretionary position toward money markets in the pursuit of a tight control of money-market liquidity which (d) further functioned as constraint on the Treasury's ability to raise RON funds domestically and (e) limited the scope for carry-trade activity on the currency market. Would it be possible at this point for Romania to seek an alternative model that does not imply a trade-off between currency stability and public-debt sustainability?

As UNCTAD (2004, 2007) pointed out, there are successful experiences with non-neoliberal approaches to economic management. Asian countries have applied variations of the following: a central bank concerned with ensuring competitive exchange rates and liquidity policies supportive of internal debt dynamics. Monetary policy ceases to be the primary tool for stabilizing inflation, instead anchored through institutionally specific income policies. All these together curtail the scope for short-term arbitraging and keep appreciations in check. Furthermore, the Asian fast recovery throughout 2009 offers an even-more-powerful reason to contemplate heterodox macroeconomic policies.

The obstacles might seem insurmountable: Romania, as its CEE neighbours, is constrained by its EU membership (and commitments to adopt the Euro), the commitments to the World Trade Organization, a highly divisive politics, a foreign-owned banking sector, and a central bank reluctant to engage into overtly political strategies that would challenge the attempts to cast policy as objective. While one must be realistic enough to think the impossible, it is undeniable that a strong state is essential for articulating a new growth model along East Asian lines. By the end of 2009, none of these reconfigurations seemed possible because central-bank practices had such detrimental effects on public finances. A state with weak public finances is not a state that can contemplate, formulate, and argue alternative approaches. If serious about its intentions to decouple currency markets from international speculative activity, the National Bank of Romania will need to renounce its susceptibility to neoliberal suspicions of government spending. It would also need to reconsider its monetary policy strategy. The inflation-targeting regime contains an unsolvable tension in the interest-rate policy because tailoring interest-rate movements to inflation targets under a flexible exchange-rate regime invariably produces exchange-rate appreciations if global liquidity conditions stimulate risk appetite.

Furthermore, as the Greek tragedy unfolds in international bond markets, the CEE countries could contemplate the heresy of remaining outside the Euro area. Surrendering policy autonomy to a supranational institution without a corresponding fiscal authority or a well-designed European mechanism for assisting countries in crisis has dented the appeal of the Eurozone.

Appendix

Liberalization of medium and long term inflows	1999	• Medium and long term international trade loans extended by non-residents to residents • Medium and long term financial loans extended by non-residents to residents
Liberalization of capital inflows with limited balance of payment impact	*2001–02*	• *Resident's real estate and direct investments abroad;* • *Romanian financial instruments* on international capital markets* • *Non-resident collaterals extended to residents;* • *Personal capital transfers (donations, inheritances, non resident short term loans extended to residents);* • *Medium and long term international trade loans extended by residents to non-residents.* • *Capital transfers linked to life and credit insurance contracts*
Liberalization of capital movements related to insurance contracts and other capital flows with a significant impact on the real sector	2003	• Resident transactions with foreign financial instruments*; • Financial loans with less than a year maturity extended by non-residents to residents; • Financial and personal loans extended by residents to non residents; • resident collaterals extended to non residents.
	2004	• Foreign financial instruments* on the domestic capital market
	11.04.2005	• Non residents domestic currency deposit account operations, held with domestic credit institutions.
Liberalization of capital inflows with a substantial balance of payment impact	*20.07.2005*	• *Current account and deposit operations of entities residing outside Romania.*
	01.09.2006	• *trading financial instruments on the money market;*

*) including mutual funds instruments (OPC)

Appendix 1 The timetable for capital account liberalization, Romania
Source: NBR (translated by author).

Notes

1. The question was asked at a congressional hearing on the deep financial turmoil unfolding in the United States in late October 2008, by the chairman of the committee, Representative Henry Waxman.
2. In the preface of his book, Niebyl (1946) put is as follows: "Inadequate theories lead to inadequate policies, and inadequate policies are 'inadequate' for the welfare of society as a whole, while at the same time they are 'adequate' – over the short run – for vested and functionally past economic interests."
3. Ricardo refused to accept that the quantity of money had any bearing on the rate of interest: "the rate of interest for money is totally independent of the nominal amount of money in circulation. It is regulated solely by the competition of capital, not consisting of money" (Ricardo 1810 quoted in Sayers 1960: 47). Later he accepted that additional notes might reduce interest rates in the short term, but he regarded this as a side point to his interest in long-run tendencies.
4. The Issue Department took the function of changing bullion for notes and inversely. Practically, any gold transactions with the Bank of England would be effected by the Issue Department. The Banking Department had as reserves only the Issue Department notes.
5. Bagehot advised that policy responses to a panic (a drain of gold) should be an interest rate rise (to attract gold inflows) while ensuring that internal demand for liquidity is satisfied given adequate collateral: "What is wanted and what is necessary to stop a panic is to diffuse the impression that, though money may be dear, still money is to be had. [..]Unless you can stop the foreign export, you cannot allay the domestic alarm" (Bagehot 1876: 9).
6. According to Menger, money is simply the most "saleable" of a set of commodities. It emerges as means of exchange resulting from spontaneous market process driven by rational economic decisions to solve the "double coincidence of wants" (Ingham 1999).
7. Gold no longer represented the reserve base of the system, instead held only for international transactions or industrial use.
8. Furthermore, the long-term (bond) rate will necessarily move in tandem with the short-rate.
9. There is ambiguity in what Wicksell held the "natural" rate to be, Marget (1938) for instance identified eight different meanings assigned to the concept.
10. "...the excess of demand (brought about by easier credit) over the supply of raw materials, labour, land and the like, and directly and indirectly of consumption goods, is the decisive factor in pushing up prices...." (Wicksell 1962: 90).
11. According to Wicksell, speculation is not an important factor in driving up prices, as the differential required by a speculator is so significant that he

would not respond to a small change (or deviation) of the monetary rate of interest.

12. "The new book on Monetary Theory which I have in preparation will, I am hopeful, throw much new light on my fundamental arguments in favour of the dogmas to which I have rashly given utterance without sufficiently substantiating them." (Keynes in Skidelsky 1992: 27).
13. Even OMOs enthusiasts like Friedman and Schwarz (1963) are surprised to note that the 1921 annual report of the Board of Governors of the Fed failed to mention the discount rates.
14. Though not in the common understanding that premised purchase or sale of debt instruments. After the 1890s new approach to policy making the Bank of England used direct borrowing from banks to make the Bank Rate effective when it wanted to attract gold inflows because its portfolio of Treasury bills was very limited.
15. This had been the case for both England and the US. While England had no legal reserve requirements, the practice of "window dressing" was in a sense similar to the US case where legal requirements see banks making recourse to the discount window or the call market to manage reserve positions.
16. Keynes explained it: "the aggregate of bank deposits (represented by M in our monetary equation), is a multiple, as nearly as possible constant, of the reserves of the member banks" (Keynes 1930: 64).
17. Along with the discount window, though this is not central to the argument since the problem is framed as a question of reserves injection.
18. In the famous IS-LM framework later developed by Hicks, this was subsequently taken by "orthodox" Keynesians to mean that monetary policy was ineffective due to the low interest elasticity of investment (Leijonhufvud 1981).
19. "Direct control of the monetary base is an alternative to fiscal policy and interest rates as a means of controlling monetary growth. [...] A precise analogy is like trying to control the output of motor cars by altering the incomes of potential purchasers and manipulating rail and air fares. Far easier to control the output of motor cars by controlling the availability of [...] say steel to the manufacturers – a precise analogy to controlling the availability of base money to banks and others" (Friedman 1980: 57).
20. Different models of how individual firms adjust prices have been suggested (see Calvo 1983).
21. The ECB approach retains some of its monetarist concerns with the dynamics of monetary aggregates, justified through the long-run link between money and prices (Woodford 2007).
22. Blinder (2001) provides an overview of the growing importance central banks attach to stabilizing expectations.
23. See Chechetti et al. (2001) for a well-developed counterargument.
24. For geopolitical considerations, the military dictator in power at the onset of the Second World War decided to join the German invasion of the Soviet Union in June 1941. During the Red Army's advance in Romania in 1944, the King staged an overthrow of the wartime military dictatorship, and brought Romania into the anti-fascist camp.
25. Attempts to recover lost territories were partly frustrated: the 1947 peace treaty only restored control over northern Transylvania, but awarded

Basarabia and northern Bukovina (now in Moldova and Ukraine respectively) to the Soviet Union.

26. Oil, ores and cereals.
27. The sectoral shifts in employment show more than 20percent of the labour force moving from agriculture to industry and services, thus closing the gap with CMEA members.
28. Interest rates on bank credit were reduced to pre-agreement levels.
29. For instance, at the end of 1992, of the US$1.3 bn short-term debt, US$1.07 bn was owed to the IMF alone (NBR 1993).
30. The report stated that: "The state will provide financial support – subsidies, preferential credit, export incentives – to sectors mostly needing structural reconversion. However it is imperious that these measures be short term, enabling these enterprises to play by market rules" Government Commission (1990: 3, own translation).
31. Products of the mining, fuel and energy sectors; metallurgy; the chemical industry; forestry; basic branches of the machine building industry; the main products of the food industry; transportation, postal and telecommunication services.
32. Partial convertibility was held to reduce exchange rate volatility.
33. Known as the first mineriada, it saw miners descending on Bucharest to "assist" the police in dealing with the protestors occupying a public square, which quickly led to a violent backlash against the opposition parties and their intellectuals.
34. At the time, Iraq debt amounted to around US$1.7 bn (1991 figures), the equivalent of the 1990-1993 IMF loans to Romania (Demekas and Khan 1991).
35. The authors were heading the IMF team negotiating the 1991 Stand By Agreement, and published an account of their experience as an IMF Working Paper.
36. The first stage in November 1990, followed by the Stand-By Agreement in April 1991, up to which point 80percent of all prices were "freed" from administrative control (Demekas and Khan 1991). After the third round, in July 1991, only 14 categories, including a few basic food items and public services – home heating, public transportation and rents, retained their administered regime.
37. The literature identifies gradual price liberalization as the root cause for unexpected, negative outcomes: explained delays in structural reforms (OECD 1993), inflationary spirals through inflationary expectations (NBR 1992); limited institutional reform (Ibrahim and Galt 2002); a sectoral segmentation of real interest rates that subsidized state-owned enterprises (NBR 1994) and reduced efficiency of monetary policy (Dragulin and Radulescu 1999: 6).
38. The creation of a foreign currency market was made a prior requirement of the 1991 SBA. It began operations in February 1991, with small volumes and substantial volatility. Thus the economy operated with a double set of exchange rates to the dollar up to November 1991: an official rate for imports of raw materials and energy (financed through a 50percent surrender requirement on hard-currency exports) and a parallel rate set "freely" in the interbank market. Supply shortages on the interbank market produced

a significant differential to the official rate, a differential which was further deployed in policy argumentation to legitimize sharp devaluations.

39. The devaluation timetable went as follows: from Lei/US$ 20 to Lei/US$ 35 in November 1990, to Lei/US$ 60 in April 1991 and Lei/US$ 180 in November 1991, when the NBR unified the two exchange rates and instituted internal convertibility on the current account operations (see figure 3.1). It further committed to a flexible regime with rates established in the interbank market.
40. As of July 1, 2005, Romania's legal tender, the leu, previously coded as ROL, has been redenominated so that ROL 10.000 were exchanged for 1 new leu (RON). The book will mirror this change, referring to the currency as ROL until June 2005.
41. This has not been the case in all formerly planned economies. Dow et al. (2008) examine the case of Uzbekistan, where specific institutional characteristics and the overall development strategy resulted in restrictions on the free convertibility of bank deposits into cash money.
42. Most analysis portrays the miners' strike as a political manipulation rather than legitimate workers' grievance (Pop 2006).
43. ROL 522 bn compared with a target of ROL 96 bn.
44. The 1992 SBA required Parliament to pass legislation strengthening financial discipline.
45. "The often invoked policy to stimulate investments through interest rates again proved illusory: during 1991, the year with the highest negative real rates, investment fell to 12percent of GDP the lowest since the second world war" (NBR 1992: 27).
46. Lei 75 bn, of which only half used for the energy sector, and lei 105 bn for the agricultural sector, all used.
47. The Romanian Commercial Bank, BCR.
48. From ROL40bn in March 1992 to ROL35bn in December 1992.
49. The largest savings bank at that time.
50. Large cash transactions were illegal, but enterprises preferred to incur the penalties associated with breaching the law while banks refused to settle payments rather than demand credit at penalty rates.
51. Credit was to be extended for three months at a 25 percent preferential interest rate.
52. For instance a large car manufacturer (ARO) reported that the debt service throughout 1992 had exceeded the wage costs for 12.000 employees (Romania Libera February 23, 1993).
53. November 1992 year-on-year figures showed a 300percent depreciation in the ROL/US$ exchange rate.
54. "The external depreciation of the ROL has followed the internal inflationary dynamics." (NBR 1993b: 31).
55. "The external equilibrium is vital for the economic independence of a country, and could thus be more important than subduing inflation; it has to be maintained even with the painful cost of internal price increases" (NBR 1993: 8)
56. This carried implications for what the NBR described the "monetary overhang" policy puzzle. The first stabilization episode was predicated on the existence of a substantial household excess liquidity. However,

throughout the first three years of transition, household ROL deposits did not fall in nominal terms. This the NBR (1993) explained as money illusion – instances when economic units overestimate the purchasing power of their nominal wealth (Kane and Klevorich 1967), failing to consider whether the collapse in real money balances could have been explained by an increased preference for liquidity in times of high uncertainty. Whether explained as economic irrationality or Keynesian liquidity preference, household behaviour invalidated the essential premise of the 1991 SBA: that household excess liquidity would be redistributed to the productive sector.

57. The SBA broad money target specified 54 percent for the first half of 1994, 35 percent in the second half.
58. The IMF (1994a) established the creation of a foreign-exchange interbank market by June 30, 1994, as a structural performance criterion.
59. Computed as the residual liability.
60. While indeed over two thirds of total refinancing was channelled through the Banca Agricola (the Agriculture Bank), only half was extended on concessional terms (amounting to 37 percent of total refinancing).
61. Directed at the agricultural, energy, and exporting sectors.
62. This explains the 4.7 percent of GDP budget deficit specified in the SBA.
63. By February 1997 the NBR reinstated the interbank currency market by reissuing licenses to all banks and further issued a directive demanding that interbank quotes be made so as to clear the market.
64. For instance, the 1995 SBA was suspended because the NBR had broken its commitment not to interfere in the foreign-exchange market.
65. In a law reminiscent of the "performance targets" during socialism, the State Ownership Fund, the entity in charge of privatization, was mandated to identify at least 50 companies per week for privatization (Meyedroff and Takhor 1997).
66. Restitution of land previously confiscated by the communist regime for collective farms.
67. Including Moody's, Thomson Bankwatch, Fitch IBCA and Standard & Poor's.
68. The debt service for 1999 rose to US$ 2.8bn, equivalent to the entire banking systems foreign reserves at the end of 1998.
69. For Romania, the terms of this arrangement envisaged a USD600 million privately-financed loan.
70. A condition of the financial and enterprise adjustment loan (FESAL) agreement with the World Bank.
71. The IMF endorsed this position, for its August 1997 SBA review recommended a waiver for non-compliance with the benchmark on arrears and did not identify exchange rate practice of interventions as contradicting its flexibility requirement. The endorsement of this policy stance is clear:

    > "The NBR at times also pursued an implicit exchange rate target as it undertook large interventions when foreign capital threatened to cause a nominal appreciation of the ROL, but interventions were fully sterilized or ceased when they threatened the reserve money target" (IMF 1997a: 4).

72. Such as in the first semester of 2002 and 2003.

73. The NBR (1997c: 23) argued that:

    "Developments in the exchange market will provide an important indicator of the stance of monetary policy. Any tendency to depreciate faster than expected will initially trigger a reduction in reserve money below target in an attempt to slow the rate of depreciation."

74. The NBR (1998a:6) report described policy in the following terms:

    The tight monetary policy stance in 1998 was instrumental in lowering inflation markedly, [...] Monetary policy was successful in alleviating substantially the inflation expectations and reducing the impact on prices of both tax adjustments and administered price increases through a severe control over monetary variables; maintaining a tight monetary policy stance, the monetary authority curbed the accelerated depreciation of the exchange rate of the ROL and cushioned its effect on inflation in the latter half of 1998.

75. A more detailed account of the banking sector developments is provided at the end of this chapter.
76. "Moreover, apart from the unfavourable influence on the conduct of monetary policy and the additional efforts of the National Bank of Romania to control liquidity, coverage of the budget deficit from domestic sources had a crowding-out effect on non-government sector and maintained or even increased interest rates because of the gap between demand and supply on the interbank market." (NBR 1998a: 56)
77. Author's translation.
78. The IMF (2004:25) country report explained that: "Monetary policy works mostly through the exchange rate, while the direct impact of the policy interest rate on inflation is modest. As continuing reliance on the exchange rate for disinflation seems unavoidable, it is imperative that monetary policy be relieved from current account considerations by wage restraint and a tight fiscal stance."
79. "As a result of lower resort by the Ministry of Public Finance to domestic resources amid substantial foreign financing in H1 2002, the need to correlate the rapidly decreasing yields on Treasury certificates with the central bank's rates was another factor underlying the monetary authority's move" (NBR 2002a: 13).
80. The reference currency shifted from the US$ to the EUR as of 3 March 2003, reflecting the large share of trade with the European Union.
81. Bancorex is a paradigmatic example.
82. The state development bank, BRD, and the state savings bank, Bancpost, were privatized at the end of 1998 and May 1999.
83. Bancorex was closed, its assets transferred to an asset recovering agency, Banca Agricola was restructured for privatization while another state-owned bank, Bankcoop was placed under special administration.
84. My translation.
85. The gaps model contains a neutral interest rate and an equilibrium exchange rate (subject to the uncovered interest parity), but the NBR has not publically disclosed where it believes these to be.
86. While the official inflation target is specified on CPI growth, policy documents (NBR 2006) suggested that the price index which monetary policy can best control should exclude both volatile prices (energy, food) and

administered prices – a measure of inflation usually referred to as "core inflation".

87. If forecasting is not done on the common assumption of a constant rate over the targeted horizon, modellers will derive the interest rate path either from market expectations of future interest rates, a Taylor rule or an optimal instrument rate projection that best reflects the central bank's preferences (Svensson, 2006). The literature converges towards supporting the last alternative (as for instance deployed in Norway), conditional on a clear communication that seeks to prevent long-term asset prices building in a more rapid tightening pace than the central bank would have wished for, and thus minimizes unnecessary volatility while increasing effectiveness of monetary policy.
88. According to one of the members of the Modelling Department of the NBR (personal communication, July 14, 2008), the GDP data used for computing the past, current and projected values of the output gap are usually subjected to revisions outside the NBR's control, as they are produced by the National Institute of Statistics. While this constitutes a source of some frustration within the Modeling Department, policy discourse has glossed over the implications of these revisions for the deployment of output gap in assessing policy stances.
89. "The expansionary effect of the interest rates only partially offsets the tightness induced by the real appreciation of the domestic currency against the euro, as a result the development in real interest rates and real exchange rate have been exerting a net contractionary effect on excess demand" (NBR 2006: 21).
90. Personal communication with a member of the NBR modelling department during July 2008.
91. In 2005, Daniel Daianu, an influential policy analyst and former minister of finance, termed as "strange the situation in which we decrease interest rates against an acceleration of inflationary pressures during the first month of 2005" (Ziarul Financiar 12/03/2005). Another analyst later explained: "The easing cycle in early 2007 occurred against a fall in inflation. Since new inflationary pressures on the economy, it is time for the NBR to reassess its policy stance". (Ziarul Financiar 18/09/2007)
92. Author's translation.
93. The Baltic countries and Bulgaria have pegged currencies to the euro, while Slovakia and Slovenia are now both members of the Eurozone.
94. The instruments used had a maturity of one-week for the Czech Republic alovakia, and two-week for Poland and Hungary.
95. The Balassa Samuelson model builds upon a two-sector economy producing tradable and non-tradable goods. Assuming wage equalization across sectors, productivity increases in the traded sector would trigger upward adjustments in both sectors, and thus higher relative prices for the non-traded sector and overall higher inflation. Since real magnitudes are derived with consumer price indices, the faster productivity growth arising from the catching-up process impacts calculations of the real exchange rate.
96. More remarkable for Hungary and Czech Republic, who registered a trade surplus for both 2006 and 2007.

97. By March 2009, the central bank of Switzerland was forced to intervene directly in currency markets to stem the franc's appreciation.
98. Mostly mortgage securities backed by government-sponsored enterprises (see New York Fed 2009 for a timeline of US and international policy measures).
99. Yet the ECB interventions were rather timid compared to the scale of the problems hitting banks. Member-state governments engaged in substantial bailout operations of national banks (e.g., in Austria).
100. Hungary, already under IMF assistance since November 2008, did not sign the statement.
101. NBR Monthly Report, March 2009.
102. Aside from macroeconomic commitments to austerity, the central banks were to perform a series of stress tests for national banking system, simulating the impact of a shock (such as a substantial devaluation) on the commercial banks' balance sheets.
103. While Latvia, the third member state that received conditionality-driven IMF support, shares several macroeconomic features with Romania and Hungary, its fixed exchange-rate regime and close ties to Nordic financial systems render it relatively less relevant in comparative terms.
104. A comparison of the relative size of swap operations to discount window loans is impossible as data on swap operations are not publicly available.
105. The MNB further introduced a series of short-term provisions for easing credit conditions. It relaxed collateral constraints, lowered reserve requirements and extended maturity of its forint loans and FX swaps (similar to the ECB).

Bibliography

Adevarul (1993a) *Ministerul Industriilor Acuza: Bancile Saboteaza Romania*, Bucharest, March 12.

Adevarul (1993b) *Faliment Cu Cecuri Bancare Legale*, Bucharest, May 16.

Adevarul (1994) *Productia Se Relanseaza, Blocajul O Demoleaza*, Bucharest, March 25.

Adevarul (2005) *Decizii Controversiale Privind Reducerea Dobanzii*, Bucharest, March 23.

Ahamed, L. (2009) "Subprime Europe," *New York Times*, March 7.

Alexeev, A. (1988) "Are Soviet Consumers Forced to Save?" *Comparative Economic Studies*, 30: 17–23.

Allen, M. and Haas, R. (2001) "The Transition in Eastern Europe: The Experience of Two Resident Representatives," *IMF Staff Papers*, 48 (3): 9–38. Washington DC: International Monetary Fund.

Alesina, A. (1994) "Political Models of Macroeconomic Policy and Fiscal Reforms," in S. Haggard and S. B. Webb (eds.), *Voting for Reform Democracy, Political Liberalization, and Economic Adjustment*, Oxford: Oxford University Press.

Amsden, A., Kochanowicz J. and Taylor L. (1994) *The Market Meets Its Match: Restructuring the Economies of Eastern Europe*, Cambridge, MA: Harvard University Press.

Andersen, C. (2009) "Agreements with Banks Limits Crisis in Emerging Europe," IMF Survey, available online at http://www.imf.org/external/pubs/ft/survey/so/2009/int102809a.htm. (accessed July 20, 2009).

Anderson, R. and Enzler, J. (1987) "Towards Realistic Policy Design: Policy Reaction Functions that Rely on Economic Forecasts," in R. Dornbusch, S. Fischer, and J. Bossons (eds.), *Macroeconomics and Finance*, pp. 291–330. Cambridge, MA: MIT Press.

Antohi, D., Udrea, I. and Braun, H. (2003) "Monetary Policy Transmission in Romania," National Bank of Romania Occasional Paper No. 3.

Apthorpe, R. and Gasper, D. (1996) *Arguing Development Policy: Frames and Discourses*, London: Frank Cass.

Arestis, P. and Caner, A. (2004) "Financial Liberalization and Poverty: Channels of Influence," The Levy Economics Institute Working Paper, No. 411.

Arestis, P. and Sawyer, M. (2004) *Re-examining Monetary and Fiscal Policies in the Twenty-First Century*. Cheltenham: Edward Elgar.

Aydin, B. (2008) "Banking Structure and Credit Growth in Central and Eastern European Countries," IMF Working Paper 08/215.

Bagehot, W. (1910) *Lombard Street: A Description of the Money Market*, London, Henry S. King & Co. First published 1876.

Ball, L. (1999) "Efficient Rules for Monetary Policy," *International Finance*, 2 (1): 63–83.

Balogh, C. (2009) "The Role of the MNB Bills in Domestic Financial Markets: What Is the Connection between the Large Volume of MNB Bills, Bank

Lending and Demand in the Government Securities Market?" *Magyar Nemzeti Bank Bulletin*, 4 (3): 6–13. Budapest: National Bank of Hungary.
Bank for International Settlements (2000) "Semiannual Over-the-Counter (OTC) Derivatives Markets Statistics," available online at http://www.bis.org/statistics/derstats.htm (accessed September 12, 2006).
Bank for International Settlements (2007) "Triennial Central Bank Survey of Foreign Exchange and Derivatives Market Activity in 2007," available online at http://www.bis.org/publ/rpfxf07a.pdf (accessed June, 25 2008).
Barro, R. J. and Grossman, H. I. (1971) "A General Disequilibrium Model of Income and Employment," *American Economic Review*, 61: 82–93.
Baumol, W. (2004) "Entrepreneurial Enterprises, Large Established Firms and Other Components of the Free-Market Growth Machine," *Small Business Economics*, 23 (1): 9–21.
Benes, J., Hurnik, J and J. Vavra (2008) "Exchange Rate Management and Inflation Targeting". *Czech Journal of Economics and Finance*, 58 (3–4): 166–194.
Berg, A., Karam, P. and Laxton, D. (2006) "A Practical Model Based Approach to Monetary Policy Analysis: Overview," IMF Working Paper No. 80.
Berglof, E. and Bolton, P. (2001) "The Great Divide and Beyond: Financial Architecture in Transition," William Davidson Working Paper, No. 414.
Bernanke, B. S., Laubach, T., Posen, A. and Mishkin, F. S. (1999) *Inflation-Targeting: Lessons from the International Experience*, Princeton, NJ: Princeton University Press.
Bernanke, B. and Gertler, M. (2001) "Should Central Banks Respond to Movements in Asset Prices?" *American Economic Review*, 91: 253–257.
Bernanke, B. and Reinhart, V. (2004) "Conducting Monetary Policy at Very Low Short-Term Interest Rates," *American Economic Review*, 94 (2): 85–90.
Bindseil, U. (2004) "The Operational Target of Monetary Policy and the Rise and Fall of Reserve Position Doctrine," European Central Bank, Working Paper No. 372.
Blanchard, O. Dell'Aricia, G. and Mauro, P. (2010) *Rethinking Macroeconomic Policy*, IMF Staff Position Note, SPN/10/03. Available at http://www.imf.org/external/pubs/ft/spn/2010/spn1003.pdf (Accessed March 12, 2010).
Blinder, A. S. (1998) *Central Banking in Theory and Practice*, Cambridge, Mass.: MIT Press.
Bloomberg (2008a) "Greenspan Concedes to 'Flaw' in His Market Ideology," October 23.
Bloomberg (2008b) "Ukraine's Hryvnia Jumps 11% as Central Bank Raises Rate to 22%," December 19.
Bofinger, P. (1996) "The Economics of Orthodox Money Based Stabilizations: The Recent Experience of Kazakhstan, Russia and Ukraine," *European Economic Review*, 40: 663–671.
Bofinger, P., Flassbeck, H. and Hoffmann, L. (1997) "Orthodox Money-Based Stabilization (OMBS) Versus Heterodox Exchange Rate-Based Stabilization (HERBS): The Case of Russia, the Ukraine and Kazakhstan," *Economic Systems*, 21 (1): 12–26.
Bolnick, R. (1999) "The Role of Financial Programming in Macroeconomic Policy," *Harvard Institute for International Development Papers*, NO. 720, pp. 1–29.
Borc, C. (2002) "Why Are Domestic Interest Rates So High?" CEROPE Working Paper No. 12.

Botel, C. (2002) "The Determinants of Inflation in Romania: June 1997–August 2001–A Structural VAR Approach," National Bank of Romania Paper Series.

Bourdieu, P. (1998) *Acts of Resistance*, Cambridge: Polity Press.

Bruno, M. (1992) "Stabilization and Reform in Eastern Europe: A Preliminary Evaluation," IMF Working Paper 92/30.

Budina, N., De Menil, C. and Turlea, G. (2002) "Money, Inflation and Output in Romania, 1992–2002," Delta Working Paper No. 15.

Buiter, W. (2009) "The Unfortunate Uselessness of Most "State of the Art" Academic Monetary Economics," *Financial Times* Blog, March 29, available online at http://blogs.ft.com/maverecon/2009/03/the-unfortunate-uselessness-of-most-state-of-the-art-academic-monetary-economics/ (accessed March 29, 2009).

Burawoy, M. and Lukacs, J. (1992) *The Radiant Past: Ideology and Reality in Hungary's Road to Capitalism*, Chicago, Ill.: University of Chicago Press.

Caballero, R. and Krishnamurthy, A. (2001) "Smoothing Sudden Stops," National Bureau of Economic Research Working Papers No. 8427.

Caballero, R. J. (2002) "Coping with Chile's External Vulnerability: A Financial Problem," Central Bank of Chile Working Papers, No. 154.

Calvo, G. (1983) "Staggered Contracts in a Utility-Maximizing Framework," *Journal of Monetary Economics*, 12: 383–398.

Calvo, G. (1991) "The Perils of Sterilization," IMF Staff Papers, December, 30 (4): 921–926. Washington DC: International Monetary Fund.

Calvo, G. and Corricelli, F. (1992) "Stagflationary Effects of Stabilization Programs in Reforming Socialist Countries: Enterprise Side and Household Side Factors," *World Bank Economic Review*, 6: 71–90.

Calvo, G., Reinhart, C. and Leiderman, L. (1993) "Capital Inflows and Real Exchange Rate Appreciation in Latin America: The Role of External Factors," IMF Staff Papers, 40 (1): 108–141. Washington DC: International Monetary Fund.

Cameron, R. (1967) *Banking in the Early Stages of Industrialisation: A Study in Comparative Economic History*, Oxford: Oxford University Press.

Capital (1999) *Bancile Duc Lupte de Gherila Cu Autoritatea Monetara*, Bucharest, April 8.

Carruthers, B., Baab, S. and Halliday, T. C. (2001) "Institutionalizing Markets or the Markets for Institutions? Central Banks, Bankruptcy Law and the Globalization of Financial Markets," in J. Campell and O. Pedersen (eds.), *The Rise of Neoliberalism and Institutional Analysis*, pp. 94–127. Princeton: Princeton University Press.

Catu, F. (2008) "ROBID/ROBOR" [Msg 25978]. Message posted to http://tech.groups.yahoo.com/group/romania-economics/message/25978

Caviglia, G., Krause, G. and Thimann, C. (2002) "Key Features of the Financial Sector in EU Accession Countries," in C. Thimann (ed.), *Financial Sectors in EU Accession Countries*, pp. 15–31. Frankfurt: European Central Bank.

Chang, Ha Joon and Grable, I. (2004) *Reclaiming Development: An Alternative Economic Policy Manual*, London: Zed Press.

Chick, V. (1983) *Macroeconomics after Keynes: A Reconsideration of the General Theory*, Cambridge, Mass.: MIT Press.

Chick, V. (1986) "The Evolution of the Banking System and the Theory of Saving, Investment and Interest," *Economies et Sociétés, Série Monnaie et Production*, 20 (3): 111–126.

Chick, V. (1999) "Karl Niebyl's Methodology: Classical Monetary Theory in Historical Context," paper presented to the History of Economic Thought Conference, Glasgow, September.
Chick, V. (2005) "Lost and Found: Some History of the Endogenous Money," in G. Fontana and R. Realfoso (eds.), *The Monetary Theory of Production*, Basingstoke: Palgrave Macmillan.
Chirot, D. (1976) *Social Change in a Peripheral Society: The Creation of a Balkan Colony*, New York: Academic Press.
Chiru, L. (2005) "BNR Considera Ca Leul S-a Intarit Prea Mult. Piata Insa Vede Loc De Aprecieri," *Ziarul Financiar*, Bucharest, October 5.
Christensen, J. (2004) "Capital Inflows, Sterilization, and Commercial Bank Speculation: The Case of the Czech Republic in the Mid-1990s," IMF Working Paper No. 04/218.
Clarida, R., Gali J. and Gertler M. (1999) "The Science of Monetary Policy: A New Keynesian Perspective," *Journal of Economic Literature*, 37 (4): 1661–1707.
Cochrane, J. and Piazessi, M. (2005) "Bond Risk Premia," *American Economic Review*, 95 (1): 131–160.
Cordero, J. A. (2009) *The IMF's Stand-by Arrangements and the Economic Downturn in Eastern Europe: The Cases of Hungary, Latvia, and Ukraine*, Washington, DC: Centre for Economic Policy Research.
Coricelli, F., Jazbec, B. and Masten, I. (2004) "Exchange Rate Policy and Inflation in Acceding Countries: The Role of Pass-Through," William Davidson Institute Working Papers Series No. 674.
Cottarelli, C. and Blejer, M. (1992) "Forced Savings and Repressed Inflation in the Soviet Union, 1968–1990," *IMF Staff Papers*, 39 (2).
Crotty, J. (2003) "The Neoliberal Paradox: The Impact of Destructive Product Market Competition and Impatient Finance on Nonfinancial Corporations in the Neoliberal Era," *Review of Radical Politics Economics*, 35 (3): 271–279.
Currie, M. (1998) *Postmodern Narrative Theory*, Basingstoke: Macmillan.
D'Arista, J. (2005) "The Role of the International Monetary System in Financialization," in G. Epstein (ed.), *Financialization and the World Economy*, Cheltenham and Northampton, Mass.: Edward Elgar, 77–110.
Daianu, D. (1994) "Inter-Entreprise Arrears in a Post-Command Economy," IMF Working Paper, No. 54/94.
Daianu, D. (1999) "Structure, Strain and Macroeconomic Dynamics in Romania," in C. Ruhl and D. Daianu (eds) *Economic Transition in Romania Past, Present, Future*, p. 5–34. Bucharest: World Bank.
Daianu, D. and Lungu, L. (2007) "Inflation-Targeting, between Rhetoric and Reality: The Case of Transition Economies," *European Journal of Comparative Economics*, 4 (1): 39–64.
Daianu, D. and Vranceanu, R. (2001) "Subduing High Inflation in Romania: How to Better Monetary and Exchange Rate Mechanisms?" CEROPE Working Paper No. 21.
Demekas, D. and Khan, M. (1991) "The Romanian Economic Reform Program," International Monetary Fund Working Paper No. 91/80.
Demir, F. (2009) "Financial Liberalization, Private Investment and Portfolio Choice: Financialization of Real Sectors in Emerging Markets," *Journal of Development Economics*, 88 (2): 314–324.

De Haas, R. and Van Lelyveld, I. (2006) "Foreign Banks and Credit Stability in Central and Eastern Europe: A Panel Data Analysis," *Journal of Banking and Finance*, 30: 1927–1952.

De La Torre, A., Gozzi, J. C. and Schmukler, S. L. (2007) "Financial Development: Maturing and Emerging Policy Issues," *The World Bank Research Observer*, 22 (1): 67–102.

De Martino, G. F. (2000) *Global Economy, Global Justice: Theoretical Objections and Policy Alternatives to Neoliberalism*, London: Routledge.

Diev, P. and Kurtz, E. (2006) "Capital Inflows, Monetary Policy and Exchange Rate Regime in New Member States: Implications for the Accession to the Euro Area," Banque de France Discussion Paper, Mimeo.

Dillard, D. (1980) "A Monetary Theory of Production," *Journal of Economic Issues*, 16 (2): 255–275.

Dow, S. C. (1996) *The Methodology of Macroeconomic Thought*, Cheltenham: Edward Elgar.

Dow, S. C. (2004) "Endogenous Money: Structuralists," in P. Arestis and M. Sawyer (eds.), *Handbook of Alternative Monetary Economics*, Cheltenham: Edward Elgar

Dow, S. C., Ghosh, D. and Ruziev, K. (2008) "A Stages Approach to Banking Development in Transition Economies," *Journal of Post Keynesian Economics*, 31 (1): 3–35.

Dragulin, I. and Radulescu, E. (1999) "Monetary Policy in Romania: Challenges and Options," William Davidson Institute Working Paper No. 234.

Dryzek, J. S. (1982) "Policy Analysis as Hermeneutic Activity," *Policy Science*, 14: 309–329.

Dumenil, G. and Levy, D. (2001) "Costs and Benefits of Neoliberalism: A Class Analysis," *Review of International Political Economy*, 8 (4): 578–607.

Dwyer, G. P. (1985) "Federal Deficits, Interest Rates and Monetary Policy," *Journal of Money, Credit and Banking*, 17 (4): 655–681.

Eatwell, J. (1982) *Whatever Happened to Britain? The Economics of Decline*, Duckworth: British Broadcasting Corporation.

Economist Intelligence Unit (1998–2005) *Romania Country Report*, London: EIU.

Edwards, S. (1994) "The Political Economy of Inflation and Stabilisation in Developing Countries," *Economic Development and Cultural Change*, 42 (2): 235–266.

Edwards, S. (2006) "The Relationship between Exchange Rates and Inflation-Targeting Revisited," NBER Working Papers No. 12163.

Egert, B. I., Drine, K., Lommatzsch, K. and Rault, C. (2002) "The Balassa Samuelson Effect in Eastern Europe: Myth or Reality?" William Davidson Working Papers No. 483.

Eichengreen, B. (2006) *The Blind Men and the Elephant*, Washington, DC: the Brookings Institution.

Elgie, R. and Thomson, H. (1998) *The Politics of Central Banks*, London: Routledge.

Ellman, M. (1989) *Socialist Planning*, 2nd edn, Cambridge: Cambridge University Press.

Epstein, G. (1992) "A Political Economy Model of Comparative Central Banking," *Review of Radical Political Economics*, 24: 1–30.

Epstein, G. (2002) "Financialization, Rentier Interest and Central Bank Policy," Paper prepared for PERI conference on "Financialization and the World Economy". available at http://www.peri.umass.edu/fileadmin/pdf/financial/fin_Epstein.pdf (accessed July 22, 2009).

Epstein, G. (2005) *Financialization and the World Economy*, Cheltenham and Northampton, Mass.: Edward Elgar.

Epstein, G. and Yeldan, E. (2006) *Developing Policy Alternatives to Inflation-Targeting, the New Façade of Neoliberal Conditionality*, Amherst, Mass.: Political Economy Research Institute.

Fabrizio, S., Leich, D. and Mody, A. (2009) "The Second Transition: Eastern Europe in Perspective," IMF Working Paper No. 09/43.

Fischer, F. (1998) "Beyond Empiricism: Policy Enquiry in Postpositivist Perspective," *Policy Studies Journal*, 26 (1): 129–146.

Fischer, S. (2001) "Distinguished Lecture on Economics in Government," *Journal of Economic Perspectives*, 15 (2): 3–24.

Fischer, S. and Gelb, A. (1991) "The Process of Socialist Economic Transformation," *Journal of Economic Perspectives*, 5 (4): 91–105.

Fontana, G. and Palacio-Vera, A. (2004) "Monetary Policy Uncovered: Theory and Practice," *International Review of Applied Economics*, 18 (1): 25–42.

Friedman, M. (1956) "The Quantity Theory of Money: A Restatement," in M. Friedman (ed) *Studies in the Quantity Theory of Money*, Chicago, Ill.: University of Chicago Press.

Friedman, M. (1960) *A Program for Monetary Stability*, New York: Fordham University Press.

Friedman, M. (1968) "The Role of Monetary Policy," *American Economic Review*, 58 (1): 1–17.

Friedman, M. (1969) *The Optimum Quantity of Money and Other Essays*, Chicago, Ill.: Aldine.

Friedman, M. (1980) *Memoranda on Monetary Control*, vol. I, HC720, London: HMSO.

Gabor, D. (2008) "From Rhetorics to Practice in Monetary Policy: A Romanian Perspective," *Comparative Economic Studies*, 50 (3): 511–534.

Gabor, D. (2010) "The IMF and its New Economics of Crisis". *Development and Change*, 41 (5): 805–830.

Galati, G., Heath, A. and McGuire, P. (2007) "Evidence of Carry Trade Activity," *BIS Quarterly Review* (September): 27–41.

Galbraith, J. K. (1967) *The New Industrial State*, Princeton, NJ: Princeton University Press.

Gale, D. (1982) *Money: In Equilibrium*, Cambridge, Cambridge University Press.

Galí, J. and Gertler, M. (2007) "Macroeconomic Modelling for Monetary Policy Evaluation," Economics Working Papers No. 1039, Department of Economics and Business, Universitat Pompeu Fabra.

Gasper, D. (1996) "Essentialism in and about Policy Discourse," in R. Apthorpe and D. Gasper (eds.), *Arguing Development Policy: Frames and Discourses*, London: Frank Cass.

Gaspar, V. and Kashyap, A. (2006) "Stability First: Reflections Inspired by Otmar Issing's Success as the ECB Economist," NBER Working Paper No. 122.

Gerschenkron, A. (1966) *Economic Backwardness in Historical Perspective*, Cambridge, Mass.: Harvard University Press.

Goldstein, J. (2009) "Introduction: The Political Economy of Financialization," *Review of Radical Political Economy*, 41 (4): 453–457.

Gomulka, S. (1995) "The IMF-Supported Programs of Poland and Russia, 1990–1994: Principles, Errors, and Results," *Journal of Comparative Economics*, 20 (3): 316–346.

Goodhart, C. A. E. (1994) "What Should Central Banks Do? What Should Be Their Macroeconomic Objectives and Operations?" *The Economic Journal*, 104: 1424–1436.

Goodhart, C. A. E. (1988) *The Evolution of Central Banks*, Cambridge, Mass.: MIT Press.

Goodhart, C. A. E. (1989) "The Conduct of Monetary Policy," *The Economic Journal*, 99: 199–346.

Goodhart, C. A. E. (2005) "The Interest Rate Conditioning Assumption," London School of Economics, Financial Markets Group Discussion Paper No. 547.

Gordon, S. (1972) "Two Monetary Inquires in Great Britain: The Macmillan Committee of 1931 and the Radcliffe Committee of 1959," *Journal of Money, Credit and Banking*, 4 (4): 957–977.

Government Commission (1990) "On the Strategy of the Transition to Market Economy in Romania" (mimeographed), Bucharest.

Gowland, D. H. (1984) *Controlling the Money Supply*, 2nd edn, London: Croom Helm.

Grenville, S. (2008) "Central Banks and Capital Flows," ADB Institute Discussion Paper No. 87.

Habermas, J. (1989) *The Structural Transformation of the Public Sphere: An Inquiry into a Category of Bourgeois Society*, Cambridge: Polity Press.

Hajer, M. (1995) *The Politics of Environmental Discourse*, Oxford: Oxford University Press.

Hall, P. A. (1986) *Governing the Economy: The Politics of State Intervention in Britain and France*, Cambridge: Polity Press.

Hall, P. (ed.) (1989) *The Political Power of Economic Ideas: Keynesianism across Nations*, Princeton, NJ: Princeton University Press.

Hart, G. (2006) "Post-Apartheid Developments in Historical and Comparative Perspective," in V. Padayachee (ed.), *The Development Decade? Social and Economic Change in South Africa 1994–2004*. p. 13–32. Cape Town: HSRC Press.

Hardie, I. and Howarth, D. (2009) "*Die Krise* but Not *La Crise?* The Financial Crisis and the Transformation of German and French Banking Systems," *Journal of Common Market Studies*, 47 (5): 1017–1039.

Hawkesworth, M. E. (1988) *Theoretical Issues in Policy Analysis*, Albany, NY: SUNY Press.

Hay, C. (1999) "Crisis and the Structural Transformation of the State: Interrogating the Process of Change," *British Journal of Politics and International Relations*, 1 (3): 317–344.

Hay, C. (2004) "The Normalising Role of Rationalist Assumptions in the Institutional Embedding of Neoliberalism," *Economy and Society*, 33 (4): 500–527.

Howarth, D. (2000) *Discourse*, Buckingham: Open University Press.

Ibrahim, G. and Galt, V. (2002) "Bye-Bye Central Planning, Hello Market Hiccups: Institutional Transition in Romania," *Cambridge Journal of Economics*, 26: 105–118.

ING Bank (2008) *Romania Money Markets Weekly Report* (October 13–20).

Ingham, G. (1999) "Capitalism, Money and Banking: A Critique of Recent Historical Sociology," *British Journal of Sociology*, 50 (1): 76–96.

International Monetary Fund (1991a) "Romania: Staff Report for the 1991 Article IV, Consultation and Request for Stand-by Arrangement," ESB/91/115.

International Monetary Fund (1991b) "Romania: First Review under Stand by Agreement," EBS/91/117.

International Monetary Fund (1992a) "Romania: Staff Report for the 1992 Article IV, Consultation and Request for Stand-by Arrangement," EBS/92/79.

International Monetary Fund (1992b) "Romania: Review under Stand by Agreement," October, EBS/92/158.

International Monetary Fund (1994a) "Stand-by Arrangement," EBS/94/87.

International Monetary Fund (1994b) "Romania: First Review under the Stand by Arrangement," EBS/94/115.

International Monetary Fund (1995a) "Review under the Stand by Arrangement," EBS/95/105.

International Monetary Fund (1995b) "Staff Report for the 1995 Article IV Consultation, Review and Request for Extension and Augmentation of Stand by Agreement," EBS/95/217.

International Monetary Fund (1996) "Romania: Recent Economic Developments and Selected Background Studies," IMF Staff Country Report No. 96/9.

International Monetary Fund (1997a) "Romania: Recent Economic Developments," IMF Staff Country Report No. 97/46.

International Monetary Fund (1997b) "Romania: First Review under the Stand by Agreement," EBS/97/167, Supplement 1.

International Monetary Fund (2001) "Romania: Selected Issues and Statistical Appendix," Country Report No. 01/16.

International Monetary Fund (2002) "Romania: First and Second Reviews under the Stand-by Arrangement, Request for Waivers, and Modification of Performance Criterion – Staff Report," staff statement, news brief on the Executive Board Discussion; and statement by the Executive Director for Romania, Country Report No. 02/194.

International Monetary Fund (2003) "Romania: Selected Issues and Statistical Appendix," Country Report No. 03/12.

International Monetary Fund (2004) *Romania: Selected Issues and Statistical Appendix*, Country Report No. 04/220.

International Monetary Fund (2006a) "Romania: Selected Issues and Statistical Appendix," Country Report No. 06/169.

International Monetary Fund (2006b) "Inflation-Targeting and the IMF," IMF Research Department.

International Monetary Fund (2007a) "Romania: Selected Issues," Country Report No. 07/220.

International Monetary Fund (2007b) "Romania: Fall 2007, Staff Visit – Aide Mémoire."

International Monetary Fund (2008) "Romania: 2008 Article IV Consultation – Staff Report," Public Information Notice on the Executive Board Discussion and Statement by the Executive Director for Romania, Country Report No. 08/208.

International Monetary Fund (2009a) "Romania: Request for Stand-by Arrangement – Staff Report," Country Report No. 09/183.

International Monetary Fund (2009b) "Hungary: Request for Stand-by Arrangement – Staff Report," Country Report No. 09/197.

International Monetary Fund, World Bank and the European Bank for Reconstruction and Development (1991) *A Study of the Soviet Economy*, Washington DC: International Monetary Fund.

Ionescu, M. (1993) "Bancile Prospera, Clientii Dau Faliment, Adevarul," Bucharest, February 23.

Isărescu, M. (2005) Speech delivered at the Conference on Inflation-Targeting, Bucharest, March 30.

Isărescu, M. (2006) *Reflectii Economice: Piete, Bani, Banci.*Academia Romana (Centrul Roman De Economie Comparata Si Consens).

Isărescu, M. (2008a) "România Nu Va Suferi O Aterizare Dură a Creşterii Economice," Agentia Mediafax, Bucharest, September 8.

Isărescu, M. (2008b) "Financial Stability in Romania," speech delivered at the Bank for International Settlements Meeting, Geneva, September.

Isărescu, M. (2008c) "Atacul Speculativ Asupra Leului a Esuat," *Ziarul Financiar*, Bucharest, October 25.

Isărescu, M. (2009) "External Deficit Financing and Macroeconomic Adjustment during the Financial Crisis: The Case of Romania," available online at http://www.bis.org/review/r100125a.pdf (accessed January 2010).

Issing, O. (2002) "Monetary Policy in a Changing Economic Environment," in *Rethinking Stabilization Policy*, a symposium sponsored by the Federal Reserve of the Kansas City.

Issing, O. (2006) "The ECB's Monetary Policy Strategy: Why Did We Choose a Two Pillar Approach?" Speech delivered at the 4th ECB Central Banking Conference "The Role of Money: Money and Monetary Policy in the Twenty-First Century," Frankfurt, November 10.

Jalan, B. (2003) "Exchange Rate Management: An Emerging Consensus?" Address of the Governor of the Reserve Bank of India, at the 14th National Assembly of the Forex Association of India, Mumbai, August 14.

Kaminska, I. (2009) "CEE's Stand Against SPECTRE-Lators," *Financial Times*, Alphaville, March 4.

Kaldor, N. (1982) *The Scourge of Monetarism*, Oxford: Oxford University Press.

Kalecki, M. (1971) *Selected Essays on the Dynamics of the Capitalist Economy, 1933–1970*. Cambridge: Cambridge University Press.

Kaminsky, G., Reinhart, C. and Végh, C. (2004) "When It Rains, It Pours: Procyclical Capital Flows and Macroeconomic Policies," NBER Working Paper No. 10780.

Katseli. L. (1983) "Devaluation: A Critical Appraisal of IMF's Policy Prescriptions," *American Economic Review: Papers and Proceedings*. 73 (2): 359–363.

Keeley, J. (1997) "Conceptualizing the Policy Process," in R. Sutton (1999) *The Policy Process: An Overview*, Working Paper 118, Overseas Development Institute.

Keeley, J. and Scoones, I. (1999) "Understanding Environmental Policy Processes: A Review," IDS Working Paper No. 89, Brighton: Institute of Development Studies.

Keller, P. and Richardson, T. (2003) "Nominal Anchors in the CIS," IMF Working Paper No. 03179.

Kemme, D. (1989) "The Chronic Shortage Model of Centrally Planned Economies," *Soviet Studies*, 151 (3): 345–364.

Kennedy, C. M. (1962) "Monetary Policy," in G. D. N. Worswick and P. H. Ady (eds.), *The British Economy in the 1950s* (Oxford: Clarendon Press).
Keynes, J. M. (1923) *A Tract on Monetary Reform*, London, Macmillan.
Keynes, J. M. (1925) *The Economic Consequences of Mr. Churchill*, London: L. and V. Woolf.
Keynes, J. M. (1930) *A Treatise on Money: Volume 2–The Applied Theory of Money*, London: Macmillan & Co.
Keynes, J. M. (1936) *The General Theory of Employment Interest and Money*, Cambridge: Cambridge University Press.
Killick, T. (1995) *IMF Programs in Developing Countries: Design and Impact*, London: Routledge.
Klein, N. (2007) *The Shock Doctrine: The Rise of Disaster Capitalism*, New York: Allen Lane.
Kolodko, G. W. and McMahon, M. (1987) "Stagflation and Shortageflation: A Comparative Approach," *Kyklos*, 40 (2): 176–197.
Kornai, J. (1982) *Growth, Shortage and Efficiency*, Oxford: Basil Blackwell.
Kornai, J. (1990) *The Road to a Free Economy: Shifting from a Socialist System–The Example of Hungary*, New York: W. W. Norton & Company.
Kornai J., Maskin, E. and Roland, G. (2003) "Understanding the Budget Constraint," *Journal of Economic Literature*, 41: 1095–1136.
Kriesler, P. and Lavoie, M. (2005) "The New View on Monetary Policy: The New Consensus and Its Postkeynesian Critique," Robinson Working Paper 05–01.
Krippner, G. R. (2005) "The Financialization of the American Economy," *Socio-Economic Review*, 3 (2): 173–208.
Krippner, G. R. (2007) "The Making of US Monetary Policy: Central Bank Transparency and the Neoliberal Dilemma," *Theory and Society*, 36: 477–513.
Laidler, D. (1991) *The Golden Age of the Quantity Theory*, Princeton, NJ: Princeton University Press.
Laidler, D. (2004) *Macroeconomics in Retrospect: The Selected Essays of David Laidler*, Cheltenham: Edward Elgar.
Lane, T. (1991) "Inflation Stabilization and Economic Transformation in Poland," IMF Working Paper, 91/70.
Larner, W. (2000) "Theorising Neoliberalism: Policy, Ideology, Governmentality," *Studies in Political Economy*, 63: 5–26.
Lee, Y. J. (1997) "Sterilizing Capital Inflows," *IMF Economic Issues No. 7.*
Leijonhufvud, A. (1981) "The Wicksell Connection: Variations on a Theme," in A. Leijonhufvud *Information and Coordination: Essays in Macroeconomic Theory*, Oxford: Oxford University Press.
Leijonhufvud, A. (2007) "So Far from Ricardo, So Close to Wicksell," paper given at Annual Conference of the Central Bank of Argentina, June.
Lemke, T. (2000) "Foucault, Governmentality, and Critique," paper presented at the Rethinking Marxism Conference, University of Amherst, Mass., September 21–24.
Lemke, T. (2001) "The Birth of Biopolitics: Michel Foucault's Lecture at the College de France on Neo-Liberal Governmentality," *Economy and Society*, 30 (2): 190–207.
Li, T. M. (1999) "Compromising Power: Development, Culture and Rule in Indonesia," *Cultural Anthropology*, 14 (3): 211–239.
Lin, S. and Osband, K. (1992) "Can the Release of a Monetary Overhang Trigger Hyperinflation?" IMF Working Paper No. 92/94.

Linden, R. H. (1986) "Socialist Patrimonialism and the Global Economy: The Case of Romania," *International Organization*, 40: 347–380.

Lucas, R. and Sargent, T. J. (1978) "After Keynesian Macroeconomics," in F. Bosworth and H. Friedman (eds.), *After the Phillips Curve: Persistence of High Inflation and High Unemployment*, Boston, Mass.: Federal Reserve Bank.

Lucas, R. E. Jr. (1976) *Econometric Policy Evaluation: A Critique*, Amsterdam: North-Holland.

Macdonald, R. (2000) "Concepts to Calculate Equilibrium Exchange Rates: An Overview," Economic Research Group of the Deutsche Bundesbank Discussion Paper No. 3.

Macmillan Committee (1978) *British Parliamentary Reports on International Finance*. First published 1931. London: H.M. Stationery Office.

Marangos, J. (2002) "A Political Economy Approach to the Neoclassical Model of Transition," *American Journal of Economic and Sociology*, 61 (1): 259–276.

Massad, C. (1997) Statement at the Joint Annual Discussion of the Latin American Governors of the International Monetary Fund, Hong Kong, China.

Mediafax (2010) "Vlădescu: Din Fiecare Miliard Încasat La Privatizarea BCR Trebuia Să Avem 100 Km De Autostradă," April 1, available online at http://www.mediafax.ro/economic/vladescu-din-fiecare-miliard-incasat-la-privatizarea-bcr-trebuia-sa-avem-100-km-de-autostrada-5797565 (accessed April 22).

Melvin, M. and Taylor, M. (2009) "The Crisis in the Foreign Exchange Market," *Journal of International Money and Finance*. 28 (8): 1317–1330.

Mckinnon, R. I. (1973) *Money and Capital in Economic Development*, Washington, DC: Brookings Institution.

Mckinnon, R. I. (1991) "Financial Control in the Transition from Classical Socialism to a Market Economy," *Journal of Economic Perspectives*, 5 (4): 107–122.

Mirowski, P. and Plehwe, D. (2009) *The Road from Mont Pellerin: The Making of the Neoliberal Thought Collective*, Cambridge, Mass.: Harvard University Press.

Mishkin, F. (1999) "International Experiences with Different Monetary Policy Regimes," National Bureau of Economic Research Working Papers No. 6965.

Mishkin, F. (2004) "Why the Fed Should Adopt Inflation-Targeting," *International Finance*, 7 (1): 117–127.

Mishkin, F. and Savastano, M. (2001) "Monetary Policy Strategies for Emerging Market Countries: Lessons from Latin America," *Journal of Development Economics*, 66 (2): 415–444.

Montiel, P. and Reinhart, C. (1999) "Do Capital Controls and Macroeconomic Policies Influence the Volume and Composition of Capital Flows? Evidence from the 1990s," *Journal of International Money and Finance*, 18 (4): 619–635.

Moore, B. (1984) "Contemporaneous Reserve Accounting: Can Reserves Be Quantity Constrained?", *Journal of Post Keynesian Economics*, 7 (1): 103–114.

Moore, B. (1988) *Horizontalists and Verticalists: The Macroeconomics of Credit Money*, Cambridge: Cambridge University Press.

Mosse, D. (2005) *Cultivating Development: An Ethnography of Aid Policy and Practice*, London and Ann Arbor, Mich.: Pluto Press.

Mundell, R. A. (1962) "The Appropriate Use of Monetary and Fiscal Policies for International and External Stability," *IMF Staff Papers*, 9 (1): 70–79.

Mussa M. and Savastano, M. (1999) "The IMF Approach to Economic Stabilization," IMF Working Paper No. 144, pp. 1–39.

National Bank of Hungary (2007) Annual Report, available online at http://english.mnb.hu/engine.aspx?page=mnben_evesjel (accessed October 5, 2008).
National Bank of Romania (1990–2008a) *Annual Reports*, Bucharest: Editura BNR.
National Bank of Romania (1992) *Politica Monetara in Perioada de Tranzitie*, Bucharest, November.
National Bank of Romania (1993) *Raport Privind Regimul Valutar Din România Şi Măsurile Necesare Pentru Stabilizarea Cursului Leului*, Bucharest, May.
National Bank of Romania (2000b–2006b) *Financial Stability Reports*, Bucharest: Editura BNR.
National Bank of Romania (2006c–2008c) *February Inflation Report*, Bucharest: Editura BNR.
National Bank of Romania (2006d–2008d) *May Inflation Reports*, Bucharest: Editura BNR.
(2005e–2008e) *August Inflation Reports*, Bucharest: Editura BNR.
National Bank of Romania (2005f–2008f) *November Inflation Reports*, Bucharest: Editura BNR.
Nicholas, H. (2003) *The Macroeconomics of Poverty Reduction: The Case Study of Sri Lanka*, New York: United Nations Development Programme.
Niebyl, K. (1946) *Studies in the Classical Theories of Money*, New York: Columbia University Press.
Nordhaus, W. D. (1990) "Soviet Economic Reform: The Longest Road," *Brookings Papers on Economic Activity*, Economic Studies Program, the Brookings Institution, 21: 287–318.
Nuti, D. M. (1986) "Hidden and Repressed Inflation in Soviet-Type Economies: Definitions, Measurements and Stabilization," *Contributions to Political Economy*, 5: 37–82.
Oana, G. (1993) "Deprecierea Cursului De Schimb Alimenteaza Inflatia," *Adevarul*, Bucharest, March 12.
Obstfeld, M. (2001) "International Macroeconomics: Beyond the Mundell-Fleming Model," Centre for International and Development Economics Research Working Paper No. C01–121, University of California at Berkeley.
Ohlin, B. (1936) "Introduction," in K. Wicksell, *Interest and Prices: A Study of the Causes Regulating the Value of Money*, London: Macmillan.
O'Neill, P. (1997) "Bringing the Qualitative State Back into Economic Geography," in R. Lee and J. Wills (eds.), *Geographies of Economies*, London: Arnold, pp. 290–301.
Onis, Z. and Senses, F. (2005) "Rethinking the Emerging Post-Washington Consensus," *Development and Change*, 36 (2): 263–290.
Organization for Economic Cooperation and Development (1993) 2002. *Economic Assessment: Romania*, Paris: OECD.
Organization for Economic Cooperation and Development (2002) *Economic Assessment: Romania*, Paris: OECD.
Orlowski, L. T. (2005) "Monetary Convergence of EU Accession Countries to the Eurozone: A Theoretical Framework and Policy Implications," *Journal of Banking and Finance*, 29 (1): 203–225.
Orphanides, A. and Williams, J. C. (2005) "The Decline of Activist Stabilization Policy: Natural Rate Misperceptions, Learning, and Expectations," *Journal of Economic Dynamics and Control*, 29 (11): 1927–1950.

Ouanes, A. and Takur, S. (1997) *Macroeconomic Accounting and Analysis in Transition*, IMF Institute. Washington DC: International Monetary Fund.

Palley, T. I. (2007) "Financialization: What It Is and Why It Matters," Levy Economics Institute Working Paper No. 525.

Paun, M. (2004) "ROL over/undervalued?" [Msg 15905] Message posted to http://tech.groups.yahoo.com/group/romania-economics/message/15905

Paun, M. (2008) "ROBID/ROBOR" [Msg. 25990] Message posted to http://tech.groups.yahoo.com/group/romania-economics/message/25990

Peck, J. and Tickell, A. (2002) "Neoliberalizing Space," *Antipode*, 34 (3): 380–404.

Persky, J. (1991) "Lange and Von Mises, Large-Scale Enterprises, and the Economic Case for Socialism: Retrospectives," *Journal of Economic Perspectives*, 5 (4): 229–236.

Polanyi, K. (1957) *The Great Transformation*, Boston: Beacon Press. First published 1944.

Pop, L. (2006) *Democratizing Capitalism? The Political Economy of Post-Communist Transformations in Romania, 1989–2001*, Manchester: Manchester University Press.

Popa, C. (2004) "The Challenges of Adopting Inflation-Targeting in Romania." Mimeo, Bucharest: National Bank of Romania.

Portes, R. (1980) "Disequilibrium Estimates for Consumption Goods Markets in Centrally Planned Economies," *Review of Economic Studies*, 47 (1): 137–159.

Portes, R. (1986) "Macroeconomic Equilibrium and Disequilibrium in Centrally Planned Economies," CEPR Discussion Paper N0.91.

Portes, R. (1994) "Transformation Traps," *The Economic Journal*, 104 (426): 1178–1189.

Portes, R. and Winter, D. (1977) "The Supply of Consumption Goods in Centrally Planned Economies," *Journal of Comparative Economics*, 1: 351–365.

Portes R., Quandt R. E., Winter, D. and S. Yeo (1987) "Macroeconomic Planning and Disequilibrium: Estimates for Poland, 1955–1980," NBER Working Papers No. 1182.

Priescu, C. (1993a) "Merg Toate: Pana La Bani," *Adevarul*, Bucharest, January 12.

Priescu, C. (1993b) "Productia Se Relanseaza, Blocajul O Demoleaza," *Adevarul*, Bucharest, January 12.

Radulescu, E. (1993) "Inflatia Slabeste Leul," *Adevarul*, Bucharest, March 12.

Rahman, J. (2008) "Current Account Developments in New Member States of the Europen Union: Equilibrium, Excess and EU Phoria," IMF Working Paper 08/92.

Reuters (2009a) "Romania Rejects All Bids in Auction to Sell 6 Month Bills," October 5.

Reuters (2009b) "Hungary Could Curb Forex Lending, OTP Disagrees," September 29.

Ricardo, D. (1821) *Principles of Political Economy and Taxation*, London: Dover Publications. First published 1817.

Ritter, L., Silber, W. L. and Udell, G. F. (1993) *Principles of Money, Banking and Financial Markets*, 9th edn, Indiana: Addison Wesley.

Roe, E. (1991) "Development Narratives; or, Making the Best of Blueprint Development," *World Development*, 19 (4): 287–300.

Romania Libera (1993) *Dobanzile Bancilor Sufoca Productia*, Bucharest, February 23.

Rose, N. and Miller, P. (1992) "Political Power Beyond the State: Problematics of Government," *British Journal of Sociology*, 43 (2): 173–205.
Roubini, N. (2009) "The Mother of All Carry Trades Faces an Inevitable Bust," *Financial Times*, November 1.
Ruziev, K. and Ghosh, D. (2008) "Banking Sector Development in Uzbekistan: A Case of Mixed Blessings?" *Problems of Economic Transition*. 52 (2): 3–42.
Sachs, J. (1996) "Economic Transition and Exchange Rate Regimes," *American Economic Review*, 86 (2): 147–152.
Sassen, S. (2003) "Globalization or Denationalization?" *Review of International Political Economy*, 10 (1): 1–22.
Sayers, R. S. (1960) "Monetary Thought and Monetary Policy in England," *The Economic Journal*, 70 (280): 710–724.
Sayers, R. S. (1976) *The Bank of England, 1891–1944*, Cambridge: Cambridge University Press.
Schadler, S. (ed.) (1995) "IMF Conditionality: Experience under Stand-by and Extended Arrangements, Part I: Key Issues and Findings," IMF Occasional Paper No. 128.
Schumpeter J. (1951) "Economic Theory and Entrepreneurial History," in R. V. Clemence (ed.), *Essays on Economic Topics of Joseph Schumpeter*, New York: Kennikat Press,
Schumpeter J. (1954) *History of Economic Analysis*, Oxford: Oxford University Press.
Scoones, I. (2003) "Making Policy in the 'New Economy': The Case of Biotechnology in Karnataka, India," IDS Working Paper, No. 196.
Serbanescu, I. (2005) "Pata" Pe…FMI. *Formula As* No. 692. Bucharest.
Serbanescu, I. (2006) "Unde Ne Duce Banca Nationala," *Adevarul*, Bucharest, March 23.
Serbanescu, I. (2009) "Criza Est-Vest: Soarta Oricarei Tari Bananiere," *Bloombiz*, September 24, available online at http://www.bloombiz.ro/finante/criza-est-vest-soarta-oricarei-tari-bananiere (accessed February 23, 2010).
Shaw, E. (1973) *Financial Deepening in Economic Development*, Oxford: Oxford University Press.
Sheng, A. and Pomerleano, M. (2009) "Zero Interest Rate Policy: Treatment May Be Expensive as the Crisis," available online at http://www.voxeu.org/index.php?q=node/4101 (accessed January 12).
Shlykov, V. (1997) "The Crisis in the Russian Economy," presentation at the US Army War College's Annual Strategic Conference.
Silberling, N. J. (1924) "Financial and Monetary Policy of Great Britain during the Napoleonic Wars," *The Quarterly Journal of Economics*, 38 (3): 397–439.
Simionescu, S. (2009) "Adrian Vasilescu: Trei Motive Pentru Care Mugur Isărescu Nu Accepta Sa Fie Premier," *Gandul*, December 9.
Skidelsky, R. (1992) *John Maynard Keynes: A Biography, Volume II: The Economist as Saviour, 1920–1937*, London : Macmillan.
Skidelsky, R. (2005) *John Maynard Keynes: 1883–1946—Economist, Philosopher, Statesman*, London: Penguin Books.
Smaghi, L. B. (2009) "Conventional and Unconventional Monetary Policy," keynote lecture at the International Centre for Monetary and Banking Studies, Geneva.
Smith, A. (2002) "Imagining Geographies of the New Europe: Geo-Economic Power and the New European Architecture of Innovation," *Political Geography*, 21: 647–670.

Spilimbergo, A., Symansky, S., Blanchard, O. and Cottarelli, C. (2008) "Fiscal Policy for the Crisis," IMF Staff Position Note.

Spulber, N. and Gehrels, F. (1958) "The Operation of Trade within the Soviet Bloc," *Review of Economics and Statistics*, 40 (2): 140–148.

Stamp, J. C. (1931) "The Report of the Macmillan Committee," *The Economic Journal*, 41 (163): 424–435.

Stone, D. (1988) *Policy Paradox and Political Reason*, Glenview, Ill.: Scott Foresman.

Sundarajan, V. (1990) "Financial Sector Reform and Central Banking in Centrally Planned Economies," IMF Working Paper 90/120.

Svensson, L. E. O. (2006) "The Instrument-Rate Projection under the Instrument-Rate Projection under Inflation-Targeting: The Norwegian Example," CEPS Working Paper No. 127.

Taylor, J. (1993) "Discretion Versus Policy Rules in Practice," *Carnegie-Rochester Conference Series on Public Policy*, 39: 195–214.

Taylor, J. (2000) "Using Monetary Policy Rules in Developing Economies," Bank of Mexico 75th Anniversary Conference. "Stabilization and Monetary Policy: the International Experience". November 14–15.

Taylor, L. (1983) *Structuralist Macroeconomics*, New York: Basic Books.

Taylor, L. (1988) *Varieties of Stabilization Experience: Towards Sensible Macroeconomics in the Third World*, Oxford: Oxford University Press.

Tesliuc, E. D. (1999) *Agricultural Policies: Achievements and Challenges*, Bucharest: Arta Grafica.

The Economist (2009) "No Panic, Just Gloom," May 14.

Thompson, G. (1986) *The Conservatives' Economic Policy*, London: Croom Helm.

Tismaneanu, V. (2003) *Stalinism for All Seasons: A Political History of Romanian Communism*, Berkeley, Calif.: University of California Press.

Togo, E. (2007) "Coordinating Public Debt Management with Fiscal and Monetary Policies: An Analytical Framework," World Bank Policy Research Working Paper, No. 4369.

Trichet, J. C. (2009) *The ECB's Enhanced Credit Support*. Kenynote address at the University of Munich (July, 13).

United Nations Conference on Trade and Development (2004) "Trade and Development Report: Policy Coherence, Development Strategies and Integration into the World Economy," available online at http://www.unctad.org/en/docs/tdr2004_en.pdf (accessed June 12, 2007).

United Nations Conference on Trade and Development (2007) *Trade and Development Report 2009*, New York and Geneva: United Nations.

Vasilescu, A. (2005) "Cum Ne-a Intrecut Trinidad Tobago," *Averea*, September 30.

Van Brabant, J. (1991) "Socialist Economics: The Disequilibrium School and the Shortage Economy," *The Journal of Economic Perspectives*, 4 (2): 157–175.

Viner, J. (1955) *Studies in the Theory of International Trade*, London: Allen and Unwin.

Wall Street (2009) "Scrisoarea FMI Nu Contine Schimbari De Politici Fata De Acordul Din 24 Martie," April 23, available online at http://www.wall-street.ro/articol/economie/63325/scrisoarea-fmi-nu-contine-schimbari-de-politici-fata-de-acordul-din-24-martie.html (accessed June 23, 2009).

Walsh, C. (2006) "The Contribution of Theory to Practice in Monetary Policy: Recent Developments," ECB Colloquium in Honour of Otmar Issing, Frankfurt.

Wicksell K. (1962) *Interest and Prices: A Study of the Causes Regulating the Value of Money*, First published 1898. London: Macmillan.
Winiecki, J. (1985) Portes Ante Portas: A Critique of the Revisionist Interpretation of Inflation under Central Planning, *Comparative Economic Studies*, 27 (2): 25–51.
Winiecki, J. (1988) *The Distorted World of Soviet-Type Economies*, London and New York: Routledge.
Winiecki, J. (1993) "'Heterodox' Stabilization in Eastern Europe," European Bank for Reconstruction and Development Working Paper No. 8.
Withers, H. (1910) "Introduction," in W. Bagehot, *Lombard Street: A Description of the Money Market*, London: Smith, Elder.
Wolf, T. (1990) "Macroeconomic Adjustment and Reform in Planned Economies," IMF Working Paper 90/27.
Wolf, T. (1991) "The Lessons of Limited Market-Oriented Reform," *Journal of Economic Perspectives*, 5 (4): 45–58.
Woodford, M. (2003) *Interest and Prices: Foundations of a Theory of Monetary Policy*, Princeton, NJ: Princeton University Press.
Woodford, M. (2007) "How Important Is Money in the Conduct of Monetary Policy?", National Bureau of Economic Research Working Paper No. 13325.
Woods, N. (2006) *The Globalizers: the IMF, the World Bank and its borrowers*. Ithaca, NY: Cornell University Press.
World Bank (1992) "Enterprise Arrears in Romania: How to Cope with the Problem of Unpaid Debts?", *The Newsletter about Reforming Economies*, 3 (10): 1–3.
Ziarul Financiar (2005) "Isarescu: sterilizam mai multi lei can pleaca speculatorii." October 6.
Ziarul Financiar (2007a) "Isarescu se Confrunta cu cea mai mare Dilema din Ultimii Doi Ani: Creste sau nu Creste Dobanda?", October 20. Available on line at: http://www.zf.ro/banci-si-asigurari/isarescu-se-confrunta-cu-cea-mai-mare-dilema-din-ultimii-doi-ani-creste-sau-nu-dobanda-3062949 (accessed October 20).
Ziarul Financiar (2007b) "Dijmarescu: BNR poate interveni pe piata valutara.," September 10.
Ziarul Financiar (2008) "Isărescu Acuza Trei Banci Ca Au Incercat Sa Introduca O Criza De Lichiditate," available online at http://www.zf.ro/banci-si-asigurari/isărescu-acuza-trei-banci-ca-au-incercat-sa-induca-o-criza-artificiala-de-lichiditate-3350431/, (accessed October 10).
Zecchini, S. (1995) "The Role of International Financial Institutions in the Transition Processes," *Journal of Comparative Economics*, 20 (1): 116–138.
Zhukov S. V. and Vorobyov, Y. V. (1991) *Reforming the Soviet Union: Lessons from Structural Experience*, Moscow: Institute of World Economy and International Relations, Soviet Academy of Science.
Žižek, S. (2009) "Lunch with FT," *Financial Times*, March 6.

Index

Lightning Source UK Ltd.
Milton Keynes UK
UKHW02f0204170418
321170UK00020B/849/P

9 781349 325054